FEDERAL BUDGET
AND
FINANCIAL
MANAGEMENT
REFORM

Federal Budget and Financial Management Reform

Thomas D. Lynch

QUORUM BOOKS

New York
Westport, Connecticut
London

Library of Congress Cataloging-in-Publication Data

Federal budget and financial management reform / [edited by] Thomas D.
Lynch.
    p. cm.
    ISBN 0-89930-538-5 (alk. paper)
    1. Budget—United States. 2. Finance, Public—United States.
3. Government spending policy—United States. 4. United States—
Appropriations and expenditures. I. Lynch, Thomas Dexter, 1942– .
HJ2052.F4 1991
353.0072′2—dc20   90–20711

British Library Cataloguing in Publication Data is available.

Library of Congress Catalog Card Number: 90–20711
ISBN: 0–89930–538–5

First published in 1991

Quorum Books, 88 Post Road West, Westport, CT 06881
An imprint of Greenwood Publishing Group, Inc.

Printed in the United States of America

∞™

The paper used in this book complies with the
Permanent Paper Standard issued by the National
Information Standards Organization (Z39.48—1984).

10 9 8 7 6 5 4 3 2 1

CONTENTS

Introduction: Call for Reform

Thomas D. Lynch

This collection of original essays addresses reform of the federal budget and financial management processes. Each essay looks at a different aspect of this topic and suggests substantive recommendations on how current processes can be improved.

THE BUDGET PROCESS

The first chapter, written by Joseph White, focuses attention on the presidential budget that is transmitted annually to Congress in late January. The word *budget* comes from the French-Norman word *bouget*, meaning "leather bag." Traditionally, the king's representative came to Parliament with a leather bag that contained the king's request for the funds he felt he needed to rule the realm. In the United States, the Budget and Accounting Act of 1921 established the executive, or presidential, budget. That budget has never been placed in a leather bag, but it is the president's request for money to run the nation.

White concludes that the once influential presidential budget, though still important, has significantly less influence today. Some critics have come to label it "dead on arrival." White argues that this shift is due, first, to the Office of Management and Budget (OMB) focusing less on management and more on policy, and second, to the changed political context in which the president's budget now exists. The OMB and its predecessor, the Bureau of the Budget (BOB), have always been concerned with policy, but BOB was known for an administrative neutrality that focused on macro management concerns. OMB became politicized in the 1970s with the use of more political and fewer career leadership appointments. Since then, OMB has become more concerned with advancing the political rather than the public management agenda of the president. The mid–1970s also saw a growth in congressional budget expertise with greatly enlarged congressional budget staffs.

Ralph Bledsoe is the author of "Coordination of Budgeting." Bledsoe's views are particularly noteworthy because not only is he a public administration scholar, but he also served in the Reagan White House developing and coordinating domestic policy. He stresses that President Reagan was not pleased with the federal budget process. Bledsoe then explains the steps that are taken in building the president's budget and subsequent executive and legislative interaction. Bledsoe concludes with a strong and perceptive set of budget process recommendations.

Bledsoe vividly describes the political duel that takes place between the president and Congress. In this duel, a tactical disadvantage accrues to the one who first offers a controversial budget option, such as increasing taxes. Bledsoe's solution to this problem is reminiscent of pistol dueling, where each opponent must be given an equal opportunity to fire the first deadly shot. In political dueling, neither side wants to be blamed for tax increases nor other politically damaging decisions. Bledsoe recognizes the problem, and his recommendation should be weighed carefully.

James A. Thurber and Samantha L. Durst have written "Delay, Deadlock, and Deficits: Evaluating Proposals for Congressional Budget Reform." They state that the political struggle between the executive and legislative branches started when the American republic was born, and it still exists today. The three Ds—delay, deadlock, and deficit—describe the current struggle. We cannot make timely or effective budgets due to executive–legislative deadlock. The results are massive federal deficits and a significantly increasing federal debt. Thurber and Durst advocate congressional budget reforms.

"Federal Budget Making: A Bipartisan Failure?" is my contribution to this compendium. Like Thurber and Durst, I discuss various budget reforms, but I pay greater attention to a workable two-stage budget process. I also discuss the related problems of unfunded liabilities, contingent liabilities, program productivity, programs tied to user fee revenues, and greater use of internal service funds. I conclude that the checks-and-balances nature of the federal budget process is a failure that can be corrected only by bipartisan action at the highest levels of national leadership.

John Forrester examines the context of forecasting in federal government budget making. He explains forecasting assumptions and how forecasts are generated for the economy, for revenues, and for expenditures. An interesting segment of his chapter addresses the problem of forecasting relative to the yearly budget deficit. Simply put—it is a methodological quagmire. We have taken a very difficult challenge and have made it even more difficult.

IMPROVED PUBLIC FINANCIAL MANAGEMENT

"Recent Developments in Federal Accounting and Financial Management" was written by Ronald Points. He stresses the challenge of financially managing the country's largest employer and consumer: the U.S. government, which has an annual cash flow of over $2 trillion. He reviews the legislation that establishes the federal financial management process and related financial management roles. Points suggests that the link missing in the existing process is a single organization that bears responsibility for directing and managing the federal government's finances.

Points also suggests that the existing process is fragmented, involving unnecessary and inappropriate overlaps between the various central agencies. He elaborates on federal financial management structure and explains financial reporting practices. He notes that fundamental managerial information is usually lacking and that the current process does not adequately provide reliable, timely, and consistent information for policy formulation and managerial control. Lack of integration is evident when, for example, budget formulation uses programs and activities as its basic units but accounting collects information using the organization and appropriations as its basic units. Other similar fundamental problems are noted.

W. Bartley Hildreth is the author of "Federal Financial Management." Hildreth builds upon the case made by Ronald Points by surveying the status of federal financial management, then highlighting where reforms are most needed. He explains the existing financial management system, including the Treasury's financial management service, appropriation and expenditure monitoring, internal controls, financial statements, cost controls, cash control, and collection control. In surveying each, Hildreth suggests significant improvements. For example, he notes that the federal government lags in defining delinquency, and this contributes to inadequate debt collection practices. He concludes that the federal government made progress during the Reagan administration, but more reform is necessary if the federal government is to keep pace with its financial management challenge.

"Data Processing in Federal Budgeting and Financial Management" was written by Stanley B. Botner. He cites various mini case examples to illustrate the current status of financial data processing in the federal government. He also cites data processing in other countries and in state and local governments to point out what can be done. Botner concludes by endorsing the recommendations of the U.S. General Accounting Office. Although major deficiencies in information technology exist in the federal government, he argues that our government should be a leader in the application of modern computers and telecommunications.

OTHER REFORM POSSIBILITIES

Lawrence L. Martin has written "Privatization and Federal Budget Reform." Martin argues that privatization is a financial management tool that should be considered in federal budget reform. He stresses that if privatization is seen in this light, the results could impact the budget deficit. Martin defines privatization by using a broad interpretation of the concept. He specifically examines possibilities for privatizing the following:

- the U.S. Postal Service
- Amtrak
- military commissaries
- power marketing authorities, such as the Tennessee Valley Authority
- the air traffic control system
- the U.S. Coast Guard
- Social Security
- federal lands and buildings, including military bases

CONCLUSION

These authors will help the reader understand the complex issues associated with federal budget and financial management reform. These issues involve the very nature of the American political process as well as technical and organizational considerations. The following essays explore these complexities and offer specific reform recommendations.

FEDERAL BUDGET AND FINANCIAL MANAGEMENT REFORM

1

PRESIDENTIAL POWER
AND THE BUDGET

JOSEPH WHITE

THE DOG THAT DIDN'T BARK

Sherlock Holmes would be curious. Virtually everybody believes the federal deficit is a crime, and they search for a culprit. Budget reform is a perennial topic in Washington. Yet there is little talk of reforming the presidential side of the budget process. It's like the dog that didn't bark in the night. The silence tells us something—but what?

Perhaps the president's budget was killed early in the story. During the 1980s it was so commonly termed "dead on arrival" that the Office of Management and Budget (OMB) delivered the fiscal year (FY) 87 plan in an ambulance, in the form of a staffer on a stretcher; he jumped up to reveal a shirt proclaiming, "The FY87 Budget Lives," while other OMB-ers in medical garb tore pages out of the document to symbolize budgetary surgery.[1] It was "dead" because the rest of the political system claimed it was useless: rejected with laughter, twenty to zero in the Senate Budget Committee in 1982; abandoned before release by President Reagan's call for negotiations in 1984; replaced by revisions that did not add up in 1989, and so on.[2]

Once upon a time its release occasioned books about "Setting National Priorities."[3] It was "a general financial and work program" for the federal government;[4] the statement of "the President's program," setting the agenda for the year's legislative battles.[5] How could the president's budget lose its function? As Naomi Caiden explains:

The place of the executive budget in the United States constitutional context has never really been clear. . . . The original concept espoused by budget reformers implied an executive budget monopoly, justified by a doctrine of administrative neutrality, at odds both with contemporary practice and the separation of powers. . . . The Budget and Accounting Act of 1921 modified this concept by retaining legislative initiative in appropriations and stressing the executive budget as a means of gaining executive responsibility and strengthening legislative budgetary control. Later the justification of policy-making capacity was added to that of administrative efficiency. . . .

Presently, neither original nor later meaning appears accurate. . . . The executive budget is now simply a bargaining counter in a complex game in which the legislature often takes the initiative and executive adopts a reactive stance. . . . Budget outcomes appear to be beyond control of either branch of government. The executive budget still exists in form, but its significance as an institution has become an enigma.[6]

To understand what has happened to the president's budget we must first address the paradox in Caiden's description of how it once fit. How, exactly, could the same process gain executive responsibility and strengthen legislative budgetary control? Most of us don't want responsibility for things somebody else controls.

We will see that there are functions which both Congress and the president legitimately want performed. Since the 1960s, however, these functions have been steadily downgraded, due to presidential disinterest, congressional institutional innovation, and a changing policy environment. As these processes reinforced each other, the president's budget has become more a presidential tool and less a part of a government by law. Neither Congress nor the president is well served, but there is little prospect of constructive reform.

HOW THE BUDGET ONCE WORKED

Originally the president would do his budget and Congress would use it, because it helped both control a third party, the executive agencies.

Restating Neutral Competence

The classic notion of neutral competence is often interpreted, by OMB staff and others, to mean personal neutrality, a willingness to serve the preferences of any president. That is too limited a notion; for OMB to be useful to both branches its *competence itself must be neutral* between the two political overseers of the bureaucracy. The clearest such competence is administrative efficiency, economy with a small "e." When General Dawes declared that "the Budget bureau keeps humble, and if it ever becomes obsessed with the idea that it has any work except to save money and improve efficiency in routine business it will cease to be useful in the hands of the President,"[7] the first budget director could have spoken for Congress' interests as well.

Efficiency meant not only scrutinizing the use of resources ("bean-counting"), but also coordinating, both by revealing if agencies were working at cross-purposes and by uncovering the "wasteful" opposite, redundancy, or overlap of functions. The coordinating function moved from budgeting to legislation with the growth of the legislative clearance process.[8] The administrative focus expanded to improving agency outputs as well as reducing inputs. As Allen Schick described it, the move was from control to management. Again, both branches could support such competence.[9]

Competence in information collection and transmission also fell under the neutral rubric. Information may favor one side in a given dispute, yet nobody wants to admit that information normally favors the other guy; that is the same as saying its own side is usually wrong. The importance of information is shown by the fact that it is central to budgeteers' notions of professionalism and to current OMB staff's definitions of their responsibilities.[10]

Both Congress and the president also want to hold agencies accountable, although often to different things. A process in which agencies set goals and explain how they might reach them sets standards for oversight and provides a base for argument about why things went wrong. In principle the original agency estimates could serve the same function, but a round of initial review and criticism *could* sharpen both analysis and presentation. OMB people still claim their work "helps the agencies make their case."[11] Compilation of estimates into a comprehensive document, with (roughly) comparable terms and divisions, must make the process more transparent to president, legislature, and public.

The final traditional function was to maintain the budget in a rough balance. Now, examination of administrative performance and "work plans" can do only so much. It can deflate agency requests for increases and raise questions about new initiatives. It can manipulate each year's definitions of the "base" at the margins, forcing agencies to absorb some cost inflation.[12] Yet it does not affect revenues and, except in the extreme case of winding down wartime programs, has only limited power to slash existing programs. After all, if a program is unsupportable, how did it survive last year's analysis? Slashing the base requires either very good new reasons or a new governing coalition.[13]

This balancing function should be stated more generally, as aligning preferences about program details and fiscal totals.[14] It involved an iterative process, in which central guidance based on aggregate preferences was challenged by agency response as to what they could and couldn't do given that constraint. In subsequent bargaining both programs and constraint might give a little. In the end the president was expected to defend his budget on both dimensions. Congress had no way to imitate the back-and-forth nature of the executive process, which depended on a modicum of confidentiality. Nor had Congress the economic expertise with which to justify its preferences for the totals. Thus the president's process seemed to do something that Congress could not. To the extent it was achieved by finding administrative efficiencies, balancing depended on a neutral competence. That, however, could not be guaranteed.

The Constitutional Context: Clerkship

A budgeting of neutral competence fit a particular pattern of presidential participation in policy making, what Richard Neustadt called the president's "clerkship."[15] It might better be described as a brokerage: in return for facilitating transactions, the president gets to charge a price. One way he facilitates is by creating an agenda of initiatives that organize the activity of the political system, and the budget "is among the cardinal services the president-as-clerk performs for Congressmen and bureaucrats and lobbyists, alike."[16] Produced at the beginning of the year; representing commitment in its most concrete form, money; emerging from a process of negotiation between the president (or at least presidential staff) and the agencies; necessarily followed by the response of appropriations bills; the budget became the year's premier initiator. It was never the sole initiator. The president could invent programs during the year and, especially in the aftermath of the Great Society, Congress proved far more capable of policy innovation than Neustadt implied.[17] Yet organizing a legislative agenda was a clear function of the president's budget process.

The president's budget served also as a target and a shield. Congress granted budgetary responsibility to the executive in part so he would take the blame for the bad news. If he proposed something they liked and constituents didn't, they could accept it and blame him; if they disapproved or constituents were really angry, members could reject the cut. In return for taking blame, the president gained greater control over agencies in less visible matters. Blame for proposals is not quite as bad as blame for actions, and Congress would share complicity in whatever finally was done (in this sense Congress was not avoiding but sharing and reducing blame). If everybody agreed hard choices must be made, the president's budget allowed him to push the choices in a direction that fit either his policy or political ends. Congress might want to cut neither law enforcement nor parks and so would accept the president's choice.

A broker works with, not against, his clients' preferences. In the "good old days" through the mid-sixties, the process worked with what now seems limited conflict because the president's budget was normally reasonably close to congressional preferences. The routines of the appropriations process as described by Fenno and Wildavsky, with Congress focusing on the budget's proposed changes to the spending base, assumed that the president accepted that base. Conversely, the focus meant that his budget did place items on the legislative agenda.[18] Argument over new initiatives could proceed without either side seeing a threat to the budget's roles in building a record for accountability or in "scrubbing" the estimates in pursuit of administrative efficiency in the existing base. The level of agreement is indicated both by the patterns of congressional consideration of requests and by the results. The Budget Bureau, both by defining the base and in its adjustments to the details, strongly influenced budget outcomes.[19]

The Collapse of Clerkship

This system came under stress trying to finance both the Vietnam War and Great Society, and it collapsed when President Nixon and Congress went to war over budget priorities from 1969 to 1973.

One difficulty was that during the late 1960s and early 1970s traditional competencies could not adjust details to totals in a way both the president and Congress would accept. The competence used for fiscal policy, though seemingly technical, is decidedly not neutral. Economists divide on partisan lines: pro- and antigovernment, willing to risk inflation to keep unemployment down, or vice versa. Therefore the recommendations of the president's economists need not be acceptable to Congress; yet, since he had economists and they didn't, the president had more reason to think he should make, not broker, policy.

Even if fiscal goals were agreed upon, changes in budget composition made the old means of accomplishing them less relevant. The growth of entitlements meant administrative savings in other accounts helped less and less.[20] And, unlike appropriated programs, there was no action agenda for entitlements; the president could propose but there was no routine of response. Along with the Vietnam War, entitlements created a fiscal crunch that spilled into a series of outlay freezes and related maneuvers that showed the breakdown of the traditional process.

In addition, neither President Johnson nor Nixon was content to be a mere clerk. Congress itself need not accept the neutral competencies of efficiency and coordination.[21] But presidents and their staffs, reinforced by the public and media, naturally wanted to do more. The routines of "setting priorities" in the extensive internal budget process, then releasing the budget to great fanfare, were seductive; after all the work performed, presidents and their staffs thought the budget should set policy, not serve Congress.

President Johnson rejected clerkship in favor of activism, loading new responsibilities on the Budget Bureau.[22] Yet he also wanted to restrain spending, so BOB was pulled in two directions, like a beagle by both ears.

Traditional competence suffered as task forces applied bureau institutional memory to new programs but took personnel from routine responsibilities. Congress would not give BOB new authority to make sense of the administrative structure of Great Society programs, a crazy-quilt of intergovernmental transfers with associated coordination problems.[23]

The Nixon administration saw the Johnson BOB as administratively ineffective and too loyal to the Great Society agenda. Thus it didn't trust the clerks, but it also meant to undo the 1921 compromise and return to the progressive reformers' executive budget monopoly. The Ash Council seems to have believed the president could actually manage the government, though nobody ever specified what "management" in this sense might mean.[24] Following the traditional separation of policy and management, the Ash Council proposed creation of a new domestic council and concentration of administrative functions in a renamed and reformed Office of Management and Budget. The plan avoided congressional veto, it seems, because management problems were real, and many members of Congress had their own grudges against the BOB. In operation, however, the administration tried to use the new OMB as a tool for "Increasing the Responsiveness of the Executive Branch."[25] In Richard Nathan's account, Nixon had concluded that "in many areas of government . . . operations is policy."[26] Roy Ash, when he became director, reorganized OMB's examining staff into four program divisions with management study groups, each under a political Program Associate Director (PAD). PADs tended to be young loyalists who were widely accused of politicizing decisions, preventing career advice from getting to the top, and lacking knowledge themselves.[27] In essence the administration used a perceived decline in administrative competence to justify reforms that further downgraded that function.

Congress would not be pleased. Here is not the place to review the unhappy history that led to the Congressional Budget and Impoundment Control Act of 1974 (1974 Budget Acts). We need only emphasize that a president with inappropriately grand ideas of the importance of his budget; preferring a more constrictive fiscal policy than much of Congress; having very different priorities from Congress; in a period of increasing fiscal constraints that could not be met through administrative savings; continually defeated in the legislature; finally, with impoundments, tried to short-circuit Congress' budgeting powers. A constitutional crisis over budget powers was avoided only because another, culminating in Nixon's resignation, took its place.

As a result, by 1973 Congress not only distrusted presidential budgets, but "cordially hated" OMB.[28] "Following vituperative hearings," it passed a bill requiring Senate confirmation of the director and deputy, retroactive to cover Ash and Malek.[29] Though able to enforce a veto on that, Nixon accepted confirmation of future appointees. Confirmation and the PADs indicated a change from OMB being anonymous career staff to a more political role, with the president and Congress expected to have different political ends. That was institutionalized further by the 1974 Budget Act.

WORKING OUT A NEW SYSTEM

Since the collapse of clerkship, the functions of the president's budget and federal budgeting itself have evolved through three stages: response to the 1974 Budget Act, the Stockman years, and the era of Gramm–Rudman.

Implications and Effects of the Congressional Budget Act

Congress created both the Congressional Budget Office (CBO) and budget committees with large staffs so it would no longer depend as much on the executive branch for information: economic forecasts, economic analyses, and estimates of program costs. The new congressional budget process also eliminated the President's monopoly of fiscal policy. Congress could justify decisions on details that differed from the president's by saying they fit its fiscal plan, not his.

Consequences for the coordinating side of clerkship were less decisive. Most especially, the congressional process could not quite imitate the president's ability to adjust details to totals, creating a budget that is internally consistent. Since totals were decided with only limited information on details, and the budget committees were far less powerful relative to other committees than OMB compared to agencies, the process, designed to imitate the president's, could not duplicate his authority. In the 1970s, favorable economic and political conditions masked this weakness by allowing the process to produce "accommodating" budgets—that is, the total was big enough to fit the details.[30] The politics of budget resolutions evolved into a largely symbolic battle, shadows made by real political forces but deciding little.[31]

The president's budget, of course, was not authoritative on either details or total, because it would be altered by Congress. Yet it was at least complete in its own terms, and if it were an acceptable starting point for Congress, alterations could be made at the margins without bringing the structure out of whack. The congressional process as originally designed did not replace the president's role in laying a template for coordinated decision.

Nor did it replace OMB's "scrubbing" of agency estimates. The 1974 Budget Act implicitly admitted as much by requiring that the president each year produce a current services budget, essentially a thorough scrub of the base, from which Congress could start if the president's own proposal was too far from their preferences. But Congress found no way to force OMB to cooperate,[32] and so current services was replaced by the CBO "current policy" baseline. The difficulty is that "current policy" is in no way an operationally justified assessment of need; it is not based on any "work plan."

Critics of the games that can be played with current policy may go too far in blaming Congress, but they demonstrate convincingly that "although current policy is often called current services, it does not measure those services in practice."[33]

Therefore the new process could help Congress check the president, but did not replace his clerical role. Nor did it alter legislative interest in giving him a chance to take blame for bad news. By seeming to require consideration of entitlements and revenues, it might even expand the area in which the president could gain power by taking blame.[34] Although it could not force action on entitlement or revenue proposals, the new process forced some consideration in budget debate, so presidential ability to put budget proposals on the legislative agenda expanded.

Yet the new process made congressional rejection of presidential proposals more public and embarrassing. Before 1974, to the extent Congress ignored proposals, they occurred quietly in widely dispersed arenas. Presidents had to ask why they should play the fool, risking their prestige and electoral credit, if Congress claimed the ability to initiate policy anyway. When a politically very vulnerable president, Jimmy Carter, faced a nasty budget crunch in 1980, rather than remaking and resubmitting his budget to meet elite calls for balance, he convened a week-long summit with congressional leaders to agree on a new plan.[35]

As the president backed off from taking blame, however, Congress altered the budget process in a way that potentially increased his influence, applying reconciliation to the first budget resolution. Reconciliation meant committees would be instructed to report specific amounts of spending cuts or revenue increases. While the budget committees had no formal recourse to deal with a noncomplying committee, it seems to have been understood by all that they could offer floor amendments, so pure noncompliance wouldn't work.[36] Reconciliation provided an action agenda and led to a process in which OMB bargained directly with congressional leadership over matters that historically had been settled at a less aggregated level. Agreements might prove hard to enforce but, relative to disaggregated bargaining, the negotiation structure clearly centralized power within Congress in the hands of party leaders and within the executive in the hands of OMB.[37] It thus restructured power within the executive branch.

The Stockman Years: Centralization, Personalization, and Growing Credibility Problems

David Stockman tried to use the new system to pursue presidential interests in opposition to both Congress and the agencies. The traditional competencies were devalued both by enormous budgetary constraint, making lower total seem more important than defensible details, and the administration's own disinterest. The resulting transformation has been sum-

marized in a raft of articles.[38] One of Stockman's top aides described it as
"OMB's adaptation from the budget as a ministerial, executive process to a
pluralistic, legislative process." OMB became the equivalent of a Hill office,
built to serve its director, the equivalent of a powerful committee chairman,
as he fought to pass his legislation.

For Stockman, an aide explained, administrative matters were interesting
only as rationales. "The notion was, if one got far enough into the truth of
how things worked, one could find reasons to fit whatever our goal might
be." And the demand for rationales and numbers was such that new learning
was hardly possible. Examiners, once "the center, the institutional weight
of the agency," became more like "research assistants" as "we brought that
system to an end in our search for centralized control." Political appointees
needed information aggregated in ways that they could trade off: pricing
estimates on a blizzard of "what-ifs" or maybe quick instruction on how a
program worked. The appointees had little use for examiners out in the
agencies studying operations and less for suggested improvements.

Centralized negotiations followed from the prevalence of cuts. Those few
agencies favored by the administration (e.g., the Pentagon) still carried their
own water on the Hill, but others had to be cut out of the bargaining loop.
Those agencies with particularly loyal leadership might support their requested cuts. But few people in OMB, political or career, expected agencies
to push hard for most of what Stockman was submitting.[39] Stockman created
a unit of "bill trackers" and a new computer system, the Central Budget
Management System (CBMS), to provide the information for his negotiations. At each stage of congressional action OMB sent letters stating objections, which the agencies and departments rarely saw in advance. Oversight
of other formal communications proliferated, with examiners spending more
time reviewing justifications, questions and answers, and even transcripts
of hearings.

As examiners functioned less as analysts and more as staff for negotiators,
OMB became a justifier of politically determined policy preferences and less
an expert on the details. When argument was made about details, as on the
outlays produced in a given year from a compromise level of budget authority, OMB was suspect. The CBMS was invented after such a fight in
1981, yet since it relied on historical algorithms, rather than details of the
proposals in question, appropriations staff scorned the data.[40] Information
was needed too fast to allow more careful analysis. "I think we don't have
as much time to get the same kind of detailed program knowledge," one
deputy associate director (DAD) reflected. "What happens is, you . . . miss
the second-order issues of how the program operates, you miss the changes
you could make that would improve operations." Each OMB veteran I interviewed agreed on that trend. At the same time, OMB negotiators might
bring examiners along for technical assistance, and another DAD worried
about neutrality:

It's a slippery slope. In the heat of a discussion it's easy to slip from a factual role into advocacy. When what's in the budget is part of an internal battle, and OMB's position has prevailed, . . . it's hard not to jump in and say why we were right. . . . My concern is, if we become advocates an incoming administration will be justifiably suspicious. . . . It hasn't happened yet, though that belief is getting out.

Stockman tried to buffer career staff from advocacy roles. In this context the PADs made sense as a way to help the director and keep the careerists out of the line of fire. In preserving some of the neutrality needed for staff to serve successive directors or presidents, however, he did little to protect the neutral competence needed to preserve credibility with Congress.[41]

Certain things, in any case, do not centralize easily. When agencies do or do not protest something, appropriators think they are learning about program needs rather than about OMB's preferences. For example, when the Pentagon refused to set priorities within its Reagan-era budgets, the subcommittees would slash in a number of areas, figuring the screams and silences that followed would answer their questions.[42] Appropriators, concerned not only with finding agreement with the executive but doing so in a way that made programmatic sense, could reject OMB positions far more easily than the agency's. And they would learn the agency's real position anyway. As many respondents put it, "the telephones work." More formally, all sides agree there were and are ways to ask questions so the answers are "technical" and OMB cannot prevent response. OMB could go no further because Congress was of one mind that agencies should be free to give information, and OMB needs appropriations too.[43]

With negotiations more centralized than the flow of information, the system in essence moved to the appropriators negotiating with OMB on the agencies' behalf. Given the overall fiscal environment, the agencies still had to do worse than in previous years.[44] Yet one had to wonder what the whole budget preparation phase was worth, especially as the proposals in the budget document had little prospect of adoption. Even when they were defensible ideas in principle, a few years of congressional deep-sixing made them look pointless. A Republican appropriations clerk, asked how the annual process began, said, "The first thing I do is write a memo to my boss about how bizarre the budget request is. He'll usually agree, and say now it's our turn." A House clerk commented, "We're not going to learn anything new in _____ or _____ , where their position hasn't changed in seven years, and there's a fundamental difference."

Some of the ideas harder to defend came from OMB's management half, which had been problematic for a long time.[45] The Reaganauts, under the name of "Reform 88," simply identified good management with reducing inputs.[46] Even my OMB respondents who claim everything *they* did to agencies had a rationale say the stuff from the management side, for which they do not feel responsible, was of dubious merit. "We argue," one said, "but, faithful unto death, we pass it back." Another recalled,

They had a formula; they would come down and say, 'we've identified that you can cut 650 FTEs, because you have xxx people doing this kind of work, which can be cut by yy.y percent.' You give that to the Department and they look at you like you're some kind of nut. It's not policy-driven, it's not programmatic, it's just added in.

Appropriations Committees Were No More Impressed

Stockman, however, was trapped; neither he nor anyone else could pursue technically reasonable budgeting (for long) given the deficit panic. The simplest definition of good budgeting is a reliable schedule, and that disappeared immediately. There were at least five rounds in 1981,[47] endless negotiations in 1982,[48] a budget renegotiated subcommittee by subcommittee in 1983, abandoned before birth in 1984. Agencies did not know whether their submissions were, in fact, administration policy, since OMB kept generating new alternatives.

The process had been personalized, and its use and status depended on the director. In spite of all the problems, congressional budgeteers respected Stockman as someone who knew his stuff and with whom they could deal. Though he had strong preferences and knowledge that is still remembered with awe, the budget is so big that analysts still felt they could contribute. Then Stockman left, to be succeeded by James Miller and Gramm–Rudman.

Budgeting Collapses: Gramm–Rudman–Hollings

Gramm–Rudman was a Dishonesty in Budgeting Act. It created a hostage game that had to fail because the policies being held were less popular than those policies (entitlements, low taxes) that were supposed to be altered in order to avoid the sequester. Politicians have not eliminated the deficit because its evils are long-term and dubious, whereas the costs of specific policies to end it are short-term and obvious. Therefore there was no legitimate alternative to shooting the hostage. Since they could neither live with the sequester nor enact an honest alternative, politicians changed the targets (in 1987), relied on windfalls (tax reform in 1986), and plain cheated.[49]

The law's failure in action stemmed from a failure in principle. Gramm–Rudman declared that budgeting was not an iterative process, in which preferences about details and totals confronted and then revised each other, but an entirely "top-down" exercise in which the total (deficit) was set and only the details could be moved. It created procedures to enforce that logic. Yet in practice, large majorities preferred to live with higher deficits to limit programmatic pain. Since they couldn't adjust the total directly, they filled in the gap with gimmicks, changing the total indirectly. As revised in 1987, the law gave OMB control of economic assumptions precisely because both branches expected OMB to provide more wiggle room. *Fraud was the only way to perform the traditional budgeting function of bringing details and totals together in an acceptable manner.*[50]

Gramm–Rudman obliterated the budget schedule: any self-interested appropriations subcommittee had to stall, because enactment of its bill before sequester left it subject to a cut of undetermined size.[51] The president's budget no longer set the agenda, because all participants looked forward, wondering what the final sequester snapshot would look like and how that would affect everybody else. The idea was to avoid commitment, as the Bush administration managed in its revisions to Reagan's FY90 plan, by specifying only the increases. If you must deal, fudging makes that much easier, as in the 1989 summit agreement that included roughly $39 billion in smoke and mirrors out of a $47 billion total.[52]

Thus the president's budget seems, as Naomi Caiden put it, a mere "bargaining counter." Substance is not only irrelevant but harmful. By 1990 the president's men could with a straight face *blame Congress for not changing his budget enough*! Chief of staff John Sununu argued that, "the failure of Congress to do any constructive revision . . . since the president sent it up is part of the problem we have."[53]

The 1989 Bush revisions were extreme even for the Gramm–Rudman years. With no attempt to even pretend to relate details to totals, it was, in the words of one House appropriations aide, "the strangest year I've ever seen. We didn't really feel we ever had a President's Budget." Jim Miller, Stockman's immediate successor, at least made his budgets add up. But he lacked Stockman's knowledge, authority, and reputation for reasonableness; he faced a Democratic Senate and a much more aggressive House in his second two years; Gramm–Rudman meant any director would be forced to less and less acceptable proposals; and as a result he faced massive credibility problems.

Given Gramm–Rudman and the ideological gap between the branches, a close aid recalls that OMB's goal became "meeting a target, that's it. . . . It was going to be dead on arrival anyway, no matter what we did. . . . Being believable in the aggregate was not an issue." Miller was less interested in managing the government or in compromising, and his style was more confrontational. It was symbolized by the famous "pork exercise," in which OMB in 1988 prepared a report of the "pork" that it would excise from appropriations if given an item veto, and suggested agencies ignore instructions in committee reports. A few of the OMB staff I interviewed think that was a good idea, but most think it was suicidal. Congressional responses are typified by a Republican Senate appropriations aide who said, "No one liked what Miller did. . . . He was bringing a questionable constitutional judgment into the appropriations process. Even if he were right, we would just write it into the law. That's just more work for us."

A DAD recalls that "as we got into more philosophical confrontations, we were stalemated legislatively and began getting more restrictions on administrative flexibility." Aside from tax reform and a few other initiatives, there was no positive "follow-on agenda. . . . It was to somehow meet Gramm–Rudman. At that point you're into the game of deficit-reduction roulette." OMB was plenty active, but at some point that activity began to cost its credibility. Thus the letters at each stage of the appropriations process are widely described as having said so much that they were not taken seriously:

Miller liked to be confrontational. He was an ideologue; he stated his views and virtually every letter had a veto threat. And to the extent he did that, they became irrelevant. You would go to a meeting and the chairman would say, "We've got the Director of OMB's letter here; he doesn't like the bill." And that was it.

A branch chief recalls that Miller "was just less politic. He said things that you could say maybe in private, but he said them in public." It is striking to listen to appropriations staff and members compare Miller to Stockman. The comparison is a bit unfair; Miller did not compromise nor attend to operations as a matter of strategy and ideology. He was not stupid, but he was handicapped by a much weaker position within his administration. Unlike Stockman, Miller acted as if he believed his own proposals. An aide recalls that "it hurt Miller that he couldn't speak for the president. We'd threaten a veto, they would call Don Regan, and he would say, 'we'll decide on that later.' . . . The letters didn't speak for anyone." Miller also had a weaker institution to work with. Stockman's cuts had gotten old, and both the use of examiners for other things and the severe turnover in the examining staff meant there was less analytical capacity than before to develop new analyses.[54]

By the end of the Miller years, therefore, there was good reason to wonder what value the institutionalized budget process added for either the president or the wider political system. If OMB commanded little institutional respect, the process could add little to the raw power of the veto. If its main function was to keep him from being embarrassed, the president would be better off without a budget. Other players, grown accustomed to rejecting the budget out of hand, could presumably live without it. It seemed that thirty years of presidential overreaching and congressional response, dividing government and increasing budgetary constraint, and a series of institutional innovations had rendered the president's budget useless, if not dead, then a zombie haunting the policy process.

OMB'S ROLE IN THE NEW BUDGET SYSTEM

Budgeting as we knew it once, an orderly process of relating parts to whole, is moribund. Yet budget decisions still are made. "The real budget," as a former OMB official remarked, "is thirteen appropriations and whatever you can get in reconciliation." When Congress passes those bills, it does pay attention to the "bottom" level, the programmatic consequences. In deciding the size of those bills Congress and the president decide on totals— even if they disguise those totals by fudging. There will be some later changes in supplementals, but in the Gramm–Rudman years they have been much smaller than in the past.[55] How, we might **ask,** does the work of the presidential budget process, including release of his budget document, influence the real budget?

Agenda-Setting and Blame Avoidance

It may seem dubious to look for patterns in a system Allen Schick has rightly called "Improvisational Budgeting."[56] Yet patterns exist, and they arise from the same factors—a need to spread blame, Congress' technical disabilities, coordination needs—that gave OMB its role in the old system.

First, and important even if ignoble, the president's budget has established each year's acceptable level of gimmickry. Congress wants the blame for doing neither less nor more. If it has more gimmicks, the president and everyone else will attack it, but if less—well, listen to a former Senate Democratic leadership aide:

If you have honest numbers, it raises the deficit. You have to cut spending more and raise taxes higher. The politicians' tendency, the whole system pushes them, to do what Stockman did, to jimmy the numbers. . . . We had guys who said, let's tell the truth, not use the rosy scenario. But then, even if we cut more from programs than the president, we have a bigger deficit. Take those [1982] phony management savings. What do you replace them with?

In this context lying is not irresponsible because it is the only way to make a budget, as he explained in contrasting the two chambers:

The House [Democrats] would adopt some of that phony stuff because *they* had to govern. . . . We said, hey, we're the minority, to hell with governing; they drove us out of office by saying they could balance the budget with tax cuts, for Christ's sake! The House felt it had to make a budget, so there was tremendous tension between Byrd and O'Neill.

Each year congressmen criticize the administration's gimmickry, and each year they adopt it. In the most telling example, Senate Democrats in their FY87 budget resolution adopted the administration's economic assumptions, for Gramm–Rudman purposes, on the first page, and then used CBO assumptions on all other pages. When double-scoring was subsequently banned, they used only the OMB forecast.

By determining each year's acceptable level of prevarication, the president determined each year's deficit, and thus fiscal policy or at least fiscal result. Because Gramm–Rudman prohibited debate over the deficit's proper level,

Congress had no way to argue; in a most backward manner, the presidential monopoly of macro policy that the 1974 Budget Act meant to challenge was restored.

The president's budget also retains some of its agenda-setting power. Within the appropriations process, the hearings are still structured as a response to the president's submission. Whether the response is serious depends on the proposal.

Budget officers talk of failure to pass "the laugh test." Some were just politically hopeless: "They say we should abolish _____ ; the . . . groups mobilize; and the committees regard it with utter disdain, with laughter. Even around this table we laugh." Some ideas have been consensually bad and politically dead: "Both the Republicans and Democrats . . . would joke about it. Sure, that's just what you want, to privatize inspections; that's putting the fox in charge of the chicken coop!" These are the cases that lead to memos about the budget's absurdity. Yet in many cases the budget's details are significant. First, the president can put increases on the agenda. Even if the appropriators have severe doubts about a project, presidential support in a tight fiscal environment where few new goodies are available guarantees a powerful claimant coalition. In this fiscal environment it is hard to imagine anybody else getting a proposed mission to Mars, a technical shield against nuclear weapons, or an $8 billion atom smasher taken seriously. In that context the entire process then looks more traditional, with much greater agency influence and OMB playing a lesser role in lobbying Congress.

Second, OMB may have found some of what one DAD called "the least provocative minuses." One examiner recalled a tax proposal for railroad retirement: "Stockman signed off on it and we worked the Hill . . . and Treasury priced it as saving $70-$80 million. . . . As it happened, a guy on Ways and Means called up and said, 'what's the idea?' He knew this issue well, and we did something like it on COBRA [the 1985–86 reconciliation]." Other things being equal, the president's proposals still can serve the old blame-deflecting function: "When you take cuts, I know that on _____ they'll have to pick them off my list. Because I'm taking the heat, I'm giving them the camouflage that they can blame it on me. . . . And know I'm the cover, so we talk [beforehand]." Even if there is a strong tendency for administration and Congress to cut a program in different ways, as on Medicare where the former is far more likely to try to shift costs to patients and the latter to providers, the president by proposing drastic cuts makes Congress look better for its approach.

I doubt any president could have met the Gramm–Rudman targets without angering Congress, but the extent of rejection depended on how sharply ideological and policy-based an approach OMB took. Further, while the decline in its credibility may place agencies in a mode of end-running the president's budget, they still have to take it seriously. It remains the structure within which they do their estimates. They also need all the help they can get under the current circumstances, and getting something in the budget is better than not. A former OMB-er remarked, "If I were in an agency now, I'd die to be in the president's budget. Because if I had to go up on the Hill alone, I'd have to go through much greater hoops in the eighties and nineties than in the sixties." A budget officer explained, "There's competition among agencies. If we don't present what we think we want or need to OMB, we'll be cut out. If we ask, we might get something."

Technical Roles

Subjective evidence—the comments of budget officers, OMB staff, and appropriations clerks—leads me to conclude that OMB's contribution to administrative efficiency has diminished. The doubts themselves reduce OMB's role. Yet some credibility remains, best evidenced by the fact that OMB staff still get good jobs on the Hill and in the agencies. Agencies have OMB horror stories, but OMB has its own about the agencies. That is particularly true in the most contentious area, personnel, where agencies see OMB imposing limits with no rationale, and examiners see agencies keeping atrocious personnel records and continually putting staff in the wrong places (usually headquarters instead of the field).[57] OMB's current credibility problems sound a lot like the self-criticisms made in a 1967 BOB staff working paper: "Workload has expanded tremendously. . . . We're overwhelmed by pieces of paper and crises. . . . The examiner's job has become a production job. . . . Staff is called upon for judgments based on less and less program knowledge. . . . Employment ceilings are arbitrary in the extreme. . . . Cutbacks are sometimes made with too little analysis."[58] And Congress has never simply deferred to budget bureau expertise.[59] Therefore it seems most accurate to say that the burden of proof has changed; if OMB has a case, it can have influence, either by making it directly or because the agency feels it cannot justify the alternative. The system is receiving less good budget review, and the decline may feed on itself. As one budget officer put it, "When you get these irrational things from OMB, then you start to get from the agencies an attitude of 'why should *we* do it right?' " But OMB still makes some technical contribution, and nobody else has taken over that function.

On one aspect of technical budgeting, scorekeeping, OMB has staged a bit of a comeback. Through the early Stockman years, OMB's influence steadily declined amid accusations of biased estimates. Much of the conflict occurred on appropriations. The issue was outlay rates, the spending in a given budget year (and thus contribution to that year's deficit) caused by budget authority provided in a bill. Unfortunately, outlays are notoriously difficult to estimate. Appropriators believe estimating the unknowable is "unprofessional," and attempts to manipulate rates lead to short-sighted decisions such as buying aircraft carriers because they spend out slowly. The

Stockman era confirmed the appropriators' view, even to OMB's political officials at the time.[60]

Gramm–Rudman, however, made outlay *estimates* the central figures in budgeting. Congress appropriated budget authority (BA) but outlay estimates determined the sequester, which in turn determined the BA agencies received.[61] Whoever kept score, therefore, could determine the budgetary pressure on any program proposal.

Congress had no intention of giving OMB such power, and the original Gramm–Rudman required that OMB and CBO both make estimates for the deficit shortfall, to be averaged or overridden by the General Accounting Office (GAO). Before that system was overruled by the Supreme Court, the FY86 sequester had to be calculated. That meant estimating outlays account by account; OMB and CBO had four weeks to prepare the report; and in the words of one central OMB player, "Nobody had a clue what this monster was." With time so short and issues so technical, he explained, the professionals in both CBO and OMB took over: "The examiner and the CBO analyst would negotiate a number. . . . The political sides weren't involved; if they had been they couldn't have got it done." A CBO participant reports that "OMB and CBO focused on a professional level in a way nobody thought was possible. There was no political manipulation." The 1987 revisions then gave OMB authority to calculate the sequester, but required that it use CBO assumptions on outlay rates. "So in constructing the '89 budget we sat down with CBO and worked out the technical assumptions at the account level. . . . And that process continues, to try to eliminate classification and conceptual differences in the procedures." The best indicator of success is the fact that House Appropriations, which hates the whole idea of outlay scoring, (grudgingly) accepts the results; a senior aide even commented that "Gramm–Rudman's forced cooperation between CBO and OMB has taken care of a lot of the problems."

OMB is not dominant, but it is a full partner in the scorekeeping process. The various players (CBO, OMB, Budget, and Appropriations staff) will disagree, but all seem to respect each others' professionalism, and see a need to avoid "having to explain technical differences to members who don't care about them and don't want to hear it." There is enough agreement that when OMB was given more authority in the 1990 agreement, appropriations staff—unlike many congressional Democrats—were concerned.

OMB also is still in the best position to handle budget issues that cross agency boundaries, such as the drug war or global warming. It will be accused of imposing a policy bias. Yet in any interagency matter there are likely to be different perspectives, and resolution in the direction of the president's preferences, if he has any that apply, seems both justifiable and a normal fee for brokerage. In practice, such matters are those on which Congress itself is most likely to be divided, so there is a role for central leadership.

To summarize, the president's budget retains the following functions that may be of use to others as well as to the president. It influences fiscal policy by defining the year's level of gimmickry. It puts proposals, particularly new initiatives, on the policy agenda. It can take some blame for cuts, has a reduced role in technical budgeting, and can provide some coordination. How these functions are performed depends greatly on the director. Mr. Darman has had fewer crosscutting mandates than Mr. Miller, takes a stand on fewer issues in his letters, has a more positive governmental agenda (mostly research) as shown in the FY90 budget, and has had support when he made veto threats.

Beyond the director, how OMB performs its functions, particularly the more technical ones, varies from division to division and branch to branch. For an outsider, that is one of the most striking aspects about interviewing within the organization. A veteran civil servant summarized that "the only part of OMB with any organizational reality is the branch." These units of seven or so examiners recruit different kinds of people, have different attitudes toward agencies, and do different kinds of analysis. Some variation stems from the different policy domains: the Energy and Sciences division hires scientists; the Veterans branch has few outside sources of analysis (only the interested study the VA); the Income Maintenance branch pays less attention to administrative efficiency because there is so much more money in program rules. But many differences are branch traditions or personalities.

Branches share, however, some attitudes towards the presidency and OMB's place in it, which have powerful implications for the future of the president's budget.

The Paradox of Serving the Presidency

Our review of OMB's influence on budget decisions suggests that Congress' more clerical needs are still the basis of OMB's power. Budgeting for details is OMB's peculiar expertise, still widely recognized as its major contribution to the rest of the political system. "I tell my examiners," a branch chief contends, "if you think nobody cares about the statutory history, or the data on whether your fifty or sixty activities are needed, *I* care, and [the DAD] does." "Somebody somewhere must get into the pricing," a division chief explained. "That's a role OMB must maintain. . . . One function of OMB will always be to ensure the taxpayer gets services for the minimal amount of money." In NASA, "if they tell us that the development of mirrors for AXAF will be a piece of cake, is that something we can believe given past experience?" On credit programs, OMB tries to call attention to contingent liabilities. If we were to start from scratch, this analytical role would be the major reason for Congress to give the president his OMB staff, and they seek this role.

Setting an agenda, taking blame, and scrubbing details give the president influence because and to the extent that they help him play the broker role with Congress. Ironically, not even OMB staff (never mind presidents) seem to see that. Instead, they are oriented to the president alone; their major purpose is to help ensure that each agency is following administration policy. In the words of one DAD:

Basically, it is to get policies developed and implemented and ensure the departments conduct their activities in ways that are consistent with the president's policies. We look at the budget as just one of the tools. . . . We look at the budget but also have responsibility for legislation. We used to have sole responsibility for regulations. Those are the three stools for implementing policies. And if the president doesn't have a policy, we look at it as our job to get him to establish a policy.

Another DAD explained, "One thing I should be doing is asking, 'Have we looked at it in terms of the policy of this administration? Are we reflecting or reminding our peers or superiors?' . . . In the Bush administration that might be carried out as, if the policy is unclear, to get it clarified." A branch chief, restating my question, said, "What do we do? We review policies and budgets. We recommend improvements, either in terms of good government or the priorities of the president of the time. . . . And, this is the benign way to put it, we work with them to ensure it is carried out."

There is a dog barking here, but it has been barking so long that it is too easily ignored. Many have written on how, since its inception, the budget bureau's role has continually expanded beyond General Dawes' "routine business." More decisive was the shift in whom it was seen as serving. Jim Pfiffner gives a wonderful example. In the 1980s a career staffer explained: "We are all fed with stories about the beginning of this institution when the first director asserted that if the president said you have to shovel garbage on the front steps of the White House, you do it." Here is General Dawes' actual statement:

Much as we love the President, if Congress in its omnipotence over appropriations and in accordance with its authority over policy, passed a law that garbage should be put on the White House steps, it would be our regrettable duty, as a bureau, in an impartial, nonpolitical, and nonpartisan way to advise the Executive and Congress as to how the largest amount of garbage could be spread in the most expeditious and economical manner.[62]

It is natural that OMB is oriented overwhelmingly towards the president. As Larry Berman wrote of the Johnson years, the BOB became a "dumping ground for all sorts of Presidential problems that should have gone elsewhere . . . because its very existence depended on its responsiveness to Presidential demands (compared to needs)."[63] But that means the budgeting needs that it can serve may be subsumed to other activities.

Thus budgeting shaded into legislative clearance, first for financial matters and then for all legislation.[64] The development of legislative clearance was somewhat replicated two decades later in the evolution of regulatory clearance, now located in the Office of Information and Regulatory Affairs (OIRA). In each case there is an argument for coordination, but by now the assumed purpose of each process is to identify the executive branch with the president. We, as much as the president's staff, are used to hearing that the actions of the executive branch should reflect presidential policies. Yet that is not obvious at all. As an individual the president could hardly have preferences on most government activity. Nor could voters have selected a president on that basis. Nor, if that means policies are to be worked out by appointees, would those logically be OMB officials rather than the cabinet officers confirmed by the Senate who actually have to run programs.

In the case of clearance, the Legislative Reference Section is still in business, managing a flow of information and clearance "to ensure that the administration speaks with a single voice to Congress . . . formally." It even remains, in Ronald Moe's assessment, "one of the last bastions of 'neutral competence' even remotely near the President." But it is "no longer the haven for generalists aggressively pursuing the presumed institutional interests of the Presidency,"[65] mainly because the rest of OMB is taking a larger role *pursuing the supposed policy interests of the president*. In Legislative Reference, a veteran recalls, "The tradition was that our people would clear the bill to Congress, then the agency would work the Hill. We'd clear testimony, but there was an awful lot of stuff that OMB was not involved in. . . . That has completely changed. Both in our division and the examiners, we monitor the bill from the beginning to the end." But in that process the PADs and higher-ups now take the lead; more neutral coordination, to avoid conflict, is now a supplement to policy-oriented intervention.

The most obvious and controversial symbol of OMB's expanded involvement in policy-making is OIRA. Regulatory clearance arose in the early 1970s for the Environmental Protection Agency (EPA), justified in part as allowing review by other agencies. This was never as clear a need as legislative clearance, as there were established procedures, such as posting in the Federal Register, to inform outsiders of proposed regs. The process evolved to a separate office (OIRA) applying a "presidential" perspective on regulatory matters.[66] A veteran of the evolution recalled that "I always felt that we should have a regulatory review. . . . It just took twenty years to get it. . . . In my wildest imagination I never thought we'd end up with what we have now. I thought that politically we couldn't pull it off." For the Carter people it was more "a good government thing"; for Reagan's it was more a matter of having "a central control mechanism."

OIRA was accused of distorting data, delay for its own sake, giving regulated industries illegitimate access, and otherwise simply sabotaging agency regulations as part of the administration's bias against government activism.[67] The Supreme Court in 1990 would rule that OIRA had greatly exceeded its statutory authority.[68] At the peak of controversy in 1986, the office's funding was eliminated in the House version of its appropriations bill. Yet the real story, here, is OIRA's survival. Abuses are charged, but the function is essentially unquestioned—even though a case may be made that, when Congress delegates authority to an agency, the president has no direct authority to override its decisions, so OMB certainly does not.[69] OIRA's existence has been endorsed by the American Bar Association and the National Academy of Public Administration. As President Carter's chief domestic policy adviser proclaimed, "Several Presidents, Democratic and Republican, have institutionalized the concept."[70] This may partly be ascribed to concerns about overregulation, but strengthening the president is hardly the only possible response. Instead, OIRA is a prime example of the legitimation of the idea that the chief executive is supposed to run agencies, as opposed to taking care that the laws are faithfully executed.[71]

CONCLUSION: REFORM IS UNLIKELY GIVEN CURRENT CONSTITUTIONAL UNDERSTANDINGS

The centralization of budget negotiations within OMB is thus a logical extension of the presidentialization of the executive. That is not quite the same as the presidentialization of government, for the structure of law and custom surrounding the power of the purse still maintains congressional dominance. Forced to choose, a departmental budget officer explained, "I'll get crosswise with OMB. It's like Willie Sutton said, where the money is. OMB hasn't appropriated ten cents!" But the fact that the president will usually lose doesn't mean there is harm in trying. His attempts to control may be bad for others, but not necessarily for him. Once he starts from the presumptions that any agency independence is illegitimate and that he is at least Congress' equal, he would be derelict if he didn't fight for control with every weapon at his disposal. And Congress cannot object to the downgrading of agencies within the executive because "the bureaucracy" has no popular (and little elite) support. Instead it supports individual programs through its own budgetary routines. To the extent it cuts out the agencies, presidential budgeting makes them even more dependent on Congress.

What has the government, as opposed to the president or Congress, lost as a consequence of the alteration of the president's budget? To begin we should dismiss any notion that either the presidential or congressional process is a significant cause of our deficit difficulties. "The process is not the problem; the problem is the problem." We have big deficits because our policy commitments exceed our resources. Short of cutting large portions of the public out of the political system, so about $150 billion in policy change could be taken out of their hides, no process fix will eliminate the deficit. The deficit, and reactions to it, have badly damaged norms of analysis and procedure throughout the budgeting world. Ultimately the regularity of the budget schedule and integrity of decisions cannot be restored without eliminating either the deficit or the panic about it.[72]

Yet whatever budget system survives the deficit must involve a large presidential role. Congress cannot quite do without the president's budget. It might imitate his ability to adjust details to totals through extremely radical reform like the Obey proposal for an omnibus spending and revenue bill. But it still could not duplicate OMB's more technical functions of program-level analysis. If we care about how well our government runs, we should want those functions performed. Even those who care most about slashing spending should prefer that it be done in a way that maintains as much programmatic output as possible.

OMB examining staff mostly believe they can still play the technical role. Their neutrality is buffered from the outside by the political level of negotiators. They believe they can protect it on the inside by submitting series of options, so that the politicos have the analysis if they choose to use it. Preparing numbers to fit the political calls they consider just part of the job.

Yet they are doing less analysis, and in any case what they do is no more important than how Congress and the agencies interpret it. That in turn depends on the chief executive's sense of his place in the process. No future president is likely to be a contented clerk or broker. But there is something to be said for not picking fights and not making all decisions on the basis of a (minority!) ideology. On balance the Darman OMB shows signs of being a more constructive institution than the Miller OMB—assuming one doesn't share Miller's preferences. President Bush himself seems far more of a broker, as on Clean Air, than was Reagan.

The 1990 budget agreement reflects more reasonable assumptions about both budgeting and institutional roles than were common for the past decade. It is a truce among the leaders of the House, Senate, and executive, with which they are trying to restore some stability to the budgeting environment. Very quietly they abolished—or at least temporarily suspended—sequesters determined by the deficit, and thus binding deficit targets. Instead of trying to force action to reduce the deficit further, thereby forcing only fraud, the new rules seek merely to prevent program expansions or tax cuts. They therefore give the budgeteers procedural reinforcement for something they are used to doing—developing technical reasons not to do something new—instead of demanding that they attack the existing budgetary base, which has always been much more difficult.

In both its numbers and rules, the 1990 agreement is the return of the appropriators to center stage. They get a small increase in domestic discretionary spending, and protection from failures of either the economy or the budget process. The rules are essentially a deal between OMB Director Darman and Senate Appropriations Chairman Byrd. So it is described in my interviews; more tellingly, it was treated as such on the Senate floor, where Byrd—not Majority Leader Mitchell or Budget Committee Chairman

Sasser—both explained and invoked his personal prestige on behalf of the enforcement provisions. Appropriations staff widely view the agreement as a victory for sensible budgeting, damping the deficit demands and priority conflicts that have distorted their own work and devastated OMB's credibility over the past decade. Accepting the status quo on discretionary domestic spending means OMB will no longer feel impelled to propose cuts that fail the laugh test. And while Darman has other reasons for doing the deal— most important, getting the deficit under political and economic control— he is also more interested than his predecessors in managing, not transforming, the government.

Thus there seems some prospect for reform from within. On balance, however, the temporary trend toward moderation seems unlikely to overcome the dominance of a president-centered understanding of the executive branch. As Jim Pfiffner's story suggests, it is too deeply imbedded in our institutional culture. Instead, we have reached an ironic position.

The congressional budget was invented as a half-baked imitation of the executive process. Given the current disincentives for agenda-setting, and relative disinterest in details, the published executive budget looks more and more like the formal congressional process. Each has some influence upon, but hardly determines, the real budget. The latter is fought out between congressional barons and presidential staff in the year's appropriations and reconciliation. The budget is probably less of a constitutional problem than in the Nixon years, because Congress is fully equipped to reject the president. Unfortunately, institutional warfare is a miserable way to plan the allocation of resources.

From a process that would help both Congress and the president oversee executive agencies, ensuring efficiency and accountability, the president's budget has been transformed into a weapon in the president's war with Congress for control of those agencies. The agencies, once players in a process that created a "work plan" for their activities, are now not so much participants as the battleground.

Congress seems unlikely ever to agree that the president's budget should give him control of the agencies. Presidents are unlikely to back off. In the resulting standoff some of the traditional budget functions will still be performed, as they were in the late 1980s. Yet they will be performed poorly, and no one is likely to be satisfied.

NOTES

Most of the unattributed quotes in this chapter are from interviews done in 1989 and 1990 with twenty-two present and former OMB staff and eleven departmental or agency budget officers. The analysis is informed, however, by the work, including interviews with executive branch and especially congressional budgeteers, done for *The Deficit and the Public Interest: The Search for Responsible Budgeting in the*

1980s (Berkeley and New York: University of California Press and Russell Sage Foundation, 1989), which I coauthored with Aaron Wildavsky, and my own forth-coming book on the appropriations process. I am grateful for their assistance; neither they nor the Brookings Institution has any connection with the judgments, never mind the errors, made herein.

1. Jeffrey L. Sheler, "Budget Skirmishing Begins," *U.S. News and World Report*, February 3, 1986, pp. 20–21.

2. These examples are taken from White and Wildavsky, *The Deficit and the Public Interest*.

3. The name of the annual Brookings Institution studies, produced from 1970 (FY71) through 1983, various editors.

4. The formulation used by W. F. Willoughby, quoted in Frederick C. Mosher, *A Tale of Two Agencies: A Comparative Analysis of the General Accounting Office and the Office of Management and Budget* (Baton Rouge: Louisiana State University Press, 1984), 21 n.6.

5. "Its money estimates and legislative program are the nearest things available to an agenda for [the] struggle over scope and shape of government." Richard Neus-tadt, *Presidential Power: The Politics of Leadership from FDR to Carter* (New York: John Wiley & Sons, 1980), 83.

6. Naomi Caiden, "Paradox, Ambiguity, and Enigma: The Strange Case of the Executive Budget and the United States Constitution," *Public Administration Review* 47, no. 1 (Jan./Feb. 1987): 84.

7. Quoted in Mosher, *A Tale of Two Agencies*, 42.

8. Richard E. Neustadt, "Presidency and Legislation: The Growth of Central Clearance," *American Political Science Review* 48, no. 3 (Sept. 1954): 641–71.

9. See Allen Schick's description of the evolution of budgeting in "The Road to PPB," *Public Administration Review* 26, no. 4 (Dec. 1966): 243–58. On administrative management, see Donald C. Stone, "Administrative Management: Reflections on Origins and Accomplishments," *Public Administration Review* 50, no. 1 (Jan./Feb. 1990): 3–20.

10. I discuss this at length in "The Two-Faced Profession," forthcoming in *Public Budgeting & Finance*.

11. The same argument is made for appropriations hearings.

12. See Mark S. Kamlet and David C. Mowery, "The Budgetary Base in Federal Resource Allocation," *American Journal of Political Science* 21, no. 4 (Nov. 1980): 804–21; also John P. Crecine, M. S. Kamlet, D. C. Mowery and M. Winer, "The Role of the Office of Management and Budget in Executive Branch Budgetary De-cision-Making," in *Proceedings of the First Annual Research Conference on Public Policy and Management*, edited by J. P. Crecine (Greenwich, Conn.: JAI Press, 1980).

13. See Joseph White, "What Budgeting Cannot Do: Lessons of Reagan's and Other Years," in *New Directions in Budget Theory*, edited by Irene S. Rubin (Albany: State University of New York Press, 1988).

14. Balance is defined as a particular task in Irene S. Rubin, *The Politics of Public Budgeting* (Chatham, N.J.: Chatham House, 1990).

15. Richard E. Neustadt, *Presidential Power*, 83.

16. Ibid.

17. See Gary Orfield, *Congressional Power: Congress and Social Change* (New York: Harcourt, Brace, Jovanovich, 1975).

18. See Joseph White, "What Budgeting Cannot Do," 180–88. Also Joseph White, *The Functions and Power of the House Appropriations Committee* (Ph.D. diss., University of California, Berkeley, 1989); Richard E. Fenno, Jr. *The Power of the Purse: Appropriations Politics in Congress* (Boston: Little, Brown, 1966); and Aaron Wildavsky, *The Politics of the Budgetary Process* (Boston: Little, Brown, 1964). For the collapse of the system from 1966 on, see chapter 1 of Allen Schick, *Congress and Money* (Washington, D.C.: Urban Institute, 1980).

19. See especially Crecine et al., "The Role of the Office of Management and Budget."

20. In FY 1962 spending essentially uncontrollable by the appropriations process was a third of the total. By FY 1974 it was half, and by FY 1989 it would be nearly three-fifths. Calculations from Congressional Budget Office, *The Economic and Budget Outlook: Fiscal Years 1991–1995* (Washington, D.C.: U.S. GPO, January 1990), Table E–5. Note that this calculation compares to the total without subtracting offsetting receipts, not the "total" column in the table. However one does the figures, the trend is a commonplace.

21. Efficiency was problematic simply because it was a *different* competence than political logic; therefore, to the extent that the president let his Budget Bureau apply it, it might lead to conflict with the legislature even if he did not intend as much. For a prescient discussion, see Aaron Wildavsky, "The Political Economy of Efficiency: Cost-Benefit Analysis, Systems Analysis, and Program Budgeting," *Public Administration Review* (Dec. 1966): 292–310. The problem was quite evident in legislative response to PPB; see White, "What Budgeting Cannot Do," 187–88; Allen Schick, "A Death in the Bureaucracy: The Demise of Federal PPB," *Public Administration Review* 33, no. 2, (Mar./Apr. 1973): 146–56.

22. Larry Berman, *The Office of Management and Budget and the Presidency, 1921–1979* (Princeton: Princeton University Press, 1979). Most of the description that follows is based on chapters four and five.

23. Congressmen feared BOB would usurp operational responsibility. See ibid., 81–85.

24. Ibid., 112. For an overview of the entire issue, see Peter M. Benda and Charles H. Levine, "OMB's Management Role: Issues of Structure and Strategy," in United States Senate, Committee on Governmental Affairs, *Office of Management and Budget: Evolving Roles and Future Issues* (99th Congress, Second Session, S. Prt. 99–134), especially pp. 88–105.

25. The title of a Fred Malek memo dated March 17, 1972. Quoted in Berman, *The Office of Management*, 119.

26. Richard Nathan, *The Administrative Presidency* (New York: John Wiley and Sons, 1983), 45.

27. "Management By Objectives," publicized in terms of rationality, was another attempt to centralize policy control in OMB. Both MBO and the PADs are widely condemned; See Berman, *The Office of Management*, 118–20; Benda and Levine, "OMB's Management Role," 101–05; Mosher, *A Tale of Two Agencies*, 112–14. We should add that bureau staff had long been concerned that their advice might be politically naive, so there was an argument for putting more political skill in OMB—but not in line positions.

28. Quotes Berman, *The Office of Management*, 121, 123.

29. Mosher, *A Tale of Two Agencies*, 131. Berman, 123, provides a page of examples.

30. See Allen Schick, *Congress and Money*; for a summary see White and Wildavsky, *The Deficit and the Public Interest*, 15–17.

31. The literature about the budget process is vast. My conclusions are based on my own research for previous citations, best summarized in "What Budgeting Cannot Do." See also Allen Schick's cited works and his "The Whole and the Parts: Piecemeal and Integrated Approaches to Congressional Budgeting," U.S. House of Representatives Committee on the Budget, print CP–3, February 1987; Joel Havemann, *Congress and the Budget* (Bloomington: Indiana University Press, 1978); Robert D. Reischauer, "The Congressional Budget Process," in *Federal Budget Policy in the 1980s*, edited by Gregory B. Mills and John L. Palmer (Washington, D.C.: Urban Institute, 1984); and the statement of Rep. David Obey in U.S. House of Representatives, Committee on Rules, *Congressional Budget Process* (Hearings, 97th Congress 2nd session, Part 1), 229–51.

32. The agencies, if they otherwise expected increases, also had no reason to be helpful.

33. Timothy J. Muris, "The Uses and Abuses of Budget Baselines," Hoover Institution Working Papers in Political Science, P–89–3, January 1989, 69–70. See also Roy T. Meyers, *Microbudgetary Strategies and Competition* (Ph.D. diss., University of Michigan, 1988).

34. For an extensive discussion of blame avoidance in entitlement politics, see R. Kent Weaver, *Automatic Government: The Politics of Indexation* (Washington, D.C.: The Brookings Institution, 1988).

35. Each side tried to stick the other with blame for an oil import fee. See White and Wildavsky, *The Deficit*, 32, 51–52. On the 1980 panic and negotiations, see chapter 2. For comments and citations on the organizational significance, see Virginia A. McMurtry, "Budget Process: OMB's Role in the Federal Budget Process," in U.S. Senate, Committee on Governmental Affairs, *Office of Management and Budget*, 38–41. Even given different circumstances, contrast this process with President Eisenhower's remaking of his own budget in 1957, described in Neustadt, *Presidential Power*, 50–53.

36. In the Senate, sending a bill to the floor inherently opens it to amendments, so once any reconciliation is there, a noncomplying committee is vulnerable. In the House, amendments depend on the rule written by the Rules Committee, which means the House leadership. Thus reconciliation is enforceable to the extent House leaders desire: it enhances their power relative to authorizing chairs. The central position of Rules was shown in disputes over civil service pensions in 1980 and 1982. See also U.S. Congress, House, Committee on the Budget, *A Review of the Reconciliation Process* (Committee Print, October 1984), 58–59.

37. Reconciliation also gave OMB far greater incentive to devote resources to analysis of entitlement programs, especially in the Health and Income Maintenance Division.

38. The most thorough is Hugh Heclo, "Executive Budget Making," in *Federal Budget Policy in the 1980s*, edited by Gregory B. Mills and John L. Palmer (Washington, D.C.: Urban Institute, 1984), 255–91. See also McMurtry, "Budget Process"; Barry Bozeman and Jeffrey Straussman, "Shrinking Budgets and the Shrinkage of

Budget Theory," *Public Administration Review* 42, no. 6 (Nov./Dec. 1982): 509–15; Bruce E. Johnson, "From Analyst to Negotiator: The OMB's New Role," *Journal of Policy Analysis and Management* 3 (Summer 1984): 501–15, and "OMB and the Budget Examiner: Changes in the Reagan Era," *Public Budgeting and Finance* 8, no. 4 (Winter 1988): 3–15; David G. Mathiasen, "Recent Developments in the Composition and the Formulation of the United States Federal Budget," *Public Budgeting and Finance* 3, no. 3 (Autumn 1983): 103–15, and "The Evolution of the Office of Management and Budget Under President Reagan," *Public Budgeting and Finance* 8, no. 3 (Autumn 1988): 3–14; James P. Pfiffner, "OMB: Professionalism, Politicization, and the Presidency" (Conference paper, Georgetown University, Dec. 1988); Irene S. Rubin, "Budget Theory and Budget Practice: How Good the Fit?" *Public Administration and Review* 50, no. 2 (March/April 1990): 179–89; Allen Schick, "The Budget As an Instrument of Presidential Policy," in *The Reagan Presidency and the Governing of America*, edited by Lester M. Salamon and Michael S. Lund, (Washington, D.C: Urban Institute, 1985), 91–125.

39. Virtually every OMB interviewee could cite cases of agencies not liking their budgets, and they felt that was to be expected. "The fact that the assistant secretary fights for major reductions for loans in rural housing at all," said one in a typical comment, "I find amazing."

40. For extensive discussion see Joseph White, *The Functions and Power*, 90–95, 456–91. CBMS also had nowhere near the error prevention capacity of the old budget preparation system, which had extensive internal checks.

41. See McMurtry, "Budget Process," 46; also my interviews. Some DADs were more likely than others to have their people deal with the Hill on back channels in an advocacy role; but even they were cautious about doing so, and in most divisions examiner involvement with the Hill was indirect.

42. This account is based on interviews with both subcommittee members and staff. The tactic is general; every guardian does it to every claimant, and much of the rationale for complex budget processes is that they serve as a sieve to force the only people who really know what is going on, the agencies, to prioritize.

43. In one well-noticed case, a branch chief, believing some testimony was inaccurate, altered the transcript rather than submitting a "correction for the record." The committee banned that branch from reviewing transcript ever again, and nobody whom I interviewed thought resistance made much sense.

44. See the data in White, *The Functions and Power*, chapter 5.

45. If it ever worked well, it was by having impressively talented staff of wide experience who responded to agencies looking for help. Any social scientist could look at the names cited in Donald C. Stone, "Administrative Management," and be impressed. Among others were Marver Bernstein, V. O. Key, Avery Leiserson, Richard Neustadt, Harold Seidman, James Sundquist and Dwight Waldo! For the fads of the 1970s, see Allen Schick, "The Budget As An Instrument," 121–22, and add reorganization.

46. It included ten objectives: to upgrade cash management, to increase debt collection, to sell more surplus property, to strengthen internal accounting, to identify unliquidated obligations, to recover funds owed to agencies, to reduce personnel, to limit wasteful spending on informational items, to save money through procurement reform (especially contracting out, the A–76 process), and to reduce government paperwork—reducing costs to other organizations. See Benda and Levine, "OMB's

Management Role," 122–31. Also see Chester A. Newland, "Executive Office Policy Apparatus: Enforcing the Reagan Agenda," in Salamon and Lund, *The Reagan Presidency*, 165–67.

47. Carter's budget; Reagan's first revisions; the Gramm–Latta 2 negotiations; the September 24 revisions; and the final formula cut.

48. A DOA Budget; the Gang of 17; Reagan with Senate Republicans; four different supplementals; TEFRA; the lame-duck session with its transportation bill and massive continuing resolution.

49. On Gramm–Rudman in principle and operation, see White and Wildavsky, *The Deficit*, chapters 9, 21, 23. For a more pointed statement of the case, see Joseph White, "Deceit on the Deficit," *Newsday*, November 26, 1989, "Ideas" section, pp. 1, 6–7. I have put some of this description into the past tense, because the 1990 agreement in a rather sneaky manner eliminated, through FY93 and at the president's discretion through FY95, the deficit-related sequester. Yet the fact that negotiators did not feel able to repeal the sequester directly, and spiraling deficits in early 1991, suggest that the law's perversities might describe budgeting's future as well as its past.

50. We might add, however, that the smoke and mirrors are so widely publicized, especially by their perpetrators, that they have more effect on the self-respect of our governors than on the governed's ability to see what is going on. The budget with all the gimmicks is very hard to follow. But it is hard to follow without the gimmicks; if anything, the gimmicks are so widely publicized that they should be the easiest part to understand.

51. See Joseph White, "A Crazy Way to Govern?" *Brookings Review* (Summer 1988).

52. See the statement of Rep. Lee Hamilton in *Congressional Record* for May 3, 1989, pp. H1553–56.

53. David Wessel and Gerald F. Seib, "White House Says It's Sincere On Deficit Talks," *Wall Street Journal*, May 14, 1990, p. A3.

54. I am privy to no statistics on turnover, but an increase is widely perceived by both OMB and agency staff. Contrary to some impressions, there is very little evidence of politicization of the examining staff. Nor do the branch chiefs and DADs (who do the hiring) report difficulty finding bright people. The challenge was keeping them.

55. Congressional Budget Office, *Supplemental Appropriations in the 1980s*, CBO Study, February 1990.

56. See chapter 6 in Allen Schick, *The Capacity to Budget* (Washington, D.C.: Urban Institute, 1990).

57. I could write a short article filled with quotes from both sides about personnel; this one is already too long for that discussion.

58. Quoted in Larry Berman, *The Office of Management and Budget*, 95–96.

59. See Richard F. Fenno, Jr., *The Power of the Purse*, 101–102.

60. For background on BA/outlay trade-offs in budgetmarking, see David C. Mowery and Mark S. Kamlet, "Games Presidents Do and Do Not Play: Presidential Circumvention of the Executive Branch Budget Process," *Policy Sciences* (1984): 303–27. For the 1980s, see White and Wildavsky, *The Deficit and the Public Interest*.

61. The House rejected outlay scoring in points of order for Gramm–Rudman enforcement, while the Senate adopted it—a consequence of the greater strength

of appropriators in the House. But the need to avoid sequester, as well as pressure from factions on the floor, forced extremely reluctant House appropriators to adopt the outlay focus in writing bills. "We've known for a long time it was coming," a senior staffer remarked, "and it finally came. The tail wagging the dog." Actual outlays, of course, matter no more than actual deficits. That's last year!

62. See Pfiffner, "OMB: Professionalism," 2 n.5.

63. Berman, *The Office of Management and Budget*, 74.

64. Richard E. Neustadt, "Presidency and Legislation: The Growth of Central Clearance," *American Political Science Review* 48, no. 3 (September 1954): 641–71.

65. Ronald C. Moe, "Legislative Clearance: Central Legislative Clearance" in U.S. Senate Committee on Governmental Affairs, *Office of Management and Budget*, 182.

66. For a history, see Morton Rosenberg, "Regulatory Management at OMB," in Senate Committee on Governmental Affairs, *Office of Management and Budget*, 197–219 in particular. See also U.S. Senate Committee on Governmental Affairs, Hearings, *Reauthorization of OMB's Office of Information and Regulatory Affairs*, 101st Congress, 2nd session.

67. Rosenberg, "Regulatory Management," 213–28. Also Margaret E. Kriz, "Kibitzer with Clout," *National Journal*, May 30, 1987, pp. 1404–408.

68. *Dole vs. United Steelworkers*, decided 2/21/90, reproduced in OIRA Reauthorization hearing.

69. Rosenberg, "Regulatory Management," 224–27.

70. Margaret E. Kriz, "Kibitzer With Clout," 1408, 1406.

71. For an analysis of the trend that makes the same point that it is much more deeply entrenched than the Reagan administration, but claims it is necessary and useful, see Terry M. Moe, "The Politicized Presidency," in *The New Direction in American Politics*, edited by John E. Chubb and Paul E. Peterson (Washington, D.C.: The Brookings Institution, 1985).

72. Allen Schick blames process more, but only in the sense that entitlements reduce the capacity to budget; he argues strongly that at present "no reform will cure budgeting's ills until substantial progress is made in reducing the deficit." See *The Capacity to Budget*, 198ff.

2

COORDINATION OF BUDGETING

RALPH BLEDSOE

When President Ronald Reagan literally dropped the forty-three-pound 1989 budget of the U.S. government on the podium of the House of Representatives during his January 1988 State of the Union speech, he was sending a message to Congress and the American people. He was fed up with a cumbersome budget process that resulted in presidential budgets being largely ignored by the legislative branch and annually labeled "dead on arrival." But, Reagan was not so concerned with the political nature of the president's budget.

Reagan objected to the ever-increasing time spent haggling over the components of the annual federal budget and the extensive congressional use of the continuing resolution (CR). The latter is used by Congress to extend its self-imposed deadlines for appropriating funds beyond the beginning of a new fiscal year. Commonly Congress enacted one or more of the thirteen appropriations bills beyond the October 1 beginning of the federal government's fiscal year. Late in 1986, for the first time, Congress passed a CR encompassing the entire fiscal year 1988 budget. Not only was this repeated in 1987, but it was passed just a few days before Christmas when it should have been passed months earlier. President Reagan had enough.

A CR, in its simplest form, directs federal government departments and agencies to continue spending for the resolution period at the same rate they were spending in the previous budget period. However, other instructions for departments and agencies are also often included.[1]

There was a redeeming feature of the fiscal year 1989 CR fiasco. A simultaneous agreement, made during a budget summit between the administration and Congress, was reached on guidelines for the subsequent year's fiscal year 1990 spending. This helped the president and members of Congress achieve rapid agreement on the features of the general budget for 1990 in early 1988 and released them for early campaigning in the 1988 elections. Even with this, however, the congressional leadership stalled some of the spending bills right up to the time of adjournment in October 1988, barely a month before the elections.

In the fall of 1990, the U.S. government again approached a deadlock between the president and Congress over the the president's budget that had been submitted the previous February. Having learned from previous interactions the difficulties that were facing them, Members of Congress and the White House staff entered into a "budget summit" earlier than usual. Memberships of the negotiating parties, the strategies, the procedures, the timetables, and other factors critical to reaching some kind of agreement were all on the table, and all were played out in the press in a highly political climate.

The political activity surrounding preparation of the budget adds increased tension to the processes of budgeting in the Congress, the White House, the departments, the agencies and the Office of Management and Budget (OMB).[2] Politics affects the timing of budget and deadlines and submittals; the workload of the men and women who labor in the budgeting vineyards checking figures, performing analyses, budget justifications, and various levels of spending; and generally affects the budget proposals submitted to the president and Congress.

As a National Academy of Public Administration research paper on "Reforming Federal Budget and Financial Management Systems" concluded, the president is "confronted with unprecedented federal budgetary problems":

1. The budget has grown 500 percent in twenty-five years.
2. In all but three of the last twenty-five years, the budget has been in serious deficit; these deficits have proven to be permanent and structural, and there is no political consensus on how deficits can be eliminated.
3. The total public debt has increased 600 percent in twenty years; in the last seven years alone, more than one trillion dollars have been added to that debt.
4. The budget has become more "locked in"—political leaders have less real discretion and far fewer policy options than they had even ten years ago.
5. More than 85 percent of federal spending is now virtually "untouchable": entitlements, commitments for national defense, other mandatory spending, and interest on the national debt.

The report concludes:

In this dangerous fiscal environment, the president and the Congress must take a new, hard look at past budget policies and practices. Budgets have increasingly become an allocation of *scarcity*, and budget cutting has proved too tough for politicians to face up to. Political motives to meet client needs or solve problems produce an unbeatable bias toward higher spending—and nobody knows how to control this bias.

The political "iron triangle" (congressional committees, strong assertive clients and constituents, and protective agencies of government) continues to exert a powerful inertia against even reasonable budget constraint and trimming.[3]

Executive and congressional budgeting is now a year-round process. The people in both branches who put together a budget once had a brief respite when a budget was "put to bed." No longer is that true. When Congress is still fiddling in October, or November, or even December, with a president's budget that was submitted the previous February it means that departments and agencies and congressional staff members are still working on a budget first submitted to OMB more than a year prior to that time. Most departments and agencies submit their initial budget proposals to OMB in September or October for the president's budget to be presented to Congress in February and for the fiscal year that would begin the next year October 1.

Budget professionals are often working on three and possibly even four fiscal year budgets at the same time. Departments and agencies ordinarily complete their analysis of a budget year just ended, make daily decisions about the budget year they are in, deal with OMB on proposals submitted for the president's budget for the next year, and begin preparation budget recommendations to be submitted for the next cycle. For a person involved in executive branch budgeting, this makes for a very active work day, work week, and work year. And with the major changes that emerged from the fall 1990 summit, OMB and CBO will be required to provide at least four kinds of sequester reports, addressing cutbacks that will be necessary because of spending targets being exceeded.[4] This will extend the workload even more. (See Table 2.1 for the Budget Enforcement Act timetable.)

ORGANIZATION OF THE BUDGET PROCESS

There are three broad steps in coordination of the budgeting process: formulation, legislative approval, and execution. Although these are separate and distinct activities, for all practicality they become simultaneous and continuing activities. (See Figure 2.1.)

Budget Formulation: OMB

The formulation of an executive budget begins well in advance of the beginning of the fiscal year to which it pertains, usually more than eighteen

Table 2.1
Budget Enforcement Act Timetable

Date	Action to be Completed
January 21	Notification regarding optional adjustment to maximum deficit amount
5 days before the president's budget transmittal	CBO sequester preview report
The president's budget transmittal	OMB sequester preview report
August 10	Notification regarding military personnel
August 15	CBO sequester update report
August 20	OMB sequester update report
10 days after end of session	CBO final sequester report
15 days after end of session	OMB final sequester report; presidential order
30 days later	GAO compliance report
End of session to July	Within session reports; presidential order
5 days after the start of the next session	Notification regarding flexibility among defense programs, projects, and activities

months prior. (See Figure 2.2.) The Office of Management and Budget formally triggers the executive budget process with its development of economic assumptions and forecasts about international and domestic events and situations. These are discussed with the president and his economic advisors, notably the Council of Economic Advisors and the secretary of the treasury. Preliminary policy guidance and budget projections are prepared by budget examiners at OMB for a so-called "spring review." Since "out year" budget projections for the target fiscal year have been included in previously submitted budgets, these are sometimes used as a starting point. The departments and agencies review their current operating programs and processes and provide OMB with initial projections about their needs for the target year.

OMB uses this information to prepare its revenue estimates and fiscal policy options. These estimates and policy options are discussed with the president. His decisions are provided to the departments and agencies as government-wide guidelines, planning assumptions, and targets. Simultaneously, OMB issues technical instructions to departments and agencies on formats for budget submissions. OMB works with the departments and agencies throughout the spring and summer to help them prepare their budget proposals.

Figure 2.1
Major Steps in the Budget Process

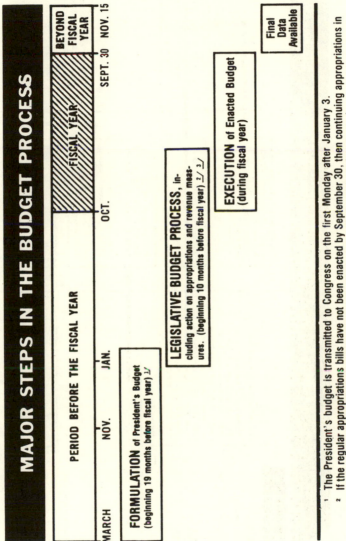

MAJOR STEPS IN THE BUDGET PROCESS

PERIOD BEFORE THE FISCAL YEAR	FISCAL YEAR	BEYOND FISCAL YEAR
MARCH NOV. JAN.	OCT. SEPT. 30	NOV. 15

FORMULATION of President's Budget
(beginning 19 months before fiscal year) [1]

LEGISLATIVE BUDGET PROCESS, including action on appropriations and revenue measures. (beginning 10 months before fiscal year) [2] [3]

EXECUTION of Enacted Budget
(during fiscal year)

Final Data Available

[1] The President's budget is transmitted to Congress on the first Monday after January 3.
[2] If the regular appropriations bills have not been enacted by September 30, then continuing appropriations in a joint resolution (commonly known as a continuing resolution) needs to be enacted.
[3] If the maximum deficit amount (M.D.A.) established in Section 251 of the Balanced Budget and Emergency Deficit Control Act of 1985 (P.L. 99-177) is exceeded, a budget reduction (i.e., sequestration) is calculated and may be executed by legislation.

Executive Office of the President/Office of Management and Budget

MAY 1988

Figure 2.2
Formulation of President's Budget

FORMULATION OF PRESIDENT'S BUDGET

APPROXIMATE TIMING

	AGENCY	OFFICE OF MANAGEMENT AND BUDGET	THE PRESIDENT

BUDGET POLICY DEVELOPMENT

MARCH
(or earlier in some agencies)

Reviews current operations, program objectives, issues, and future plans in relation to upcoming annual budget. Submits to the Office of Management and Budget projections of requirements that reflect current operations and future plans, supporting memoranda and related analytic studies that identify major issues, alternatives for resolving issues, and comparisons of costs and effectiveness.

Develops economic assumptions. Obtains forecasts of international and domestic situations. Prepares fiscal projections.

Discusses budgetary outlook and policies with the Director of the Office of Management and Budget. Council of Economic Advisers, and with the Cabinet as appropriate.

**APRIL
MAY**

Issues policy guidance on material to be developed for Spring planning review.

Discusses program developments and management issues, and resulting budgetary effects, with agencies.

MAY

Compiles total outlay estimates for comparison with revenue estimates. Develops recommendations for President on fiscal policy, program issues, and budget levels

Discusses with the Director of the Office of Management and Budget and others as necessary, general budget policy, major program issues, budgetary planning targets, and projections.

Establishes general guidelines and agency planning targets for annual budget.

JUNE

Issues internal instructions on preparation of annual budget estimates.

Issues technical instructions for preparation of annual budget estimates.

COMPILATION AND SUBMISSION OF AGENCY ESTIMATES

Conveys President's decisions to agency heads on Government wide policies and assumptions, the application of policies, and budgetary planning targets to individual agencies.

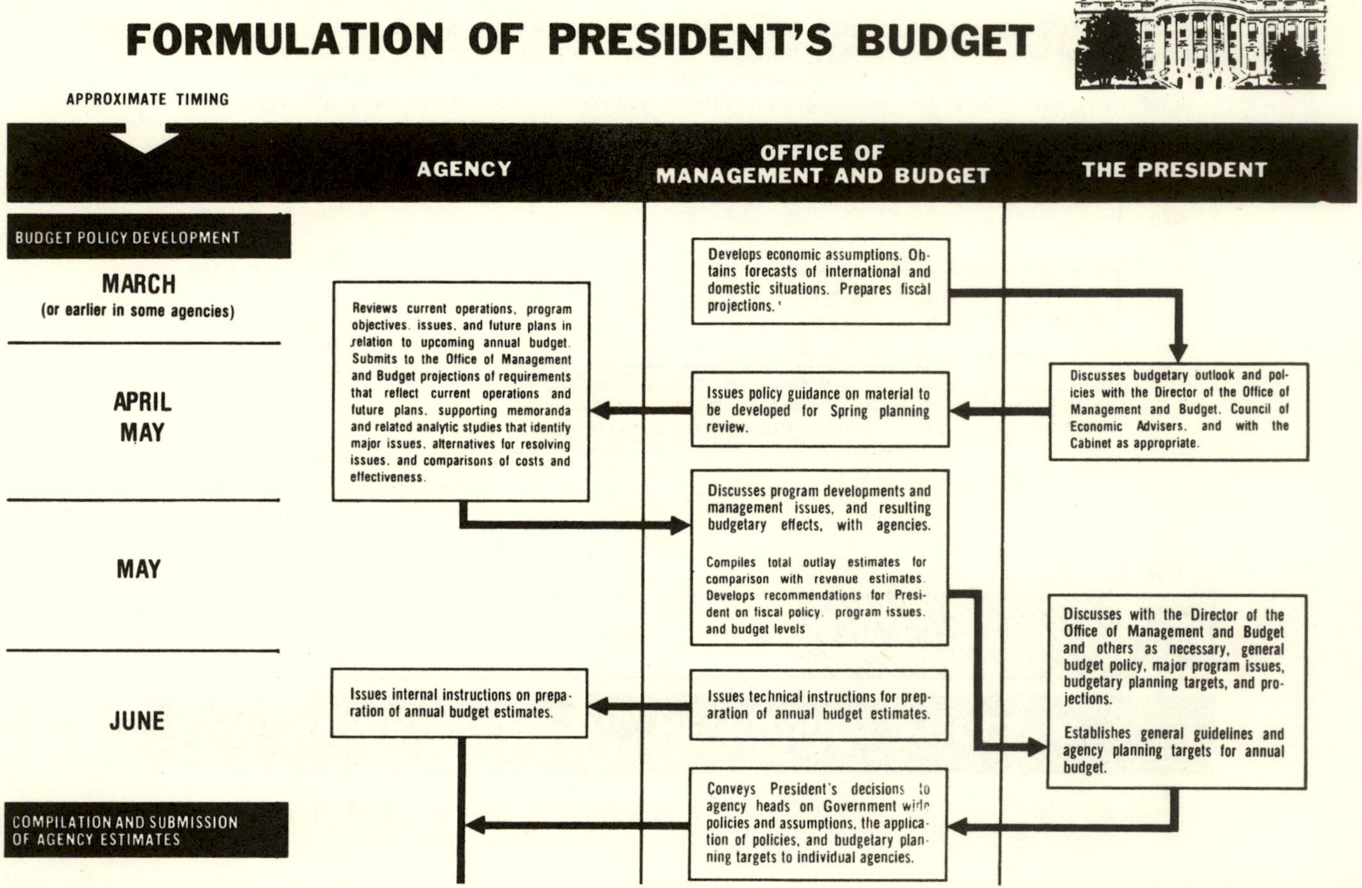

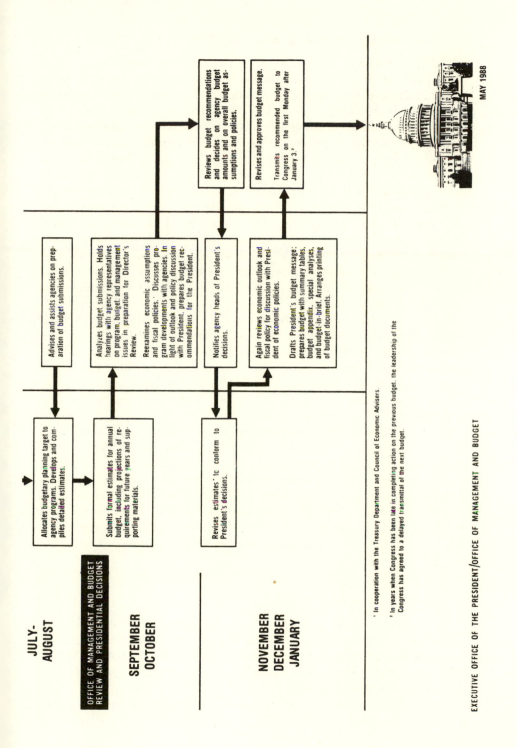

JULY-AUGUST

OFFICE OF MANAGEMENT AND BUDGET REVIEW AND PRESIDENTIAL DECISIONS

SEPTEMBER OCTOBER

NOVEMBER DECEMBER JANUARY

Advises and assists agencies on preparation of budget submissions.

Allocates budgetary planning target to agency programs. Develops and compiles detailed estimates.

Analyzes budget submissions. Holds hearings with agency representatives on program, budget, and management issues in preparation for Director's Review.

Reexamines economic assumptions and fiscal policies. Discusses program developments with agencies. In light of outlook and policy discussion with President, prepares budget recommendations for the President.

Submits formal estimates for annual budget, including projections of requirements for future years and supporting materials.

Reviews budget recommendations and decides on agency budget amounts and on overall budget assumptions and policies.

Notifies agency heads of President's decisions.

Revises estimates to conform to President's decisions.

Revises and approves budget message. Transmits recommended budget to Congress on the first Monday after January 3.²

Again reviews economic outlook and fiscal policy for discussion with President of economic policies.

Drafts President's budget message; prepares budget with summary tables, budget appendix, special analyses, and budget-in-brief. Arranges printing of budget documents.

¹ In cooperation with the Treasury Department and Council of Economic Advisers.

² In years when Congress has been late in completing action on the previous budget, the leadership of the Congress has agreed to a delayed transmittal of the next budget.

MAY 1988

EXECUTIVE OFFICE OF THE PRESIDENT/OFFICE OF MANAGEMENT AND BUDGET

Federal Departments and Agencies' Activities

Within departments and agencies, budget staff members use the OMB policy guidance and subsequent instructions as the basis for their more specific guidelines to program line managers. These may cover deadlines and formats for budget proposals. Usually budget proposals are submitted to department and agency budget staffs fifteen to sixteen months prior to the beginning of the target year. This is necessary so that cabinet department secretaries, agency directors, and other key administrators have ample time to review their proposals prior to sending them to OMB. They are due approximately twelve to thirteen months before the beginning of the fiscal year. This is when strategies and analyses for supporting budget projections are developed by the chief executives of the departments and agencies.

This part of the process has become burdened with paperwork and procedures. Departmental and agency strategies and analyses are often more focused on the process for obtaining the funds needed for the programs than on the means for carrying out the programs once the funds are appropriated.

The precise budget formulation process for departments and agencies is usually designed by the budget director, following OMB guidance. The schedule calls for budget submittals to be prepared early enough for cabinet secretaries, agency administrators, and directors to review them and discuss changes with other policy-level officials. Some then meet simultaneously with all their program managers, while others work one-on-one with policy-level officials and program managers.

In some instances, there are so-called "mock" budget reviews prior to a department or agency budget being submitted. These might include OMB budget examiners and department or agency budget officials and program managers. At these reviews the budget proposals are discussed, and suggestions are made about changes that might be considered. Signals are sent to each side about positions on proposals that will be taken in the later budget interactions. Many departments and agencies hold these mock hearings to refine their strategies for presenting budget proposals and analyses to OMB.

OMB Budget Examination

After a department or agency budget is submitted to OMB, budget examiners in OMB review the submittals and prepare a budget review document for the director. It identifies the primary issues and potential policy differences, especially "budget-buster" items. Hearings are held with agencies on their budget proposals.[5]

After one or more review sessions on each department's or agency's budget submittals, the OMB director returns a "budget mark" to the department or agency, along with explanations of what is being accepted and rejected. This normally sets in motion another series of negotiation sessions between OMB and agencies. In some years the previous guidance by the OMB director or the president strongly advises the department or agency head against the use of that procedure. However, this appeal process, usually called a "reclama," is sometimes planned for and well organized.

Appeals

A small appeals group may be established in the White House to hear department and agency arguments and make recommendations to the president. The final step might include an opportunity for the cabinet member or agency administrator or director to make a personal appeal to the president. However, many cabinet members will choose not to appeal to the president, because they are generally satisfied with their treatment by OMB or they feel their case is futile, given budget constraints. Strategically they may wish to let Congress do their appeals work for them in subsequent congressional budget hearings. Regardless, when the appeals process has been exhausted, the department or agency head is notified of the president's decisions, and the budget formulation goes "underground." This simply means that, within OMB and the White House, decisions must be made to meet targets set by the president, or the Gramm–Rudman–Hollings congressionally imposed deficit process.

The Economic Report

Simultaneous to developing the budget, OMB, the Council of Economic Advisors, and the Treasury Department prepare and issue a report in the late fall. It covers the overall economic assumptions that are to be used in the president's budget. Assumptions in the economic report are subject to great debate, especially after the Congressional Budget Office's analysis of the report is reviewed by almost every member of Congress. The administration is usually accused of presenting a "rosy scenario." This sets the stage for Congress to be critical of the figures in the president's budget that will be released in January. The administration will defend its economic numbers, by either pointing to its "good" revenue and expenditure forecasting, or by identifying the factors it believes justify its figures.

The Presidential Budget Proposals

In the final days of preparing the president's budget, arrangements are made for the printing of the document(s) that support the budget. For the fiscal year 1991 budget, the president's budget was bound into a single volume, replacing the five or six documents produced for previous years' budgets.[6] During this period many changes are made as OMB attempts to produce a budget that the president can finally adopt and defend before Congress and the American people. Since it does not legally authorize spending until enacted into law by Congress, the president's budget submitted to Congress in January is merely his proposed federal budget. Its contents are referred to as the president's proposals. In addition, OMB must prepare for the president to include in his budget a preview sequester report that indicates discretionary spending limits for each spending category, information on any net deficit increase, and the sequester that would be necessary to bring the spending back into line.

On the first Monday following January 3, the president submits his proposed budget for the fiscal year beginning October 1 of that year. Once the president has made public his budget proposals, the interactions with Congress begin. Normally a cabinet meeting is held just prior to the release of the budget document. Cabinet members are presented with the administration's strategy on how to proceed with their public appearances and their congressional testimony when the president's proposal budget is defended. Rarely will a cabinet member deviate from defending the president's budget at this point, except at great peril to his or her position as a member of the administration. Presidents expect great loyalty from their cabinet members during this period because the presentation and defense of the budget is a significant leadership action by any president.

Coordination of the defense of the budget is done by the White House, with major assistance from OMB. The OMB director is usually the lead administration witness before Congress. The director sets the tone to be followed by cabinet members as they defend their individual departmental and agency budgets. The chairman of the Council of Economic Advisors and the secretary of the treasury usually provide the administration's defense of its economic assumptions. As the budget bills are "marked up" by the various appropriations committee, OMB usually keeps score on how the individual bills are faring and what is happening to the overall spending levels. OMB has an official role under Gramm–Rudman–Hollings to determine the final size of the deficit, after all bills (or more likely a CR) are passed. Gramm–Rudman–Hollings requires OMB to define any sequestration (across the board cutting) that may be necessary.

When departments and agencies are defending the previously submitted budget before Congress in the spring, they are also reviewing the fiscal year they are about half-way through and are beginning to prepare the next year's budget that will be submitted to OMB in September. In August, just prior to completing the budget for the fiscal year that begins in October, OMB must also submit an update report to reflect any new information on spending that may exceed target levels and the impact of any sequestration that may be necessary.

The Legislative Process

Upon receipt of the president's budget and the sequester preview reports, members of Congress immediately begin claiming the president has asked for too much or too little for the programs of special interest to them and their constituents and complain about specific sequestration information. (See Figure 2.3.) Some even suggest the president's budget is "dead on arrival," and they proclaim that Congress must put its own budget together with spending priorities and sequestrations more desirable than those of the president. The House and Senate budget committees immediately begin preparing the first budget concurrent resolution. They work with all committees on the drafting of such a resolution. Throughout the spring, they will hold "mark up" sessions in which an attempt is made to produce the resolution by their self-imposed deadline (usually April or May). The first concurrent resolution, which is usually worked out in a conference committee of the two houses, should produce budget totals that are in accord with established ceilings. They are then communicated to the various appropriations committees as guidance for completing appropriations legislation.

Appropriations Committees

Appropriations committees will have already held hearings with the OMB director, the chairman of the Council of Economic Advisors, and the secretary of the treasury on the administration's economic assumptions. This is all a prelude to countering the president's budget proposals and sequestration reports. Thereafter, the committees begin hearings with administration officials in which specific budget proposals by the president are reviewed and discussed. Appropriations committees use the guidance from the budget committees as they attempt to address spending proposals and limits. The full committee usually gives spending targets to subcommittees which attempt to remain within these targets as they conduct their hearings.

As committees and subcommittees complete their reviews of the president's proposals, they attempt to reach agreement on appropriations legislation, including sequestration, and to pass spending bills. A spending bill is similar to other legislation, in that it must go through a congressional process before it becomes a law. Following subcommittee and committee approval, the House of Representatives considers and approves spending bills and forwards them to Senate. If the Senate approves an identical bill, it is forwarded to the president. If the Senate does not concur with the House bill, it is taken up by a conference committee in which the disagreements are resolved. Action under law should be completed by September 30. However, rarely is the deadline met. That is why a continuing

Figure 2.3
Congressional Budget Process

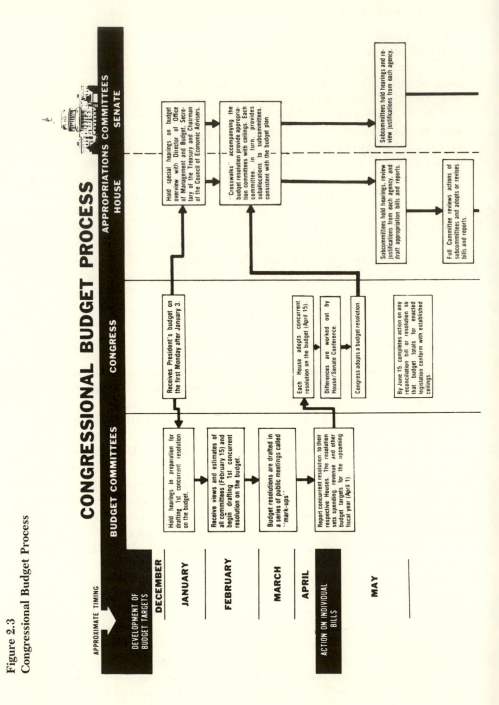

CONGRESSIONAL BUDGET PROCESS

APPROXIMATE TIMING	BUDGET COMMITTEES	CONGRESS	APPROPRIATIONS COMMITTEES HOUSE SENATE

DEVELOPMENT OF BUDGET TARGETS

DECEMBER

JANUARY

Hold hearings in preparation for drafting 1st concurrent resolution on the budget.

Receives President's budget on the first Monday after January 3.

Hold special hearings on budget overview with Director of Office of Management and Budget. Secretary of the Treasury and Chairman of the Council of Economic Advisers.

FEBRUARY

Receive views and estimates of all committees (February 15) and begin drafting 1st concurrent resolution on the budget.

''Crosswalks'' accompanying the budget resolution provide appropriation committees with ceilings. Each committee, in turn, provides suballocations to subcommittees consistent with the budget plan

MARCH

Budget resolutions are drafted in a series of public meetings called ''mark-ups''

APRIL

Report concurrent resolution to their respective Houses. The resolution sets spending, revenue and other budget targets for the upcoming fiscal year (April 1).

Each House adopts concurrent resolution on the budget (April 15).

Differences are worked out by House/Senate Conference.

Congress adopts a budget resolution.

ACTION ON INDIVIDUAL BILLS

MAY

By June 15, completes action on any reconciliation bill or resolution so that budget totals for enacted legislation conform with established ceilings.

Subcommittees hold hearings, review justifications from each agency, and draft appropriation bills and reports.

Subcommittees hold hearings and review justifications from each agency.

Full Committee reviews actions of subcommittees and adopts or revises bills and reports.

42

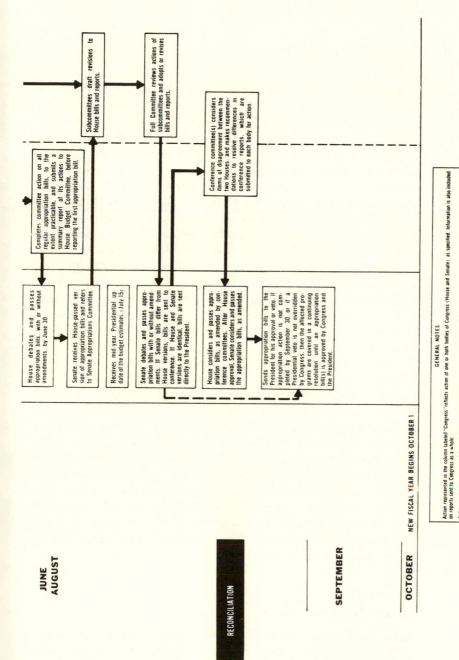

JUNE
AUGUST

House debates and passes appropriation bills with or without amendments, by June 30

Senate receives House passed version of appropriation bills and refers to Senate Appropriations Committee.

Receives mid year Presidential update of the budget estimates. (July 15)

Senate debates and passes appropriation bills with or without amendments. If Senate bills differ from House versions, bills are sent to conference. If House and Senate versions are identical, bills are sent directly to the President.

Completes committee action on all regular appropriation bills, to the extent practicable, and submits a summary report of its actions to House Budget Committee, before reporting the first appropriation bill.

Subcommittees draft revisions to House bills and reports.

Full Committee reviews actions of subcommittees and adopts or revises bills and reports.

Conference committee(s) considers items of disagreement between the two Houses, and makes recommendations to resolve differences in conference reports which are submitted to each body for action.

House considers and passes appropriation bills, as amended by conference committees. After House approval, Senate considers and passes the appropriation bills, as amended.

Sends appropriation bills to the President for his approval or veto. If appropriation action is not completed by September 30 or if a Presidential veto is not overridden by Congress, then the affected programs are covered in a continuing resolution until an appropriation bill(s) is approved by Congress and the President

RECONCILIATION

SEPTEMBER

OCTOBER   NEW FISCAL YEAR BEGINS OCTOBER 1

GENERAL NOTES

Action represented in the column labeled "Congress" reflects action of one or both bodies of Congress (House and Senate; as specified. Information is also included on reports sent to Congress as a whole.

Action on revenue measures follows the same general procedure as action on appropriation bills, except that revenue measures are reported by the Ways and Means Committee in the House, and by the Finance Committee in the Senate.

MAY 1988

EXECUTIVE OFFICE OF THE PRESIDENT/OFFICE OF MANAGEMENT AND BUDGET resolution is needed to permit departments and agencies to operate until a new appropriations bill is passed by Congress.

The Gramm–Rudman–Hollings Law

During the presidency of Ronald Reagan (1981–1989), major budgeting priority changes were made. Without going into the details of President Reagan's and Congress' battles over their respective priorities, the results during the Reagan term were higher budget deficits. Greater spending occurred with only slightly higher income due to tax rate reductions in the earlier Reagan years. With an outlook for a steadily increasing deficit facing the federal government, Congress passed and the president signed into law the Balanced Budget and Emergency Deficit Control Act of 1985, also identified by its principal authors, Senators Gramm, Rudman, and Hollings.

The primary aim of the law was to reduce the size of the deficit each year until a balanced budget was reached. Deficit targets set for subsequent fiscal years were FY 1988—$144 billion; FY 1989—$136 billion; FY 1990—$100 billion; FY 1991—$64 billion; FY 1992—$28 billion; FY 1993—$0. The Gramm–Rudman–Hollings law called for across-the-board sequestration (cuts) if the administration and Congress reached a budget stalemate. Half of the sequestration was to come from defense and half from nondefense programs, projects, and activities. The president was required to issue the sequestration order.

Although many believe that across-the-board decisions are never a good policy or management practice, this process was viewed as a means to force Congress and an administration jointly to make tough budget decisions. Of course this law, like all others, can be changed or skirted. For example, the Omnibus Reconciliation Act of 1990, in which the Budget Enforcement Act of 1990 was included as Title XIII, significantly changed discretionary spending limits and maximum deficit amounts. This law also changed concepts and definitions, how inflation would be addressed, and credit cost reestimates. The discretionary spending limits and maximum deficit amounts in Table 2.2 illustrate the drastic kinds of changes that were made at the fall 1990 budget summit. As with all processes of this type, it is a near certainty that further changes will be made each year on into the foreseeable future. Technical adjustments are considered to be a given among those who participate in these arenas.

Congressional Micromanagement

Throughout this process, members of Congress rely on their own experiences and those of administration sources and special interest groups in making spending decisions. In recent years, congressional committee and subcommittee staffs have been expanded to permit far more oversight of

Table 2.2
Discretionary Spending Limits and Maximum Deficit Amounts ($ in Millions)

Discretionary spending limits:

	New Budget Authority	Outlays
Defense Discretionary:		
1991	288,918	297,660
1992	291,643	295,744
1993	291,785	292,686
International Discretionary:		
1991	20,100	18,600
1992	20,500	19,100
1993	21,400	19,600
Domestic Discretionary:		
1991	182,700	198,100
1992	191,300	210,100
1993	198,300	221,700
Total Discretionary:		
1994	510,800	534,800
1995	517,700	540,800

Maximum deficit amounts:

1991	327,000
1992	317,000
1993	236,000
1994	102,000
1995	83,000

administration spending proposals. In addition, the General Accounting Office (GAO) and other congressional agencies have grown in size and stature. They provide Congress with more analyses and reports on executive branch operations.

This has led to some criticism that Congress is "micromanaging" the executive branch. Examples of this are found in appropriations bills that call for special controls on executive branch spending. For example, in one appropriations bill, the U.S. Department of Labor was precluded from spending funds to *study* a possible field restructuring that *might* result in one or more field offices being closed. In the appropriations legislation for the Department of Transportation, the department was prohibited from spending funds for any efficiency study that *might* result in more than three people being terminated. Bills containing similar restrictions have been proposed by many appropriations committees and subcommittees.

BUDGET EXECUTION

The coordination of budget execution pretty much lies with the departments and agencies. However, a number of controls are administered by OMB and the Treasury Department to ensure that the budget is executed according to its enactment provisions. (See Figure 2.4.) Although OMB budget examiners usually are already working on the president's next budget and are not able to exert extensive controls on the spending processes, there are procedures that they must follow regarding spending budgeted funds.

Apportionment

A budget examiner monitors the execution of the budget through the apportionment process. Through the act of apportioning funds, OMB makes funds available for obligation by the executive branch agency. Generally, funds must be apportioned by OMB before they can be obligated. The apportionment document is prepared by the budget examiner. This allows OMB to control allocation of spending authority for the departments and agencies.[7] The Treasury Department also compiles reports on the spending of budgeted funds. These are reviewed by OMB, the department, and the agency involved.

In the last few years, OMB's apportionment powers have come under renewed congressional scrutiny. The apportionment process can serve pro forma monitoring functions as well as discretionary purposes. Congress restricted or eliminated OMB's apportionment powers, or threatened to do so, in several instances where it believed congressional policy preferences were being thwarted by OMB apportionment actions.

When an appropriation bill is passed by Congress and signed by the president, the department or agency must request OMB to issue a warrant so that spending can begin. OMB reviews and approves the warrant based on the approved appropriation. It forwards the approval to the department or agency. The department or agency can revise its operating budget and request an OMB apportionment of the funds approved in the appropriation. OMB may then determine how much of appropriated funds should be apportioned, withheld, or deferred.

Departments and agencies allot their apportioned funds to the various program activities. They report periodically to OMB on spending plans that may result in improved operations or the need for reprogramming efforts. OMB must also prepare within-session sequester reports to Congress, reflecting any appropriation that causes a breach in a discretionary spending limit. This report will contain similar information to that in the preview sequester reports.

Figure 2.4
Execution of Enacted Budget

EXECUTION OF ENACTED BUDGET

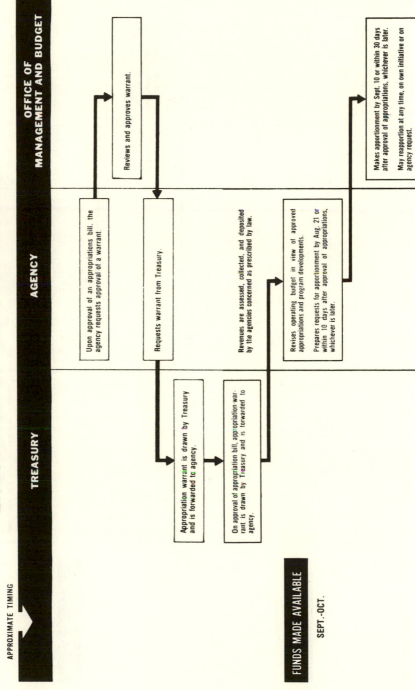

APPROXIMATE TIMING

TREASURY

AGENCY

OFFICE OF MANAGEMENT AND BUDGET

Upon approval of an appropriations bill. the agency requests approval of a warrant.

Reviews and approves warrant.

Requests warrant from Treasury.

Appropriation warrant is drawn by Treasury and is forwarded to agency.

On approval of appropriation bill, appropriation warrant is drawn by Treasury and is forwarded to agency.

Revenues are assessed, collected, and deposited by the agencies concerned as prescribed by law.

Revises operating budget in view of approved appropriations and program developments.

Prepares requests for apportionment by Aug. 21 or within 10 days after approval of appropriations, whichever is later.

Makes apportionment by Sept. 10 or within 30 days after approval of appropriations, whichever is later.

May reapportion at any time, on own initiative or on agency request.

FUNDS MADE AVAILABLE

SEPT.-OCT.

Figure 2.4 (Continued)

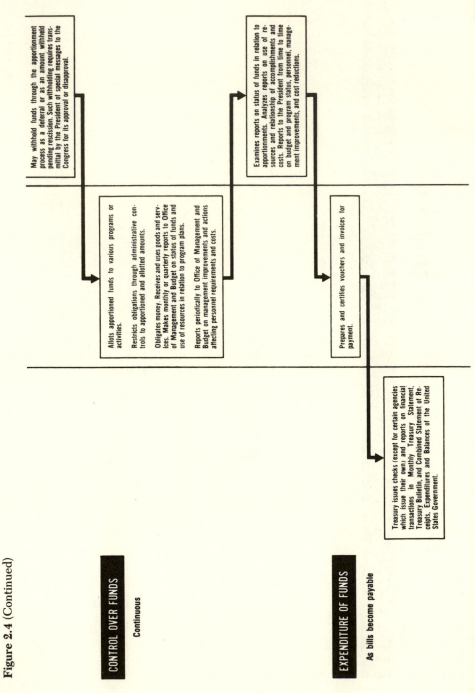

CONTROL OVER FUNDS

Continuous

May withhold funds through the apportionment process as a deferral or as an amount withheld pending rescission. Such withholding requires transmittal by the President of special messages to the Congress for its approval or disapproval.

Allots apportioned funds to various programs or activities.

Restricts obligations through administrative controls to apportioned and allotted amounts.

Obligates money. Receives and uses goods and services. Makes monthly or quarterly reports to Office of Management and Budget on status of funds and use of resources in relation to program plans.

Reports periodically to Office of Management and Budget on management improvements and actions affecting personnel requirements and costs.

Examines reports on status of funds in relation to apportionments. Analyzes reports on use of resources and relationship of accomplishments and costs. Reports to the President from time to time on budget and program status, personnel, management improvements, and cost reductions.

EXPENDITURE OF FUNDS

As bills become payable

Prepares and certifies vouchers and invoices for payment.

Treasury issues checks (except for certain agencies which issue their own) and reports on financial transactions in Monthly Treasury Statement, Treasury Bulletin, and Combined Statement of Receipts, Expenditures and Balances of the United States Government.

EXECUTIVE OFFICE OF THE PRESIDENT/OFFICE OF MANAGEMENT AND BUDGET

MAY 1988

Expenditures

Throughout the year, agencies prepare vouchers for payments and forward them to the Treasury Department for issuance of checks. Treasury also prepares periodic statements on receipts, expenditures, and balances in various accounts. Under the Budget and Impoundment Control Act of 1974, the president must report to Congress for its approval or disapproval of any spending that is to be deferred or funds that are to be withheld.

This act was passed during the presidency of Richard Nixon (1969–1973), when the administration felt that Congress had appropriated more funds than were needed to run the federal government. President Nixon simply did not wish to spend the funds and returned them to the Treasury. This angered Congress. It resulted in the passage of the 1974 act, which required the president to inform and receive approval by Congress before appropriated funds could be rescinded, deferred, or otherwise impounded.

There are extensive regulations covering spending and obligations processes. Inspectors General watch over spending practices. Congressional oversight is exerted by various congressional committees. The General Accounting Office can investigate spending if asked to do so by a member of Congress or on its own initiative. Also various internal controls are put in place by many executive branch managers. The Federal Managers' Financial Integrity Act requires each cabinet secretary and agency administrator to attest each year that the organization's financial management controls are free from possible fraud, waste, or mismanagement.

RECOMMENDATIONS FOR IMPROVED COORDINATION

Several recommendations are offered here for improving the coordination of the federal government's budgeting practices:

1. *The movement toward multiyear budgeting should be continued and even speeded up.* Multiyear budgeting and variations in spending authorities (e.g., the use of "no-year" funding) have been used for several decades, but Congress has never formally enacted into law a full multiyear appropriation. The processes used in Congress and the executive branch would be more efficient, and decision making would be enhanced by a longer-term perspective on the budget. A biennial budget, consistent with the tenure of each new Congress, would be a major reform. Annual updates and modifications would be possible, and elimination of the need for a complete new budget cycle each year would likely save millions of dollars.

2. *"Full-cost" budgeting should be expanded.* There is merit in the view of some members of the National Academy of Public Administration[8] that "full-cost" budgeting should be expanded. Life-cycle costing for some programs has been used for many years and should be extended significantly, especially for the many programs that commit the federal government to

expenditures and risks that cover a long time period. Federal insurance, loan guarantees, and bailouts are notable examples. By not facing up to these huge potential debts during the budget process, Congress and the executive branch are gambling with the people's money.

3. *Public confidence in the budgeting process must be improved.* In a system of free, democratic governance, a demands-supports relationship is essential. Taxpayers should demand government efficiency and "truth in budgeting" and should support the government with tax funds. Government must, in turn, demand the necessary taxes from its citizens to protect the freedoms and provide the services outlined in the Constitution. When the public loses confidence in either the budget process or the competence or sincerity of the participants in the process, their support for government will diminish. This directly affects the important relationship between a government and its peoples. Recent budget coordination, negotiation processes, and political strategies foster a loss of confidence in government and in its effectiveness in society.

4. *Capital budgets should be made to work.* This type of budgeting practice is needed to fund the major improvements needed in our highway system, airports, water treatment and control facilities, and numerous other major public construction projects. The current practice of having an annual budget cover the total cost of a project, instead of spreading out the payments, is based on the fear that this approach will be misused by one or more parties involved in the budget process. This includes Congress as well as federal departments and agencies. Long-term financing is often a money-saving approach used to take advantage of current lower costs for projects. By postponing capital expenditures, there is a risk of higher construction costs and more expensive replacement and repair costs in maintaining an often antiquated facility. A fresh look at capital budgeting is needed.

5. *The budget structure needs work.* The current structure of the budget is complicated and difficult for many to understand. This contributes to the length of time it takes to formulate a budget and sometimes places program managers at the mercy of budget specialists and examiners. When the budget becomes something other than a political or managerial instrument, its value is lessened. There are currently too many categories and a fragmentation of budgetary definitions and terms. These make the understanding of the nation's budget nearly impossible, which contributes even further to the loss of public confidence in government.

6. *Finally, a proper balance of tension is needed for the budget approval process.* Too much hostility and distrust has characterized recent interactions in budget formulation and execution. Interactions between OMB and federal departments and agencies have not always been smooth. "Gaming" is more the rule than the exception. What is needed are higher professional standards of conduct to govern these exchanges. Interactions between the adminis-

tration and Congress will always be fraught with political tension, and rightly so. This tension creates strength and balance through healthy differences of opinion about priorities. However, when the political hostility reaches a state where an impasse is reached, the nation suffers. We are too close to that condition.

The president and Congress each seem to posture themselves so that neither is first to commit itself to a rigid budget position. Otherwise, the other can then attack politically. Currently, the president is the first to submit his budget proposals each year. In an attempt to keep options open, the proposals usually include few innovations. Thus, they are usually followed by predictable rejection by Congress. Anticipation of rejection could be the reason few innovations are offered. One way to break this cycle might be for Congress to prepare a set of budget proposals simultaneously with the administration. At what is now becoming an annual "budget summit," the proposals could be exchanged and negotiations begun. A deadline for reaching agreement must be set. This reform would continue the proper checks and balances tension but lower the tension to a more appropriate level to avoid negative political gamesmanship.

The fall 1990 budget summit was fraught with tension, creating much frustration among the American people because of the petty games they felt were being played. The participants were equally frustrated, with splits emerging within political parties and between those with usually similar leanings. The mechanics of the budget process were more than tinkered with, and were crafted to suit the styles of the participants. As the participants change or are changed, new processes will surely be formulated and utilized. Such is the foreseeable future for budget coordination within the national government.

NOTES

1. Louis Fisher, "Continuing Resolutions: Can't Live With 'Em, Can't Live Without 'Em," *Public Budgeting and Finance* 8, no. 2 (Summary 1988): 101–4.

2. Aaron Wildavsky, *The Politics of the Budgetary Process* (Boston: Little, Brown and Company, 1964).

3. Charles F. Bingman, Herbert N. Jasper, Ronald C. Moe, and John Young, "Reforming Federal Budget and Financial Management Systems" (Paper for the National Academy of Public Administration, May 1988).

4. U.S. Congress, Omnibus Reconciliation Act of 1990. Title XIII, Budget Enforcement Act of 1990, Washington, D.C., October 1990.

5. Bruce Johnson, "OMB and the Budget Examiner: Changes in the Reagan Era," *Public Budgeting and Finance* 8, no. 4 (Winter 1988): 3–21. This article explains the traditional role of budget examiners and trends that affect their abilities to perform their roles.

6. Prior budget submittals have included separate volumes containing the budget,

a budget in brief, a budget appendix, special analyses, historical tables, and a management report.

7. Johnson, "OMB and the Budget Examiner."

8. Bingman, et al., "Reforming Federal Budget and Financial Management Systems."

3

Delay, Deadlock, and Deficits: Evaluating Proposals for Congressional Budget Reform

James A. Thurber and Samantha L. Durst

Throughout American history there has been a struggle between the executive branch and Congress over "the power of the purse" and recent years have been no exception. The debate over deficits, debt, and the size and composition of government taxing and spending goes back to the first Congress and the first secretary of treasury, Alexander Hamilton. This struggle continues to be at the center of American politics, but the dynamics of the budgetary process have changed dramatically in recent years.

Since the passage of the Budget and Impoundment Control Act of 1974 (P.L. 93–344), delay, deadlock, deficits, and ever increasing debt have been a regular feature of congressional budgeting. As a result, several hundred budget reforms have been proposed in the last decade, but few major changes have been made except the Gramm–Rudman–Hollings Deficit Reduction Act in 1985 (GRH), the GRH amendments in 1987 (GRH II), and the Budget Enforcement Act of 1990. Blaming Congress for unbalanced and late budgets, Presidents Reagan and Bush have pushed for enhancements to their budgetary power. Members of Congress have resisted presidential proposals for budget process changes and called for their own reforms. Scholars and journalists have also suggested ways to improve the budget process; in 1988 Rudolph Penner and Alan Abramson concluded that, "It is obvious that the budget process invented with such promise in 1974 [the Budget and Impoundment Control Act] is no longer working effectively. It will have to be mended if there is to be any hope that it can deal with the political conflicts over spending and taxation that are sure to be with us for many years to come."[1] Some reformers call for procedural changes, others for changes in the basic budgetary power of the president and Congress, and still others for major tax and spending policy change as a way to solve the problem of deficits, delay, and deadlock in the congressional budget process.

The purpose of this chapter is to describe and evaluate six major proposed changes to the budget process. To put these reforms into a political context, the existing congressional budget process and the institutions that surround it are discussed. The six reforms are:

1. Revisions to the deficit targets and deadlines in Gramm–Rudman–Hollings
2. Change in the use of the Social Security trust fund surplus
3. Pay-as-you-go proposals
4. The presidential line-item veto
5. Enhanced rescission authority
6. A constitutional amendment requiring a balanced budget[2]

Although none of these reforms have been adopted, the six proposed changes are selected based on their prominence in public debates and in the budget process reform literature on congressional budgeting. The concluding section of this chapter briefly assesses each proposed reform based on a common set of criteria:

1. Impact on presidential budgetary power
2. Impact on congressional budgetary power
3. Impact on distribution of power within Congress
4. Effect on the complexity of the budget process
5. Effect on the timeliness of the budget process

THE CONGRESSIONAL BUDGET PROCESS

Defining Roles

The congressional budget process is only one part of the financial system that governs federal revenues and outlays. The president is responsible for formulating and transmitting a proposed federal budget to Congress. For the formation of the budget, the president relies on his staff and advisors, the Office of Management and Budget (OMB), the Council of Economic Advisors, the Department of Treasury, and the government agencies that administer federal programs. The president's budget includes an accounting of how funds have been spent in the past, the president's recommendations and estimates of receipts and outlays for the coming fiscal year (FY), the current services budget, and economic and technical assumptions for the new fiscal year.

After the president submits his budget to Congress (on the first Monday after January 3rd each year), the congressional budget process formally begins. The 1990 Budget Enforcement Act allows for the president to delay the submission of his budget proposal until the first Monday in February, but it stipulates that "this increased flexibility be used very rarely to meet only the most pressing exigencies."[3] The actual level of federal receipts and outlays is determined by Congress through the use of various kinds of legislation. Even though the president submits the budget, Congress is under no obligation to accept that budget. Congress is free to alter the president's budget in any way it wishes or to pass its own budget.

Taxes and other revenue-raising methods are specified by legislation that follows the normal legislative process with major committee responsibilities lying with the budget committees in each chamber of Congress, the Ways and Means Committee in the House, and the Finance Committee in the Senate. All revenue legislation must originate in the House of Representatives, although in recent years this procedure has been sidestepped.

Legislative authorizations and appropriations, which designate how expenditures will be spent, have to be passed by Congress and signed by the president before they can take effect. Authorizing legislation establishes the federal agencies that will administer federal programs or allows existing agencies to continue to exist. Authorizing legislation is typically enacted for only a limited amount of time, after which new authorizing legislation must be passed by Congress. Authorizing legislation is developed for every federal program by the legislative committee with jurisdiction over that program or programs. Sometimes authorizing legislation even stipulates the maximum amount of federal funds that can be appropriated to a given federal program.

Appropriation legislation grants federal agencies budgetary authority, which allows them to incur debts. As with authorizations, budget authority can be granted for varying periods of time. Under the current budget process, most agencies must be given budget authority each year. Appropriation legislation falls within the jurisdiction of the House and Senate appropriation committees, but, like revenue legislation, it is usually first to be considered by the House. Once the House has passed appropriation legislation, it is sent to the Senate for consideration. If the legislation passed by the Senate differs from the House version, a conference committee meets to resolve the differences, just as with other forms of legislation. Once the differences are resolved, and both houses of Congress have passed the same legislation, it is sent to the president for his signature. The president can either sign or veto the legislation. All of this is supposed to be accomplished prior to October 1, the beginning of the fiscal year; however, in recent years that task has been difficult or impossible.

1974 Budget Reforms

A number of important budget reforms expanding the existing congressional budget process were established by the 1974 Congressional Budget and Impoundment Control Act (also referred to as the Congressional Budget Act).[4] The Congressional Budget Act created standing budget committees in the House and in the Senate which are responsible for setting overall tax and spending levels. It also required Congress to annually establish levels of expenditures and revenues with prescribed procedures for arriving at those spending and income totals. The procedures include three important elements. First, a timetable was established which set deadlines for action on budget-related legislation. This timetable was intended to ensure completion of the budget plan prior to the start of each fiscal year (see Table 3.1). Second, the Congressional Budget Act required the annual adoption of concurrent budget resolutions (which do not require presidential approval). Initial concurrent budget resolutions establish targets for total budget authority, budget outlays, and revenues for the upcoming fiscal year. Then, a final "binding" resolution with ceilings on budget authority and outlays and a floor on revenues is adopted. Finally, the act instituted a reconciliation process to conform revenue, spending, and debt legislation to the levels specified in the final budget resolution.[5]

The reconciliation process is the procedure under which the budget committees may direct other committees to determine and recommend revenue and/or spending actions deemed necessary to conform authorization and appropriations to the determinations made in the budget resolutions. The budget committees have the option of mandating that House and Senate committees "report" legislation that will meet budget authority, outlays, and revenue targets.[6] The reconciliation process allows the budget committees to direct one or more of the legislative committees to make changes in existing laws to achieve the desired budget reductions. The budget committees submit the recommended changes to each house "without any substantive revision".

The reconciliation process as contemplated in the 1974 Budget Act was to be a relatively brief and simple exercise. By most interpretations, reconciliation measures were to be in second concurrent resolution (not the first) and applied only to appropriations. However, the House and Senate budget committees turned the process around and included reconciliation directions for authorization and appropriations committees in the first budget resolutions for FY 1981. Even though the intent of the Budget Act was clearly that reconciliation was to be used for the second "binding" resolution, the strategy of placing ceilings on the first resolution worked. The budget committees were successful in invoking the reconciliation process for FY 1981 by requiring several congressional committees to reduce spending by about $6.2 billion and for the tax-writing committees to recommend revenue increases of $4.2 billion. The FY 1981 reconciliation bill (Public Law 96–499) established an important precedent and resulted in savings for fiscal years 1981–1985 of more than $50 billion in outlays (not budget authority) and $29 billion in additional revenues for the same period.

Table 3.1
Budget Timetable

Action to be completed	Previous Deadline	GRH Deadline
President submits fiscal year budget to Congress	15 days after Congress reconvenes	First Monday after January 3
CBO submits report on fiscal policy to budget committees	April 1	February 15
Congressional Committees submit "Views and Estimates" to budget committees	March 15	February 25
Senate Budget Committee reports budget resolution	April 15	April 1
Congress completes action on budget resolution	May 15	April 15
Annual appropriation bills may be considered in the House	May 15	May 15
Congressional committees report new authorizing legislation	May 15	No Provision
House Appropriations Committee reports all appropriations bills	No Provision	June 10
Congress complete action on reconciliation legislation	No Provision	June 15
House completes action on all appropriation bills	No Provision	June 30
'Snapshot' of fiscal deficit taken by CBO and OMB	No Provision	August 15
CBO and OMB issue report to GAO on fiscal deficit and initial sequestration order	No Provision	August 20
GAO issues fiscal deficit and sequestration report to president (now unconstitutional)	No Provision	August 25
House and Senate must vote on joint resolution. If passed by both houses, it is sent to president for signature or veto.	No provision	August 30
President issues initial fiscal sequestration order based on GAO report	No Provision	September 1

Table 3.1 (Continued)

Action to be completed	Previous Deadline	GRH Deadline
Congress completes action on all appropriation bills	7 days after Labor Day	No Provision
Congress completes action on second budget resolution	September 15	No Provision
Congress completes action on reconciliation legislation from second budget resolution	September 25	No Provision
Fiscal sequestration takes effect	No Provision	October 1
Fiscal year begins	October 1	October 1
CBO and OMB issue a revised report to GAO reflecting final congressional action	No Provision	October 5
GAO issues a revised report to the president	No Provision	October 10
Final fiscal sequestration order based on revised report becomes effective	No Provision	October 15
GAO issues a compliance report on sequestration order	No Provision	November 15

Source: Adapted from James A. Thurber "Budget Continuity and Change: An Assessment of the Congressional Budget Process," in Studies of Modern American Politics, by D.K. Adams (Manchester, England: Manchester University Press, 1987), 81. Although these dates are in the Balanced Budget and Emergency Deficit Control Act, they have not been met in the past few years. More often the process has been delayed or changed informally.

The budget reforms established by the 1974 Congressional Budget and Impoundment Control Act have focused attention on the budget process in Congress. However, its ability to enable Congress to control the size of the budget and the deficit are questionable. Since the act's implementation, the deficit has continued to grow and budgets have been late in all but three years. In addition, the effect of the act has been to increase the complexity involved in formulating a budget and the difficulty of gaining congressional support for the final budget because many of Congress' favorite programs risk having their funding limited.

CONTROLLING THE BUDGET PROCESS THROUGH GRAMM–RUDMAN–HOLLINGS

Congress is increasingly concerned with its seeming inability to control the budget process, resulting in missed budget deadlines and large deficits, as emphasized by U.S. Representative Dan Rostenkowski, chair of the House Ways and Means Committee:

The unified budget deficit of $74 billion in FY 1980 increased to $152 billion in FY 1989. As a result, the total federal debt has more than tripled from $709 billion to $2.2 trillion over this period. The annual interest payments on our national debt have increased from $52.5 billion to $170 billion. Today interest payments are the third largest spending item in the federal budget, trailing only defense and social security.[7]

By the early 1980s, projected budget deficits were in the $200 billion dollar range, far more than had ever been experienced before. This concern led to the passage in 1985 of the Balanced Budget and Emergency Deficit Control Act (P.L. 99–177) sponsored by Senators Phil Gramm (R–Texas), Warren Rudman (R–New Hampshire), and Ernest Hollings (D–South Carolina). The goal of the Gramm–Rudman–Hollings (GRH) plan was to balance the federal budget by establishing statutory guidelines (maximum levels) for the federal budget deficit over a number of years. The legislation revised established budgetary deadlines for each of the major aspects of the congressional budget process in order to bring more discipline to congressional budgeting, to make the process more efficient, and to focus attention on reducing the deficit.[8] The timetable established by GRH is listed in Table 3.1. Table 3.1 indicates each major action to be completed in the budget process, the budget guidelines that governed the process under the 1974 Congressional Budget and Impoundment Control Act, and the GRH guidelines. Many aspects of the budget process did not have guidelines prior to the passage of GRH.

Sequestration

The central enforcement mechanism of GRH is a series of automatic spending cuts that occur if the federal budget does not meet or fall within ten billion dollars of the deficit targets (these automatic spending cuts are commonly referred to as sequestration).[9] Sequestration requires federal spending be cut automatically if Congress and the president do not enact laws to reduce the deficit to the maximum deficit amount allowed for that year. The GRH deficit targets for each fiscal year are listed in Table 3.2. If the proposed federal budget does not meet the annual deficit targets established by Gramm–Rudman–Hollings, then the president must make across-the-board spending cuts evenly divided between domestic and defense programs until those targets are met. However, most entitlement programs (approximately 43 percent of the budget) and interest payments (approximately 14 percent of the budget) are partially or totally exempt from the potential cuts.

The 1985 GRH legislation gave the General Accounting Office (GAO) the responsibility for triggering the across-the-board cuts. In 1986, the Supreme Court declared that part of the legislation to be unconstitutional because it gave the GAO, a legislative support agency, executive functions.[10] The Supreme Court's decision would have prevented the implementation of GRH, but Congress responded with the passage of the Balanced Budget and Emergency Deficit Control Reaffirmation Act of 1987 (GRH II). The GRH II legislation altered the original GRH Deficit Reduction Plan by directing the Office of Management and Budget (OMB), an executive agency, to issue the report that would trigger sequestration if deficit reduction targets were not met. GRH II also revised the original deficit reduction targets in accordance with more realistic economic assumptions (see Table 3.2). In the years since its adoption, the GRH deficit reduction plan has brought the constraints of fiscal austerity to Congress and has dominated the budget process. However, since the Gramm–Rudman–Hollings balanced budget legislation was enacted, the deficit never has been as low as the law requires.

ENFORCING GRH DEFICIT TARGETS

The Unmet Promise of Targets and Sequestration

The Gramm–Rudman–Hollings plan for deficit reduction seemed to promise long-term progress toward lower deficits and a balanced budget. However, the GRH I and II goals have proven to be elusive. The GRH mechanisms have increased presidential and congressional attention on each budget year in isolation, instead of on long-term budgetary goals. Even though GRH II revised the original deficit targets, the new targets proved to be out of reach in early 1990 (see Table 3.2).[11]

Sequestration was supposed to threaten the interests of all participants in

Table 3.2
Gramm–Rudman–Hollings Deficit Targets

Fiscal Year	Deficit Reduction Target* (in billions of dollars)			
	1985 GRH Limits	1987 GRH Limits	1990 Budget Enforcement Act	Deficits
1986	172	——	——	221
1987	144	——	——	150
1988	108	144	——	155
1989	72	136	——	152
1990	36	100	——	195
1991	0	64	327	——
1992	——	28	317	——
1993	——	0	236	——
1994	——	——	102	——
1995	——	——	83	——

*CBO estimates of the deficit taken from An Analysis of the President's Budgetary Proposals for Fiscal Year 1991 (Washington, D.C.: Congressional Budget Office, March 1990), 8; and The Economic and Budget Outlook: An Update (Washington, D.C.: Congressional Budget Office, July 1990), x.

Source: Adapted from James A. Thurber, "Budget Continuity and Change: An Assessment of the Congressional Budget Process," in Studies of Modern American Politics, edited by D.K. Adams (Manchester, England: Manchester University Press, 1987), 85. 1990 deficit targets are taken from Title XIII, Section III, "Revising and Enforcing Deficit Targets," of the Budget Enforcement Act of 1990, Conference Report, 6.

Note: The budget figures include Social Security, which is off-budget but is counted for the purposes of the Balanced Budget Act targets. For comparability with the targets, the projections exclude the Postal Service, which is also off-budget.

the congressional budget process enough to make them want to avoid it. However, the penalty of sequestration has not had the intended effect. In some years, the expected sequestration was so large that it ceased to be an effective threat. In other years, participants in the process have compared the projected impacts of sequestration on their favored programs with the potential impact of cuts from regular legislative process and decided that their interest were best served by delaying the passage of bills until after sequestration occurred.[12]

Two characteristics contribute to the failure of the threat of sequestration to force deficit reductions. First, and most important in practice, sequestration has been avoided by using optimistic economic and technical assumptions as substitutes for actual policy changes. In the past, the administration tended to underestimate federal outlays, largely by underestimating the current services outlays.[13] For example, in FY 1987, the administration's current services outlay estimates were $27 billion below the Congressional Budget Office "current policy" outlay estimates. The difference in estimates was due almost entirely to differences in economic or technical assumptions. Interest accounted for 64 percent of the difference between estimates of the current services outlays by the administration and Congress, and lower OMB estimates of inflation accounted for almost all of the remaining difference. Second, enforcement of the deficit targets is not effective after the final budget "snapshot".[14] After the snapshot is taken, indicating that the deficit target has been met, legislation can be then adopted that raises the deficit in the current year and following years as well.[15]

Four proposals to deal with these problems are currently under consideration.[16] These are:

1. To use fixed deficit reduction targets for amounts due to policy changes
2. To "look back" and add-on last-minute spending to deficit reduction goals
3. To target the structural deficit for reduction
4. To modify the sequestration formula

Add Deficit Reduction Targets for Policy Changes

One proposal for revising the GRH deficit targets is that instead of fixed targets for the maximum level of the deficit each year, there should be fixed yearly targets for the amount of deficit reduction related to policy changes each year until the balanced budget is actually achieved. It would not work to specify fixed reduction only from the previous year, which could still be largely evaded by using optimistic assumptions and by loading spending into the current year's budget after the final snapshot of budget revenues and expenditures. Instead, the reductions would have to reflect a continuous, long-term evaluation of the impact of the budget on the size of the deficit. Under this proposal, new spending enacted after the final "snapshot" would automatically affect the deficit targets for the next year. GRH II worked this way for FY 1988, when $23 billion in deficit reduction was required. This proposal would not, however, require a balanced budget or zero deficit at a specific future date. This proposal also risks contributing to the propensity for temporary tax and entitlement changes, so that the same changes could be counted in each year's deficit reduction goal without making a cumulative contribution to deficit reduction. However, such evasions could be controlled by mandating that tax and entitlement changes achieve similar savings in the year following the budget year, or by a comparable modification of the baseline of the budget.[17]

"Look Back" Requirements

Because Congress evaluates the budget only once a year to ascertain whether it is meeting the GRH deficit targets, after that evaluation it is relatively free to add on new expenditures to the budget, often increasing the actual level of the deficit. The current budget process bases enforcement exclusively on the OMB projection of next year's deficit. The projections can be wrong. Since 1985, when Gramm–Rudman–Hollings was first enacted, the actual budget deficit never has been cut to the legal limit (see Table 3.2). Under current law, if OMB projects in early October that the deficit in the upcoming fiscal year will exceed the legal limit, the president must implement sequestration on October 15. The sequester deadline having passed, nothing happens. Nobody seems to be held accountable for past sins. Congress and the president simply pretend that they are solving the problem, but they do not look back.

"Look back" legislation enacted in the 1990 Budget Enforcement Act (BEA) would require that any amount added to the current year's deficit by policy changes made after the final budget snapshot would also be added to the following year's deficit reduction target. This would eliminate incentives for post-snapshot deficit increases and for schemes that reduce the budget deficit by shifting spending into the next fiscal year, but it would reduce the flexibility of fiscal policy in case of emergencies.

The Committee for a Responsible Federal Budget argues that if last year's actual spending exceeded the limits in the budget agreement by more than 1 percent, and unless Congress passed and the president signed legislation to eliminate the overage within thirty days, sequestration would be triggered. Sequestration would cut the difference between last year's actual spending and the targets, and would reduce total federal outlays. It would control real spending.

Target the Structural Deficit Only

The deficit targets could be fixed to structural deficit rather than on the total budget deficit. "Structural" deficits adjust for the strength of the economy by estimating expenditures and revenues that would exist when the economy was at "full employment," usually a figure around 5.5 percent. The structural deficit would presumably have to be estimated by OMB, just as GRH deficit targets currently must rely on OMB's estimate of the total deficit, to avoid separation-of-powers problems. Although this reform cannot deliver a balanced budget at a specific date, it may provide for steady and permanent deficit reduction. This reform would not likely eliminate problems caused by optimistic productivity and interest rate forecasts and by overly positive technical or economic assumptions.

Modify the Sequestration Formula

Under Gramm–Rudman–Hollings I and II, if the proposed federal budget does not meet the annual deficit targets, the president must make across-the-board spending cuts evenly divided between domestic and defense programs until those targets are met. However, there is basic disagreement over where sequestration cuts should be made. Some argue that some programs are more essential than other programs and should be protected. Others are opposed to a deficit reduction strategy based only on cuts in existing programs, without any tax increases. Very few people, in or out of Congress, are completely satisfied with the current sequestration procedure, resulting in a number of proposals for sequestration reform.

Several members of Congress have argued that, if a sequestration becomes necessary, some portion of the amount required should come from an automatic tax increase, like a uniform percentage surtax on corporate and/or personal income taxes. Other members of Congress have called for sequestration cuts only for "physical" capital; if sequestration is triggered, domestic capital funding, such as the construction of highways, mass transit, aviation, and water treatment plants, should be cancelled. Others have advocated a broadened domestic base of programs eligible for sequestration including the elimination of the 2 percent cap on cuts in health care programs, the elimination of the exemption of low-income and other transfer payments (e.g., Aid to Families with Dependent Children, child nutrition, food stamps, Medicaid, and veteran's compensation), and the elimination of federally sponsored retirement programs (other than Social Security).

Deciding where the sequestration cuts will come from has tremendous implications for the entire nation. Not only will it make a financial statement about the limitation of federal expenditures, it will also make a political and social declaration of what the nation's priorities are now and will be in the years to come. Unfortunately, this plan also fails to correct for lowballing of assumptions, spending, and revenues.

THE SOCIAL SECURITY SURPLUS AND BUDGET REFORM

Trust Fund Surplus

As a result of the 1977 and 1983 Social Security amendments, there is a growing annual Social Security Trust Fund surplus, which is financed through payroll taxes. The surplus will be about $68 billion in 1990 and $103 billion in 1983. Reserves will build up rapidly, probably reaching a peak of nearly $3 trillion measured in constant 1989 dollars in about 2020. Thereafter, with the retirement of the postwar baby boomers, surpluses will turn into deficits, and reserves will have to be drawn on to pay benefits.

The build-up in Social Security reserves is intended to be an advance response to future demographics. Because of the baby boom and subsequent baby bust, the burden of Social Security benefits will rise. Now there are 3.3 workers paying Social Security taxes to support 1 retiree; in 48 years there will be only about 1.9 workers to support 1 retiree.[18] Because we literally cannot hoard and 'set aside' food, clothing, shelter and medical care for the baby boomers' retirement, the inescapable economics of our demographic future and the benefit promises of the Social Security system is that a higher proportion of future national product will go to retirees and a lower proportion will go to future workers. This transfer will most likely require higher taxes of some kind on future workers or reduced benefits for retirees.

The Moynihan Proposal to Eliminate the Surplus

Senator Patrick Moynihan (D–New York) has argued that the current Social Security Trust Fund surpluses are being used to finance the federal deficit (through the investment of Social Security funds in Treasury bonds) and to hide the true size of the deficit. Senator Moynihan and others have proposed a number of reforms designed to alter the Social Security Trust Fund surplus and the way in which these surpluses are analyzed during the congressional budget process. Changes that might result from these proposed reforms would impact on our perception of the size of the deficit and the ability of the government to meet GRH deficit targets. In addition, changes could limit much of the remaining flexibility that members of Congress have to address budgetary issues and increase the complexity of the budget process itself.

In January 1990, Senator Moynihan proposed that the Social Security system return to the pay-as-you-go financing that was the basis of the system prior to 1983.[19] Under this financing method, payroll tax rates are scheduled at the level necessary to finance and maintain a reserve of roughly one year's worth of Social Security benefits. The Moynihan reform provides for cutting the Social Security tax rate from 6.2 percent to 6.06 percent in 1990 and to 5.1 percent in 1991. It also provides for a series of rate increases in 2012 (to 5.6 percent), 2015 (to 6.2 percent), 2020 (to 7.0 percent), 2025 (to 7.7 percent), and 2045 (to 8.1 percent). These tax rates will be enough to finance benefits and maintain a fund roughly equal to a year's worth of benefits for the next seventy-five years. The retroactive cut in the Social Security tax rate in 1990 and 1991 would result in a $55 billion dollar tax cut for working people.[20] Senator Moynihan contends that such a cut, used and invested by people working now, is a better use of the money, potentially aiding the economy and making current and future workers more affluent.

Stop Counting the Social Security Surplus

Senator Phil Gramm (R–Texas) and others have argued that the Social Security surpluses should not count as part of the deficit as of 1994, and that the non-Social-Security budget be balanced in 1994 and beyond.[21] Not only does this proposal require even greater deficit reduction, but by taking Social Security "off-budget" it also takes off the table major ways of reducing the deficit, such as Social Security cost of living adjustments (COLA) restraints. Furthermore, if Social Security COLAs are not restrained, it will be politically difficult to restrain other COLAs.

There are numerous drawbacks to this proposal. Because Social Security would be "off-budget" (excluded from the unified federal budget), there would be less discipline over the Social Security Administration and its use of Social Security funds. The Social Security Administration could use the existing surpluses to increase benefits, and then the system would be unable to support retirees as demographic changes take place. It could also be used as a precedent to set other trust funds off-budget. The surpluses in other major trust funds will be about $62 billion in 1993, according to CBO. Exclusion of these funds from the unified budget would further increase the necessary deficit reduction and at the same time, reduce the potential sources of saving. Restraints on spending from these trust funds would be loosened at the same time as these trust fund program areas could still be receiving general fund support and competing with general fund programs lacking the protection of trust fund status. In the 1990 Budget Enforcement Act both Social Security Revenues and Expenditures were, in fact, moved off-budget.

Count Social Security But Require a Budget Surplus

With the adoption of this proposal, Social Security would continue to be counted as part of the unified federal budget. However, beyond 1994, it would require additional deficit reduction of about $36 billion a year until the total surplus equals the amount by which the Social Security surplus exceeds 1 percent on GNP. This is about the average size of deficits in the 1960s and much less than the average for the 1970s. This approach does not take Social Security off the deficit-reduction negotiation table and would not lead to the Social Security surplus being used to increase benefits.

This reform seems to be more acceptable politically in some ways because it does not set a precedent for putting other trust funds (such as the highway and airport trust funds) off-budget. The fundamental deficit and Social Security problem—balancing the budget while preparing the nation for higher retirement costs—can then be solved by moving the total budget into surplus as soon as possible. But this is a difficult political venture, since this would be a task full of conflict. Political (rather than economic) judgments are the key to a solution to the deficit/Social Security problem. The government could shift its spending away from public consumption toward public investment. Obviously, if living standards grow in the next forty years, future workers may be able to afford sharing more with retirees (i.e., Moynihan's tax reduction-increase proposal).

At this time each of these alternatives seems unrealistic, but we should bear in mind that taking Social Security off-budget is not the same as taking it off-government.[22]

PAY-AS-YOU-GO PROPOSALS

Revisited Fiscal Conservatives

Pay-as-you-go reforms harken back to a more tight-fisted era when fiscal conservatives such as the late Harry F. Byrd (D–Virginia) insisted that the federal government should not write a check unless there was cash in the treasury. That cannot happen for some time, because of the huge budget deficit. But various plans are making their way through Congress that would insist that new spending be paid for by either deeper cuts in old programs or higher taxes.[23] In 1989, for example, Representative Les AuCoin (D–Oregon) introduced a "Drug Wars for Star Wars" swap, and this appears to be only one of many that will be proposed in the future.

All pay-as-you-go reforms are based on the notion that any increase in outlays above the previous year's "base level" must be paid for by offsetting outlay reductions or by tax increases. Advocates say any kind of pay-as-you-go approach would be an improvement over the 1980s, when a Republican president and a Democratic House allowed the huge explosion in defense spending and entitlement programs that were paid for with borrowed money.

Pay-as-you-go reforms are not necessarily intended to reduce the deficit, but to limit growth in existing budgets and deficits by requiring that new expenditures be linked to cuts in expenditures for existing programs or to tax increases.[24] With pay-as-you-go reforms, the ceiling for each year's new budget would be set as if every program except Social Security had been frozen at the previous year's amount. If members of Congress proposed higher expenditures for existing programs or expenditures for new programs, they would also have to propose tax increases or cuts in existing programs in order to produce the revenues required to fund their new or more expensive programs.

The Rostenkowski Proposal

Representative Rostenkowski (D–Illinois) has proposed a budget reform, similar to pay-as-you-go reforms, that is a combination of spending reductions and revenue increases designed as a solution to the existing deficit. This plan is targeted at reducing deficit within five years, but not at controlling federal spending over the long term. Spending cuts account for 60 percent of the plan's deficit reduction. The Rostenkowski plan calls for freezing most federal spending—including Social Security benefits—at current levels for one year and for cutting defense spending by $150 billion over five years. Spending on all nondefense discretionary programs (except means tested programs) would be frozen for one year (FY 1991). Means tested programs, which protect the poor, would be unaffected. Defense spending would be frozen in FY 1991 and budget authority would fall three percent below inflation in each of the next four years. The plan would increase excise taxes on gasoline, tobacco, and alcohol and raise the top marginal income tax rate paid by the wealthiest from 28 to 33 percent. It would also rule out President Bush's plan to reduce the capital gains tax and a Democratic proposal to cut the Social Security payroll tax (like the one proposed by Senator Moynihan). This plan is intended to reduce spending by $24.4 billion in FY 1991 and by $254.5 billion over the next five years. The Bush administration gave a warm welcome to Rostenkowski's deficit reduction plan.[25]

The pay-as-you-go reform, in whatever form, could lead to a different composition of deficit reductions with more cuts in direct spending and more revenue increases. Pay-as-you-go shifts the penalty for not reducing the deficit to an earlier stage in the process (when spending is first proposed); it forces legislators to consider the budgetary implications of various federal programs prior to the final stages of the budget process (after the proposed budget and deficit are totaled). But, as is the case with other budget process reforms, you must have effective enforcement procedures to prevent committees from producing deficit-increasing legislation.

PRESIDENTIAL LINE-ITEM VETO

New Presidential Power

The president currently has the constitutional power to veto any bill or joint resolution, subject to the constitutional power of Congress to override that veto by a two-thirds vote of those present and voting in each chamber. Item veto or line-item veto proposals are based on the presumption that the president is unable to veto specific provisions of a measure—he must accept or reject the legislation in its entirety. Whether the president should be allowed to veto individual items in appropriations bills and/or other budget legislation, including revenue bills and authorizations for direct spending, is the central question related to the line-item veto.

Generally, an item-veto mechanism provides that, in signing a bill, the chief executive would be empowered to designate the appropriations and budget provision(s) to which he objects and return a copy of such appropriations and provision(s), with his objections, to the house in which the bill originated. The legislature would then consider the veto message under the procedures applied to a general veto. The item veto would give the president a substantial increase in power vis-à-vis Congress.

The item veto was first proposed by President Grant in 1873 and has, over the years, been advocated by a number of presidents including Presidents Hayes, Arthur, Franklin Roosevelt, Truman, Eisenhower, Reagan, and, most recently, Bush. President Ronald Reagan consistently called for a line-item veto as stated in his last budget message to Congress: "My successors should be given the authority, subject to congressional override, to veto line-items in annual appropriations bills, in authorizing legislation that provides for or mandates programs, and in revenue bills. Such authority would permit the elimination of substantial waste and would be an effective instrument of enforcing budget discipline."[26] As early as 1876, a constitutional amendment to grant the president an item veto was proposed in Congress and over 200 similar proposals have been introduced in subsequent Congresses.

Shifting Power to the President

The use of an item veto has been advocated for a variety of reasons, including the need to right the balance of power between the executive and legislative branches, and as a procedural tool to be used in the face of persistent federal budget deficits. Generally, item-veto proposals are directed toward appropriations measures only, but some proposals would also give the president item-veto authority over other kinds of budget-effecting legislation. In his February 1989 budget submission, President Bush proposed line-item veto authority which "should cover not only appropriations bills but also bills that create spending authority (including mandatory or entitlement spending) and revenue bills".[27]

The adoption of an item-veto or a line-item veto mechanism would give the president the same power that many governors already possess. Interestingly, even though forty-three state governors already have item-veto authority of one form or another, experience at the state level suggests the veto affects not so much the growth of spending as its composition.[28] Moreover, the line-item veto at the state level does not give the executive clear-cut powers over the details of *revenue* legislation.

A presidential item-veto power could have significant implications for Congress and for congressional-presidential relations. It might simplify the appropriations process by forcing Congress to concentrate solely on provisions pertinent to spending bills rather than complicating the appropriations process by attaching nongermane "riders" (amendments) to authorization and appropriations legislation because the president could simply veto those items. A presidential item veto might replace negotiations between the leadership and the president over spending measures, weakening the power of the majority party and Congress as an institution. A line-item veto could also lessen Congress' feelings of social or moral responsibility in the appropriations process, as there would be little incentive to reject controversial or special-interest provisions which could easily, but might not, be vetoed by the president.

The line-item veto would make the president a more powerful player in the shaping of the details of legislation determining the priorities of the nation, raising new concerns about the balance of power between the branches of government as provided for by the U.S. Constitution. The item veto proposed by Presidents Reagan and Bush would give the president legislative authority not envisioned by the framers of the U.S. Constitution by allowing the president to substitute his judgment for that of the legislature, thwarting the will of the majority in the Congress. The power to tax and spend is a constitutionally protected congressional power, and a line-item veto could alter this arrangement.

The potential for an expansion of presidential powers based on new item-veto authority is tremendous. The president already has authority to propose impoundments (rescissions and deferrals). These impoundments provide the president ample authority over the budget process. Additionally, the president's existing veto authority (and the threat of its exercise) already provides him with tremendous influence over the course of legislation. When the veto is used, it is rarely reversed. A review by the Congressional Research Service at the end of the 100th Congress showed that Congress has overridden only 103 of 2,455 presidential vetoes.[29]

Enhanced Rescission Authority

Closely related to the line-item veto are proposals to grant the president enhanced rescission authority. Rescissions are one form of presidential impoundment authority. Such authority would allow the president to cancel the expenditure of funds after they have been appropriated by Congress. Under this reform, rescissions would become effective automatically in the absence of a specific disapproval of the president's request by a vote in Congress. Enhanced presidential rescission power is a viable statutory alternative to a line-item veto. This would be a shift toward more presidential power to force Congress to consider separately spending which the president believes to be unnecessary or wasteful.

The president's impoundment authority collapsed in the early 1970s with the attempts by President Nixon to withhold congressionally appropriated funds on an unprecedented scale. Judicial challenges to Nixon's impoundment actions resulted in a series of cases uniformly ruling that the funds had to be released. The enactment of the Congressional Budget and Impoundment Control Act of 1974 divided impoundments into categories of rescissions (permanent cancellations of spending) and deferrals (temporary postponements of the availability of funds).

Congress created a procedure for checking the use of impoundments, but through the use of rescissions the president was given the power to eliminate individual items in the budget considered wasteful or unnecessary. Currently, the rescission procedure provides that the president may submit a special message to Congress proposing a cancellation of spending authority; this is referred to Senate and House Appropriation Committees. Unless both chambers complete action approving the president's rescission bill within forty-five legislative days, the budget authority must be made available. During the forty-five-day period, the authority can be withheld from obligation.[30] Under the enhanced rescission proposal, Congress would need to muster a two-thirds vote to overcome a rescission. If Congress does not vote to disapprove the rescission, the president could continue to withhold the funds indefinitely. This would greatly weaken the role of Congress relative to that of the president in the budget process.

A CONSTITUTIONAL AMENDMENT REQUIRING A BALANCED BUDGET

The Proposal

President Reagan urged Congress to adopt a balanced budget amendment in his annual messages: "I remain committed to and urge approval of a constitutional amendment requiring a balanced budget. The amendment should require a super-majority vote [at least 60 percent] in the Congress to increase taxes."[31] President Bush, numerous members of Congress, and others have suggested a variety of proposals urging the adoption of a constitutional amendment to require a balanced budget similar to President Reagan's proposal. The resolution with the largest number of cosponsors in the U.S. House of Representatives in the 101st Congress (H.J. Res. 268) was introduced by Representative Stenholm (D–Texas). This proposal provides for a constitutional amendment requiring Congress and the president, prior to each fiscal year, to agree upon an estimate of total receipts (excluding those derived from borrowing) for that fiscal year by enactment of a joint single subject resolution. The bill would prohibit outlays for the upcoming fiscal year (except those used for repayment of debt principal) from exceeding the estimated receipts for that year unless Congress, by a three-fifths roll call vote in each house, authorized outlays to exceed receipts.

Failed Acceptance Test

While interest in a constitutional requirement to balance the budget has increased since 1980, the high-water mark for such an amendment in both houses was 1982. In 1982, the Senate passed by the necessary two-thirds vote S.J. Res. 58, a balanced budget/tax limitation amendment. In that same year, the House failed to adopt a similar amendment, although a discharge petition was successful in bringing the issue to a vote, and a majority voted in favor of the amendment. In 1986, the Senate voted on a similar amendment mandating a balanced budget (S.J. Res. 228), but the measure failed to gain the necessary votes for passage. In 1988, the Judiciary Committee did not complete its markup of an amendment, thus, the Senate did not vote on the proposal in the 100th Congress. The national drive to gain additional state petitions for a constitutional convention to approve such an amendment continues to lack support by the necessary thirty-four states. In fact, momentum is gaining for a counterdrive so that states can recall earlier petitions for such a convention, with two states voting to do so in 1988.[32]

Those advocating a constitutional amendment to balance the budget argue that it could succeed in eliminating the federal deficit. Adoption of a balanced budget amendment has worked at the state level.[33] Only a constitutional amendment can ensure that Congress will adopt and enforce a balanced budget for each fiscal year. Advocates also argue that only the mandate of the people through a constitutional amendment can curb overspending and bring adequate fiscal discipline to the federal government. There are, however, a number of potential problems associated with a balanced budget amendment. The primary problem is that of defining a balanced budget. The problem of incorporating economic theories, policies, and definitions into the Constitution are virtually insurmountable. Absolute definitions of complex budget terminology and procedures would be difficult to develop. Loose definitions could crowd the courts with challenges each budget session. The courts would become the ultimate arbiters of the nation's budgetary policy, which encroaches on the constitutionally based authority of congressional spending power.

One problem raised by a constitutional amendment would be determining when, if ever, the budget could be out-of-balance. For example, assuming the president proposes and Congress adopts a budget in compliance with the constitutional limitation, most spending would still occur outside Congress' or the president's direct control. Revenues can be less or spending more than expected due to economic changes. In such a case, even the most faithful adherence by Congress and the president to a balanced budget plan might not prevent a deficit. How could this problem be dealt with constitutionally? Moreover, a constitutional amendment requiring a balanced budget would eliminate the flexibility which the federal government needs to address critical economic problems, such as recessions. In such circumstances, deficit spending may be appropriate.[34] The adoption of a balanced budget requirement would likely result in creative financing approaches to keep some spending from being subject to the limitations. For example, states which have constitutional spending limitations often have two budgets, one for current expenditures and one for capital expenditures. Recent analyses suggest that the much-praised experience with such constitutional requirements at the local level has not prevented a rate of growth in government spending and taxing since World War II in excess of the federal growth rate in these areas.[35]

Enforcement is another complex issue which would have to be addressed, either in the text of the amendment itself or through the enactment of separate legislation. Procedures for reaching the balanced budget, remedial measures (if a balanced budget were not achieved), and punitive sanctions would need to be specified and could present difficult policy choices. The experience of Congress and the president in implementing the GRH deficit targets illustrates the difficulty of making the choices necessary to achieve deficit reduction. A balanced budget amendment would only make the congressional budget process more contentious, pressured, and difficult. If there were conscientious adherence to the deficit targets set forth in GRH, a balanced budget amendment might not be needed at all and the tremendous dislocation and inflexibility which could occur through implementation of a constitutionally mandated balanced budget could be avoided. Even if the other problems associated with adopting and implementing the balanced budget amendment were worked out, the length of time necessary to obtain the passage of a constitutional amendment puts this budget reform well beyond the category of a near-term deficit solution.

EVALUATING THE PROPOSED CONGRESSIONAL BUDGET REFORMS

Delays, deadlocks, and deficits—these are the problems that have characterized the congressional budget process in the past two decades. This chapter has outlined six proposals for improving the congressional budget process. Whether any of these changes (GRH revisions enforcing deficit targets, changes in the use of the Social Security Trust Fund surplus, pay-as-you-go proposals, the presidential line-item veto, enhanced rescission authority, and a constitutional balanced budget amendment) would be able to eliminate the problems currently associated with the congressional budget process is questionable. However, it is possible to analyze the potential impact of these reforms on the budget process, Congress, and the president.

Table 3.3 outlines the hypothesized impact of each proposed reform of five structural and process factors. These factors or evaluation criteria are presidential power, congressional power, the distribution of power within Congress, the complexity of the budget process, and the impact of the reform on congressional ability to meet existing budget timetables. This table summarizes an assessment of the impact of each reform on the structure and power of the presidency and Congress and on the budget process.

Presidential and Executive Branch Budgetary Power

Generally all of the reforms would increase the power of the president relative to the power of Congress in the budget process. (See column one of Table 3.3.) However, the reforms would affect presidential and executive branch power in different ways. Several reforms, such as those that impose deficit targets, affect the Social Security surplus, establish pay-as-you-go provisions, or install a balanced budget amendment, do not affect the president's power to act directly in the budget process. However, they do increase the president's resources to negotiate budget policies and priorities with Congress. Those structural and policy changes could indirectly increase the president's power. In contrast, the presidential line-item veto and enhanced rescission authority would directly increase the power of the president to influence the size of the budget and the deficit and the composition of programs funded by the budget; if the president opposed a program, set of programs, or the level of federal funding (for political or economic reasons), he could veto or rescind them. This represents a significant expansion of presidential powers. All of the reforms described in this chapter would increase the power of the president in the budget process relative to the power of Congress. Such an increase in presidential power may be unacceptable to those in Congress who want to protect their constitutional "power of the purse." Senate Appropriations Committee Chairman Robert C. Byrd (D–West Virginia) described it this way: "If you turn over control of those purse strings to the man downtown [the president], whether he is a Democrat or Republican, you eliminate the need for a Congress. . . . The president will not only be the chief executive, he will be the chief legislator."[36]

Congressional Budgetary Power

The potential impact of the proposed reforms on congressional power over the budget process is substantial and mixed. (See the second column of Table 3.3.) Currently, Congress has substantial flexibility in budget decision making, in spite of the self-imposed limitations by the Congressional Budget Act and the GRH Act. New or enhanced deficit targets, changes to the Social

Table 3.3
Evaluating Proposed Congressional Budget Reforms

Reforms	Presidential/ Executive Branch Power	Congressional Power	Power within Congress	Budgetary Complexity	Budgetary Timeliness
			Evaluation Criteria		
Deficit Targets	Increase	Decrease	Centralize	More Complex	More Time Consuming
Social Security Surplus	Increase	Decrease	Centralize	More Complex	More Time Consuming
Pay-As-You-Go	Increase	Increase	Decentralize	More Complex	More Time Consuming
Line-Item Veto	Increase	Decrease	Centralize	More Complex	More Time Consuming

Table 3.3 (Continued)

Reforms	Presidential/ Executive Branch Power	Congressional Power	Power within Congress	Budgetary Complexity	Budgetary Timeliness
		Evaluation Criteria			
Enhanced Rescission Authority	Increase	Decrease	Centralize	More Complex	More Time Consuming
Balanced Budget Amendment	Increase	Decrease	Centralize	More Complex	More Time Consuming

Source: The format and evaluation criteria for this table are adopted and reformulated from *Proposed Budget Reforms: A Critical Analysis*. Prepared for the Committee on Governmental Affairs of the U.S. Senate. Washington, D.C.: CRS and CBO, April 1988.

Security Trust Fund, pay-as-you-go proposals, or a balanced budget amendment could decrease the ability of Congress to appropriate the level of
funding it might wish to, unless the appropriations are tied to tax increases,
thus decreasing one of the most significant powers of Congress. Although
raising taxes to pay for existing programs or new programs is unpopular,
President Bush and congressional leaders in mid–1990 agreed to increase
revenues to help reduce the deficit. Pay-as-you-go proposals would especially
limit the prospects for new programs because they would require funding
for new programs to be taken from existing programs. If a presidential line-
item veto or enhanced rescission authority were adopted, it would substantially decrease congressional power to control budget outcomes. Not only
would the president gain a powerful tool for actually preventing funds from
being distributed in accordance with the wishes of Congress, but the president would also be able to use the threat of a line-item veto or the rescission
of funding to negotiate and build coalition around his budget.

Power inside Congress

The proposed reforms would have a mixed consequence for the distribution of power within Congress. (See column three of Table 3.3.) Pay-as-
you-go reforms would decentralize power within Congress because the reforms encourage individual members to initiate their own "budget proposals"
by recommending cuts and revenue enhancements in a variety of programs
in order to save their own programs. Stricter enforcement of deficit targets
and/or taking the Social Security Trust Fund Surplus "off-budget" would
increase the public's understanding of the actual size of the federal deficit,
increasing pressure on members of Congress to make cuts. This could force
Congress to centralize more of its budget activities around the leadership
and the budget committees. The enactment of a balanced budget amendment
would have similar centralizing effects. Enactment of the line-item veto and
the enhanced rescission authority provisions would also result in more centralization of power within Congress as the congressional leadership was
forced to pursue negotiated budget solution with the president, in light of
his new power in the budget process.

Budgetary Complexity and Timeliness

All of the proposed reforms would increase the complexity of the budget
on Capitol Hill. (See column four, Table 3.3.) Increased budgetary complexity refers to an increase in the multiplicity of budget process steps and
the elaborate decision-making elements necessary to pass a budget. Complexity and timeliness are directly related. The more complex the process,
the more time consuming it is. The impact of the proposed reforms on the
ability of Congress to complete its budget work on time is substantial. (See

column five of Table 3.3.) All of the proposed reforms would make it more difficult to pass budgets on time. Use of the line-item veto or enhanced rescission authority would extend the budget progress over a longer period of time by forcing Congress to react to presidential actions. The cycle of actions and reactions by Congress and then the president and then Congress again would add another time-consuming step to an already overly complex process. Other reforms would be more time consuming by increasing the number of confrontations in Congress and between Congress and the president. These confrontations would also increase in complexity as more financial cuts were made to the budget or as pressure grew to raise taxes. Already difficult budget decisions would be made more difficult if Congress had to respond to enhanced deficit targets, changes in the Social Security Trust Fund, new pay-as-you-go proposals, or a balanced budget amendment.

THE 1990 BUDGET PROCESS REFORMS

Some of the issues addressed by the reforms discussed in this chapter were recently incorporated into the congressional budget process by the Budget Enforcement Act (BEA) of 1990. In the Budget Enforcement Act significant changes were made to the way federal budgets will be evaluated by Congress in the 1990s. The BEA passed on October 27, 1990, after months of "budget summit" negotiations and amid rapidly changing political and economic conditions. During these months, the deficit projections for FY 1990 and FY 1991 rose far above the figures that had been projected in President Bush's February budget proposal. The cost of the savings and loan bailout contributed significantly to the change in projections, as did changing assumptions about the health of the American economy.[37]

When it became apparent that the president's budget package was already obsolete and that Congress was settling in for a long and complex battle over federal spending, budget priorities, the state of the economy, and the size of the deficit, the Bush administration proposed a "budget summit." The budget summit was largely the brainchild of OMB director Richard C. Darman.[38] The bipartisan summit, comprised of congressional leaders and top administration officials, was intended to ease potential conflicts over the budget, negotiate compromises to difficult economic and political questions, and provide "political cover for unpopular election-year decisions."[39] After months of negotiation, all of the "summitteer's" efforts proved futile when the House of Representatives rejected the summit's budget proposal on October 5, 1990. Democrats and Republicans in both houses of Congress began to believe the summit proposal was so full of political compromise that it was a political disaster. After the defeat of the summit's budget package, Congress returned to its traditional form of decision making by congressional committee rather than to the extralegislative summit process. There was a flurry of legislative activity to develop a new budget plan before the November 5 congressional elections (where it appeared likely that the American public would react strongly and negatively in light of the budget crisis and the state of the economy) and to prevent the government from having to furlough employees or shut down completely. The result of this legislative activity was the FY 1991 budget and the Budget Enforcement Act of 1990.

The final FY 1991 budget envisions an estimated $40 billion reduction in the deficit. In addition, the FY 1991 budget is linked to a multiyear budget plan to reduce the federal deficit by $492 billion over the next five years (1991–1995).[40] The multiyear plan is intended to reduce the deficit through revenue increases roughly equal to $137.2 billion and outlay reductions of about $281.4 billion. The remainder of the deficit reduction will come principally from debt service savings. These savings and the estimated reduction in the deficit are achieved through the provision of the BEA that alters Gramm–Rudman–Hollings and incorporates a number of reforms into the congressional budget process.

In the BEA, the GRH deficit targets are extended through 1995, new deficit targets are established, and existing deficit targets are revised to reflect current economic and technical assumptions. The law provides for OMB to make additional adjustments in the targets based on changes in economic and technical assumptions, prior to the FY 1992 and FY 1993 budget cycles. OMB also has the option of making adjustments to the targets in FY 1994 and FY 1995.[41]

The law also changes the process of sequestration, which had been the hallmark of the GRH legislation. The 1990 act requires a specified amount of savings each year, for each of the years covered by the multiyear budget plan. Through FY 1993, sequestration is not linked to the total budget but to discretionary spending (i.e., spending for programs that must be appropriated each year) "ceilings" in three categories of government programs (defense, domestic, and international).

The ceiling of each discretionary spending category is enforced by end-of-session sequestration applied across-the-board to all of the programs within a category that exceeds its spending limit. For example, if the ceiling for discretionary spending in the international category is exceeded, the end-of-session sequester would apply to all programs within the international category. This process is referred to as "categorical sequestration." Categorical sequestration would only be triggered if the spending limits of any or all of the categories are exceeded due to changes in legislation (e.g., an extension of program benefits or of the number of people eligible to receive benefits or tax cuts). If the spending limits are exceeded because of changes in economic conditions (or, as is the case with many domestic programs, because the number of eligible recipients increases), sequestration would not be triggered. In FY 1994–1995, the system will return to fixed deficit targets enforced by the same sequestration rules used prior to the 1990 act, unless OMB exercises its option to fully adjust the FY 1994 and FY 1995 deficit targets in light of more up-to-date economic and technical estimates. There will be a single ceiling for all discretionary spending in FY 1994–1995. The law provides for a "look-back" at each legislative session to insure that legislation does not cause the spending limits to be exceeded. However, the law also provides for exemptions to spending ceilings due to "emergency needs."

As part of the 1990 Budget Enforcement Act, a number of the programs that are part of the budget (like the savings and loan bailout and the military operations in the Persian Gulf) will not be counted against the spending limits of their categories. In addition, Social Security receipts and disbursements are taken completely off-budget, and none of their transactions are included in estimates of the deficit or the calculations for sequestration. In both the House and Senate, the Social Security Trust Fund will be protected by "fire wall" points of order against legislation that would reduce trust fund balances.[42] An immediate consequence of this action is to increase the projected deficit to an unprecedented $317 billion for FY 1991.

Another major reform included in the 1990 Budget Enforcement Act is a pay-as-you-go (PAYGO) procedure that will cut nonexempt entitlement spending automatically to make up for any increase in the deficit due to the passage of legislation that increases entitlement benefits, extends benefits to more people, or would lead to revenue reductions. Under the new budget act, increases in direct spending (or reductions in revenues) must be paid for by offsetting spending reductions (or revenue increases). If the increase or decrease is not offset, there will be a special reconciliation to eliminate any net revenue loss and a sequester to eliminate any deficit increase. Notably, the law does not require that each individual bill be deficit-neutral, only that the net result of all the bills for each session of Congress be deficit-neutral. In addition, as was the case with the categorical spending limits, legislation can be exempted from the pay-as-you-go provision if there is an emergency need. However, since the new PAYGO rules force the authorizing committees to pass revenue-neutral bills, it shifts power within Congress, and between Congress and the president. Because OMB decides whether a bill meets the revenue-neutral test, its cost estimates will help to shape policy, giving new power to the president.

In addition, under the BEA provisions, the economic and technical assumptions made by OMB and used in estimating the president's budget proposal each January, will be locked-in for purposes of the sequestration projection to be made later in the year, giving OMB and the president new power in the budget process. Congress will no longer be aiming at "moving targets" as the president alters his estimating assumptions during the year.

The 1990 budget agreement also requires that all new revenues go to reduce the deficit. If the economy grows faster than anticipated, and revenues therefore exceed projections, the increased revenues would not be available to pay for increased spending.

The effect of the 1990 Budget Enforcement Act on the congressional budget process is substantial. It shifts the focus of the debate on the congressional budget process away from a discussion of the deficit to a discussion of statutory limits on spending, tax cuts, and "savings." As noted by John Yang: "The latest incarnation of the Gramm–Rudman–Hollings law–its third since it was enacted in 1985—would shift the emphasis from reducing the deficit to a specific target each year to achieving a designated amount of savings each year, regardless of the resulting deficit."[43] The intent here is clearly to decrease the emphasis on the federal deficit during the annual budget debates, which have become more heated in recent years as the deficit has grown in size and become more visible to the American public. Budget power has potentially been taken away from the budget committees. Through the five-year deal now in place, the budget committees may have little to do and the appropriations committees may gain more power over spending. The ability of OMB to modify the deficit targets and of Congress to exempt costly programs from the categorical spending limits may make the deficit targets impossible to miss and, as a result, make them useless in the struggle against higher deficits. However, the ability of the 1990 act to refocus attention away from the deficit, to decrease the deficit, or to increase savings within categories of the budget, remains to be seen.

CONCLUSIONS

While the Congressional Budget and Impoundment Control Act of 1974, the Gramm–Rudman–Hollings Deficit Reduction Act of 1985 and 1987, and the 1990 Budget Enforcement Act reforms are attempts at improving the budget process, they have not been able to prevent budgetary delay, deadlocks, or deficit spending in Congress. The responsibility for these problems does not lie solely with either the American electorate or their elected officials. The American electorate has wanted new programs and increased federal spending without the burden of higher taxes. It wanted social problems solved, but has been unwilling to make a commitment to eliminating them. In those situations, the federal government has stepped in and met the needs and demands of the people. By the same token, elected officials have been torn between their genuine desire to serve the needs of their constituents (the potential beneficiaries of federal programs and higher federal spending), their own desire to win reelection by sending federal dollars back to their districts, and their need to legislate in the best economic and political interests of the country. The result of all of this has been larger budgets and higher deficits.

Some responsibility for current budget problems must be taken by each side. If the electorate had possessed the political will to pay for the programs they wanted or needed, the means for directing and controlling Congress has always been at its disposal. The public could make their views known to their elected officials, be more aware of the stated positions of their officials, and find out how their representatives vote on budget legislation. Most importantly, the electorate has always been able to either vote for candidates that support greater fiscal responsibility or vote out elected officials who fail to make sound budgetary decisions. A newfound commitment and display of political will may soon become evident as public concern over the deficit and the state of the American economy grows, and when all new revenues must be used to reduce the deficit. A poll, taken before passage of the FY 1991 budget and the 1990 Budget Enforcement Act, indicated that "Americans overwhelmingly expect their federal taxes to go up to reduce the budget deficit, and they are willing to accept some new taxes."

Change must come from the will of the American electorate through their representatives in Congress. If voters want a balanced budget through expenditure cuts and new taxes, Congress will pass a balanced budget with or without additional reforms. The 1990 budget process reforms may be the first indication that such political will exists. If the American electorate wants programs, but without increased taxes (through deficit financing), no reform will change the budget process or the choices made by Congress. Process reforms can not make up for the lack of political will. In the past, neither the American electorate nor their elected officials in the White House or on Capitol Hill have had the political will necessary to make revenues match outlays. A clear example of this lack of political will was the struggle over the 1991 budget when the hard deficit reduction targets of GRH I and II were dropped in favor of a new five-year deficit reduction plan, which may just have been a way of putting off difficult budgetary decisions for four or five years.

Policy outcomes and budget process reforms cannot be separated from political issues or the political arena, as was shown in the 1990 budget negotiations. Most members of Congress are simply unwilling to let a few high-level officials control the budget process; the budget's impact on the nation and on political careers is simply too great for members of Congress to dismiss. However, Congress must demonstrate that it has the political will necessary to eliminate the budget deficit and to budget responsibly and intelligently for the benefit of both its various constituencies and the country as a whole. Some members are already doing that by working toward reforming the budget process (as demonstrated by the FY 1991 budget and the 1990 Budget Enforcement Act) and by reevaluating the way they think about the budget. However, the 1990 Budget Enforcement Act may be just another means by which Congress temporarily avoids deadlock over the budget, by delaying the time by which they must come to grips with the deficit. Whether the 1990 Budget Enforcement Act will affect any real change in the congressional budget process remains to be seen.

NOTES

1. Rudolph G. Penner and Alan J. Abramson, *Broken Purse Strings: Congressional Budgeting 1974–1988* (Washington, D.C.: Urban Institute Press, 1988).

2. This chapter summarizes several 1990 Budget Process Revisions and other proposed reforms to the budget process, but does not attempt to discuss all 1990 changes and proposed reforms. In addition, the description of each general type of reform may contain references to a number of specific reform proposals that fall within that type.

3. From Title XIII, Section II, "President's Budget Submission," of the Budget Enforcement Act of 1990, conference report, 15.

4. One of the important reforms instituted by the 1974 Budget Act was the creation of the Congressional Budget Office (CBO). This agency serves as Congress' principal source of information and analysis on the budget and on spending and revenue legislation. The CBO has a specific mandate to assist the House and Senate budget committees and the spending and revenue committees; secondarily it responds to requests for information from other committees and individual members of Congress. Prior to the creation of CBO, Congress was forced to rely on the president's budget estimates and economic forecasts and the annual analysis of the economy and fiscal policy done by the Joint Economic Committee.

5. James A. Thurber, "Budget Continuity and Change: An Assessment of the Congressional Budget Process," in *Studies of Modern American Politics*, edited by D. K. Adams, (Manchester, England: Manchester University Press, 1987).

6. See Allen Schick, *Reconciliation and the Congressional Budget Process* (Washington, D.C.: American Enterprise Institute, 1981); D. Tate, "Reconciliation Breeds Tumult as Committees Tackle Costs: Revolutionary Budget Tool," *Congressional Quarterly Weekly Report* (Washington, D.C.: Congressional Quarterly, May 23, 1981), 887–91.

7. "The Rostenkowski Challenge," prepared by the Office of Representative Dan Rostenkowski, press release. March 12, 1990.

8. These deadlines significantly altered prior budget process deadlines. Notably, the new deadlines have been delayed or modified informally each year since GRH I and GRH II were passed.

9. See Penner and Abramson, *Broken Purse Strings*, 97.

10. *Bowsher v. Sinar*, 106 S. Ct. 3181 (July 7, 1986).

11. The fiscal year (FY) is the government's yearly accounting period, which begins on October 1 and ends on the following September 30. The fiscal year is designated by the calendar year in which it ends; i.e., fiscal year 1992 begins October 1, 1991 and ends on September 30, 1992. See *An Analysis of the President's Budgetary Proposals for Fiscal Year 1991* (Washington, D.C.: Congressional Budget Office, 1990). As of May 15, 1990, some authoritative sources estimated that the deficit would be $200 billion, so a "budget summit" with congressional leaders was called by President Bush to determine the steps necessary to meet the GRH II target.

12. U.S. Congress, House, Committee on the Budget, *The Fiscal Year 1991 Budget*, February 2, 1990, committee print.

13. Current services outlays are the costs associated with maintaining existing government services and programs.

14. At the present time, Congress evaluates the budget only once a year to ascertain whether it is meeting the GRH deficit targets. The result is the budget "snapshot." After that evaluation, Congress is free to add on new expenditures to the budget, which often increase the deficit.

15. See U.S. Congress, Senate, Committee on Government Affairs, "Proposed Budget Reforms: A Critical Analysis," in *Proposed Budget Reform: A Critical Analysis*, prepared by Allen Schick (Washington, D.C.: Congressional Research Service and the Library of Congress, April 1988), 52.

16. The selection of these proposals comes from discussions with House and Senate budget committee staff, September 1989, and an unpublished staff memo, July 25, 1989.

17. Interviews with House and Senate budget committee staff, September 1989.

18. House budget committee staff memo, July 25, 1989.

19. See *A Bill to Cut Social Security Contribution Rates*, a statement to the press by Senator Daniel Patrick Moynihan on Tuesday, January 23, 1990.

20. Ibid.

21. The required 1993 deficit reduction is $235 billion under realistic economic assumptions.

22. These other options include: (1) "take the medicine now" (stop counting the *net* surplus beginning in 1992 and do not extend GRH beyond 1993); (2) protect Social Security funds through a "protection act" (have points of order against proposals to transfer Social Security assets to the general fund of federal funds); and (3) remove Social Security and medicare from the unified budget and exclude it from GRH calculations, but also end the Medicare subsidy over three years (1993–1996). There are a number of other proposed reforms which involve the Social Security Trust Fund. However, at this time there is little political support inside or outside of Congress for these reforms.

23. " 'Pay as You Go'; Democrats Sense New Opportunities in Old Ideas," *The Washington Post*, March 28, 1990, A21.

24. U.S. Congressional Budget Office staff memo; *Pay-as-You-Go Budgeting* (Washington, D.C.: Government Printing Office, March 1990).

25. *The Washington Post*, March 13, 1990, A1.

26. U.S. Office of Management and Budget, Executive Office of the President, *The U.S. Budget in Brief: Fiscal Year 1990* (Washington, D.C.: Government Printing Office, 1989), 11–12.

27. Fiscal Year 1990 Budget Message to Congress.

28. Penner and Abramson, *Broken Purse Strings*, 121.

29. House budget committee staff memo (Washington, D.C.: unpublished, July 25, 1989).

30. Thurber, "Budget Continuity and Change."

31. OMB, *U.S. Budget in Brief, Fiscal Year 1990*, 11.

32. House budget committee staff memo, (Washington, D.C.: unpublished, July 25, 1989), 144.

33. U.S. Congress, *Proposed Budget Reforms: A Critical Analysis*, 18.

34. This is a summary of views expressed by House budget committee staff, September 1989.

35. Penner and Abramson, 124.

36. In John E. Yang, "Republicans Seek Big Trade-offs for any Tax Hike," *The Washington Post*, May 15, 1990, A5.

37. John E. Yang and Steven Mufson, "Package Termed Best Circumstances Permit," *The Washington Post*, October 29, 1990, A4.

38. Ibid.

39. Ibid.

40. John E. Yang, "Gramm–Rudman–Hollings Redux," *The Washington Post*, October 30, 1990, A19.

41. Ibid.

42. The "fire wall" points-of-order provisions provided for in the 1990 Budget Enforcement Act differ between the House and the Senate. In the House the provision

creates a 'fire wall' point of order (as free-standing legislation) to prohibit the consideration of legislation that would change the actuarial balance of the Social Security trust funds over a 5-year or 75-year period. In the case of legislation decreasing Social Security revenues, the prohibition would not apply if the legislation also included an equivalent increase in Medicare taxes for the period covered by the legislation.

The Senate

also creates a fire wall to protect Social Security financing but does so by expanding certain budget enforcement provisions of the Congressional Budget Act of 1974. The Senate amendment expands the prohibition in Section 310(g) of the Budget Act to specifically protect Social Security financing, prohibits the consideration of a reported budget resolution calling for a reduction in Social Security surpluses, and includes Social Security in the enforcement procedures under Sections 302 and 311 of the Budget Act. The Senate amendment also requires the Secretary of Health and Human Services to provide an actuarial analysis of any legislation affecting Social Security, and generally prohibits the consideration of legislation lacking such an analysis.

From Title XIII, Section 6, "Treatment of Social Security," of the Budget Enforcement Act of 1990, conference report, 10.

43. Yang, "Gramm–Rudman–Hollings Redux," A19.

SELECT BIBLIOGRAPHY

Aberbach, Joel. *Keeping a Watchful Eye: The Politics of Congressional Oversight.* Washington, D.C.: Brookings Institution, 1990.

Axelrod, Donald. *Budgeting for Modern Government.* New York: St. Martin's Press, 1988.

DiLorenzo, Thomas J. "Putting Off-Budget Federal Spending Back on the Books." Washington, D.C.: Heritage Foundation, January 30, 1985.

Downs, George W., and David M. Rocke. "Theories of Budgetary Decision Making and Revenue Decline." *Policy Sciences* 16 (1984): 329–47.

Eisner, Robert. *How Real Is the Federal Deficit?* New York: Free Press, 1986.

Ellwood, J. W., and J. A. Thurber. "The New Congressional Budget Process: The Hows and Whys of House-Senate Differences." In *Congress Reconsidered*, 2d ed., edited by L. C. Dodd and B. Oppenheimer. Washington, D.C.: Congressional Quarterly, 1981.

Ferejohn, John, and Keith Krehbiel. "The Budget Process and the Size of the Budget." *American Journal of Political Science* 31 (May 1987): 296–320.

Fisher, Louis. "The Budget Act of 1974: A Further Loss of Spending Control." In *Congressional Budgeting: Politics, Process and Power*, edited by Thomas W. Wander, F. Ted Hebert, and Gary W. Copeland, 170–89. Baltimore, Md.: Johns Hopkins University Press, 1984.

Gist, John R. " 'Stability' and 'Competition' in Budgetary Theory." *American Political Science Review* 76 (December 1982): 859–72.

Haas, Lawrence J. "Line-Item Logic." *National Journal*, June 9, 1990, 1391–94.

Kamlet, Mark S., and David C. Mowery. "An Analysis of Congressional Macro-budgetary Priorities and the Impact of the Congressional Budget Act." Paper presented at the annual meeting of the American Political Science Association, September 1–3, 1983.

Kenworthy, Tom. "Moynihan Attacks Rostenkowski's Benefits Cuts." *The Washington Post*, March 17, 1990, section 1, p. A9.

LeLoup, Lance T. "Discretion in National Budgeting: Controlling the Controllables." *Policy Analysis* 4 (Fall 1978): 455–75.

Lynch, Thomas D. *Public Budgeting in America*, 2nd edition. Englewood Cliffs, N.J.: Prentice Hall, 1985.

McAllister, Bill. "White House Warmly Greets Rostenkowski Deficit Plan." *The Washington Post*, March 13, 1990, A1, A4.

Moran, Donald W. "Perspectives on Proposals for Budget Process Reform." *National Tax Journal* 37 (September 1984): 377–84.

National Economic Commission. *National Economic Commission: Staff Papers, Background Papers, and Major Testimony*, compiled by Margaret D. Chisholm, Peter T. Nakahata, Margaret R. Shaw, and Arthur W. Stigile. Washington, D.C.: Government Printing Office, March 1989.

———. *Report of the National Economic Commission*. Washington, D.C.: Government Printing Office, March 1, 1989.

Office of Management and Budget, Executive Office of the President. *United States Budget in Brief: Fiscal Year 1990*. Washington, D.C.: Government Printing Office, 1989.

———. *Budget of the United States Government: Fiscal Year 1991*. Washington, D.C.: Government Printing Office, 1990.

Penner, Rudolph G., ed. *The Congressional Budget Process after Five Years*. Washington, D.C.: American Enterprise Institute, 1981.

Penner, Rudolph G., and Alan J. Abramson. *Broken Purse Strings: Congressional Budgeting 1974–1988*. Washington, D.C.: Urban Institute Press, 1988.

Peterson, Paul E. "The New Politics of Deficits." In *The New Direction in American Politics*, edited by John E. Chubb and Paul E. Peterson, 365–97. Washington, D.C.: Brookings Institution, 1985.

Rivlin, Alice M. "The Political Economy of Budget Choices: A View From Congress." Paper presented at the American Economics Association, December 29, 1981.

————. "Economics and the Political Process." *The American Economic Review* 77 (March 1987): 1–10.

Rivlin, Alice M., and Robert W. Hartman. "Control of Federal Credit Under the Congressional Budget Process." In *Reconstructing the Federal Budget: A Trillion Dollar Quandary*, edited by Albert T. Somers. New York: Preager, 1984.

Rostenkowski, Dan. "Cold Turkey: How to End the Deficit in 5 Years." *The Washington Post*, March 11, 1990, section 2, pp. B1, B4.

————. "The Rostenkowski Challenge." Press release, March 12, 1990.

Rubin, Irene S. *The Politics of Public Budgeting: Getting and Spending, Borrowing and Balancing*. Chatham, N.J.: Chatham House, 1990.

————. ed. *New Directions in Budget Theory*. Albany, N.Y.: State University of New York Press, 1988.

Schick, Allen. *Congress and Money*. Washington, D.C.: Urban Institute, 1980.

————. *Reconciliation and the Congressional Budget Process*. Washington, D.C.: American Enterprise Institute, 1981.

————. ed. *Perspectives on Budgeting*. Washington, D.C.: American Society for Public Administration, 1987.

Shuman, Howard E. *Politics and the Budget: The Struggle Between the President and the Congress*. Englewood Cliffs, N.J.: Prentice Hall, 1984.

Thurber, James A. "Congressional Budget Reform and New Demands for Policy Analysis." *Policy Analysis* (Spring 1976): 198–214.

————. "Assessing the Congressional Budget Process under Gramm–Rudman–Hollings and the 1974 Budget Act." Paper presented to the annual meeting of the American Political Science Association, 1986.

————. "Budget Continuity and Change: An Assessment of the Congressional Budget Process." In *Studies of Modern American Politics*, edited by D. K. Adams. Manchester, England: Manchester University Press, 1987.

U.S. Congress, House, Committee on the Budget. *The Whole and the Parts: Piecemeal and Integrated Approaches to Congressional Budgeting*. Washington, D.C.: Government Printing Office, February 1987.

U.S. Congress, House, Committee on Rules. *Issue Presentations before the Rules Committee Task Force on the Budget Process*. Washington, D.C.: Government Printing Office, October 1984.

U.S. Congress, House and Senate, Committees on the Budget. *Reducing the Deficit: Spending and Revenue Options—Part II*, prepared by the Congressional Budget Office. Washington, D.C.: Government Printing Office, 1990.

U.S. Congress, Senate, Committee on Finance. "Remarks of Robert S. Strauss." February 27, 1990.

U.S. Congress, Senate, Committee on Governmental Affairs. "Proposed Budget Reforms: A Critical Analysis." In *Proposed Budget Reforms: A Critical Analysis*, prepared by Allen Schick. Washington, D.C.: Congressional Research Service and Congressional Budget Office, April 1988, 1–70.

U.S. Congressional Budget Office. *New Approaches to the Budgetary Treatment of Federal Credit Assistance*, prepared by Marvin Phuap. Washington, D.C.: Government Printing Office, March 1984.

————. *The Economic and Budget Outlook: Fiscal Years 1991–1995*. Washington, D.C.: Government Printing Office, January 1990.

————. *Pay-As-You-Go Budgeting*, a CBO staff memorandum. Washington, D.C.: Government Printing Office, March 1990.

U.S. Congressional Research Service. "Legislation, Appropriations, and Budgets: The Development of Spending Decision Making in Congress," prepared by Allen Schick. Washington, D.C.: Government Printing Office, May 1984.

————. *Manual on the Federal Budget Process*, prepared by Allen Schick, Robert Keith, and Edward Davis. Washington, D.C.: Government Printing Office, March 31, 1987.

Wander, Thomas W. "Patterns of Change in the Congressional Budget Process, 1865–1974." *Congress and the Presidency* 9 (Autumn 1982): 23–49.

Weaver, R. Kent. *Automatic Government: The Politics of Indexation*. Washington, D.C.: Brookings Institution, 1988.

————. *The New Politics of the Budgetary Process*. Glenview, Ill.: Scott, Foreman and Company, 1988.

4

FEDERAL BUDGET MAKING: A BIPARTISAN FAILURE?

THOMAS D. LYNCH

Most U.S. citizens are not pleased with the inability of the president and Congress to deal effectively with the yearly deficit budget.[1] The federal government has a three trillion dollar debt and $180 billion is needed to pay the yearly interest on it. Interest is now the third largest expense in the fiscal year (FY) 1991 $1.3 trillion federal budget.

Even the authors of the Gramm–Rudman–Hollings (GRH) budget reform declare that the federal budget process does not work correctly. Rarely are timely appropriation bills enacted. Each year the budget continues to be unbalanced, and the interest payments consist of 14 percent of the projected federal outlays. Worse, the budgets that are passed are misleading in terms of the true yearly deficits. The tension between a Democrat-controlled Congress and a Republican president contributes to delay and disagreements.

Related but largely ignored is the alarming problem of unfunded and contingent liabilities. The Congress and the president commit the federal treasury to billions and even a trillion dollars of future expenses in a manner considered unacceptable in the private sector. For example, the federal government does not set aside funds to cover its pension liability for its own work force in spite of the fact that the federal government requires that private employers do so. Instead, the federal government makes an implicit pledge that its future pension obligations will be honored. Obviously this practice significantly distorts the yearly budget figures.

Contingent liabilities are related distortions. They are called loan guarantees—pledges made by the federal government to pay the loans of others (e.g., students, farmers, homeowners) if the original debtor defaults. Such guarantees tend to lower interest costs for debtors thus giving them an important benefit. There is often no drain on the federal treasury if the original debtors pay their obligations. However, if the economy weakens, then the federal costs can become significant. A problem which occurred in the 1980s (and may again in the 1990s) was that federal loan guarantee programs were run in an unsound manner. Both the student loan and the federally guaranteed savings and loans programs illustrate that contingent liabilities can dramatically increase the national deficit.

In 1990 Congress passed and the president signed the Budget Enforcement Act of 1990, which significantly changed the federal budget process. Those changes and their likely impact shall be discussed in this chapter. In brief, the new law moved the focus of congressional and presidential attention away from lowering the federal deficit to achieving yearly adjusted targets for savings designed to control federal spending. However, there were some major exceptions set out in that law. The current fiscal year deficit is higher after the bill passed. Even with a booming rather than a recession economy, the 1992 deficit will be $315 billion plus and the $3 trillion deficit will grow by at least another three quarters of a trillion dollars by mid-decade. The complaint with the law was not that too much was done but rather that Congress is now under little pressure to address the true problem. The new law scrapped the Gramm–Rudman–Hollings disciplinary machinery until 1993.

This chapter explores the yearly federal deficit and related problems. The sections will examine the national debt, claims that the debt really is a nonissue, proposed budget reform and related liabilities problems, and several financial management ideas designed to increase productivity.

CAUSE FOR CONCERN

The Price of Interest

During the Reagan and early Bush terms, the inflation rate has been low, the unemployment rate has been moderate to low, and the economy has grown at a slow but acceptable pace. Given that record, what if there is a large yearly federal government deficit? True, the newspapers make headlines about the large yearly deficits. But don't the true economic indicators tell us that the economy is doing fine, or in a mild recession, and that the deficit is not really a significant problem? Let us look at the economic impact of the deficit.

The U.S. government's annual borrowing for its three trillion dollar debt increases the demand for available savings and investment capital. This increases the cost of borrowing money for individuals, companies, state and local governments, corporations, and other countries. Particularly hurt is the marginal borrower who finds loan money unavailable or very expensive.

This has negative economic and social implications, such as harming American international trade competitiveness. The United States is in its fourth decade of declining trade competitiveness and relative loss of quality of life. If people measure corporate size by stock market value, they discover that two of the ten largest corporations are American and eight are Japanese. Of the fifty largest corporations in the world, only 24 percent are American but 70 percent are Japanese. Part of that unfortunate economic reality is due to America's government debt. The national debt causes high interest rates which discourage businesses from investing in improved capital to increase their productivity and which drive up the value of dollars in international markets.[2]

Limiting Policy Options

A large yearly interest payment limits the policy options available to future Congresses and presidents. As interests and principle paid on the national debt constitutes a continually larger percent of the federal government's budget, future policy makers can not respond to other national needs and emergencies because they must first service the national debt. The only alternatives to meeting the yearly debt payment are default or renegotiating the loan terms. Subsequent to exercising such an option, the government would find fewer institutions and people willing to loan it money at favorable terms. Thus, a nation, which is facing high debt service payments, must decide between (1) default or loan renegotiations with the likelihood of higher future interest payments and less credit available or (2) not meeting emergencies or critical economic and social needs.

Governments, like individuals, normally do not reach a credit crisis within a short time. The federal government fits the classic pattern of irresponsible spending associated with individuals, corporations, and nations that go bankrupt. Certainly, the United States can afford a debt service payment of 14 percent and even higher. However, as the percentage climbs each year, there is less money available for defense, social welfare, and other needs. Under these circumstances, the desires for higher program funding could lead to printing excess money and to hyperinflation.

Another threat is that the U.S. Treasury will not find investors for its new bonds or refinanced old bonds. Until recently the United States has attracted foreign investors to buy its bonds, but now economic and political factors have changed to encourage both Japanese and European investors to keep their money at or near home. If the U.S. Treasury has difficulty in finding investors for its bonds, then it is forced to increase its interest rates to attract investors. However, if the Treasury attempts to refinance its existing debt and it can not find investors, then a major world financial crisis exists. A more likely circumstance is that the Treasury will have to pay double digit interest rates and force others in America also to pay higher interest rates due to market pressures.

Trade Deficit

The United States trade deficit is also a major concern. A deficit means that jobs for American workers are lost to workers in other countries because American goods and services are not competitive compared to those of other countries. This leads to lower national growth and a lower standard of living in the United States. Because of the trade deficit, a shift in the value of the U.S. dollar occurs. For example, Americans find their currency buys less in Europe and Japan.

The key to solving the trade deficit is having a competitive economy in which quality American goods can be produced for less than the current effort. The Council on Competitiveness (a group representing many of America's leading corporations) believes that at least part of the answer for increasing competitiveness lies in (1) more research and development, (2) better education, and (3) increasingly substituting machines for human power. Each of those reforms requires greater government investments or favorable tax policy. Both are difficult to achieve because of the limits imposed by the budget deficit.

Transfers of Wealth

Charles A. Bowsher, U.S. Comptroller General, noted that servicing the national debt is the largest transfer of American wealth in U.S. history. American workers, who are the major taxpayers, are having their money transferred to institutional investors and wealthy individuals who purchase U.S. Treasury securities. In 1988, 13 percent or more than $27 billion was paid to foreign owners of U.S. Treasury securities.[3] Essentially, the middle and working class in America are enriching the wealthy with high interest rather than using those resources for better schools, for more research and development that will produce better jobs and higher living standards, or for infrastructure improvements.

RECENT HISTORY

GRH and the Sequestration Fix

In 1990, the president and Congress were locked in a dramatic budget crisis that literally shut down many government services and continually threatened a longer government shutdown as Congress disagreed and President Bush threatened a veto. In this crisis circumstance, a remarkable budget law was passed that not only increased taxes but also substantially changed the budget process at the same time the federal budget was being enacted. The budget reform portion of the new law had 141 pages of "enforcement" language. The law was passed with few members having read it, no hearing being conducted, and no debate. The law was literally passed in the dead of the night. To understand the new law, a discussion of the previous law is necessary, and that discussion follows.

The 1985 Balanced Budget Act (GRH) established an automatic, across-the-board procedure for cutting programs called sequestering. The GRH set deficit reduction targets for subsequent years with the Office of Management and Budget which is responsible for estimating the revenue and expenditures in the budget. For example, in FY 1991 the deficit was to be no more than $64 billion. If that target could not have been met by Congress, many domestic and defense programs would have received an automatic, across-the-board cut so that the $64 billion target was met. When the GRH law was passed, the law makers felt the prospects of an across-the-board cut would be sufficiently unpleasant so that Congress and the president would act responsibly. However, a review of FY 1989 and FY 1990 budgets proves this assumption to be false.[4]

The deficit reduction targets were not irrevocable. The GRH permitted Congress to revise the targets if there was a recession. Also, the law including the deficit reduction targets could have been amended at any time unless the president vetoed the change. Also, supplemental appropriations could ignore the GRH targets. According to the former House Budget Committee Chairman, Jim Jones, most members of Congress consider the targets a farce.[5]

One accounting trick to meet the deficit reduction targets under GRH, but not possible under the new law, has been the use of surpluses in the federal government's trust funds. Without the trust fund surpluses, the FY 1989 deficit would have been $204 billion rather than the reported $152 billion. This is essentially a loan from the trust funds to the general fund.[6] This obfuscatory trick was challenged by Senator Moynihan with his proposal to put Social Security on a pay-as-you-go basis. Under his bill, there would be no surplus to loan to the general fund. Removing the Social Security trust fund surpluses makes meeting the old deficit reduction targets very difficult to achieve, but those old targets have been revised.

Adopting a tax increase of significant proportions is practically impossible if the president will use his veto to stop new taxes. President Bush did accept new taxes and revisions in tax in 1990. The most unlikely future type of tax increase is a return to higher, or somewhat higher, progressive rates on the income tax. An unlikely but possible additional tax increase is the value-added tax advocated by Senator Hollings. This tax, common in industrialized countries, raises significant money by placing a sales-like tax on the increase in value of a product in every step in its evolution. This regressive consumption tax can be added on products and services at the border; thus it does not harm America's international economic competitiveness as does the income tax.

The 1990 budget reforms were largely the product of OMB Director Richard Darman and Senator Robert Byrd, who achieved the changes with minimum debate during an extremely heated and difficult tax increase and revision legislation debate. The 1990 act included such highly emotional subjects as revising slightly the higher progressive tax rates, increasing gasoline taxes and various excise taxes, and lowering deductibles for high-income people. The budget reform portion was essentially not debated in spite of its complexity and significance to the federal budget process.

The key aspect of the 1990 legislation was to eliminate the GRH focus on lowering the federal deficit and replace it with controlling federal spending. Some important programs were exempted from the process. In place of deficit reduction targets, adjustable targets for proposed savings in four categories for FY 1991 through 1993 were defined to force Congress to live within those yearly targets. Starting in 1994, the four categories will be collapsed into one category just as in GRH. This FY 1991 through 1993 procedure essentially prevents Congress from reordering military versus domestic budget priorities and makes the yearly budget resolution process less significant until FY 1994.

The law creates three discretionary spending categories (i.e., defense, international aid, and domestic programs). Operation Desert Storm is not covered in any category and thus is exempt. If Congress chooses to increase discretionary spending in most other programs, it must cut other spending programs in the appropriate category and live within the yearly category target. For the fourth category—entitlement spending programs—Congress must remain "revenue neutral" in terms of costs or tax benefits to meet the yearly target. If Congress fails to make the offsetting reduction in a category according to OMB, an automatic sequester cuts all category programs to stay within the ceiling. Social Security remains exempt from the process as in the earlier GRH legislation. The new law creates a schedule that permits sequestering several times a year for discretionary programs and once a year for entitlement and tax cuts.

The 1990 law strengthens the power of OMB in the budget process. The various annual federal spending category targets can be adjusted by OMB for economic and technical reasons established in the law. OMB has the responsibility to monitor legislation and determine if spending is likely to exceed the ceiling and the amount of the sequester if that is necessary. Due to a mistake in the 1990 appropriation bill for the State Department, the funding measure was about $403 million over the category ceiling and OMB announced a 2 percent sequester to insure spending stayed within the cap. Thus the new act was tested almost immediately after it passed. OMB can also recommend to the president when a situation is an emergency. If the president and Congress agree, then emergency spending falls outside the ceilings. Another OMB power is to determine what category a program or portion of a program properly belongs under the law. This gives OMB added flexibility.

The 1990 law has important exceptions that lessen its significance as a deficit reduction measure. Important and very expensive programs such as Social Security, Desert Storm, and deposit insurance guarantees are not included. These are expensive programs that often significantly add to the yearly deficit. In addition, the president and Congress can declare an emergency for any program, and that program also would be exempt from the 1990 provisions. The ability of OMB to adjust the yearly ceiling targets is limited by legal guidelines, but this nevertheless gives OMB some additional power such as the ability to adjust ceilings to further the political interests of the White House.

The 1990 Darman–Byrd reforms include three noteworthy changes. First, Senator Moynihan's concern over the false impression given by accounting the Social Security Trust Fund has been resolved by not allowing the surplus to be used in calculating the federal deficit total. Second, the new law requires the executive branch to estimate the budget authority needed to meet yearly contingent liability and includes that amount in the ceiling except for the deposit insurance programs. Third, a "look back" provision in the new law reduces discretionary spending limits based on the actual previous year's breaches. Thus the ceilings are based on actual rather than estimated numbers that tend to be manipulated for political reasons. This adjustment means that politically inspired optimistic estimating is a less useful ploy, as any forecasting errors will be adjusted according to the look-back provision.

POSSIBLE BUDGET REFORMS

Debated Reforms

The following discussion reviews the various budget reforms seriously being considered in Washington plus some additional reforms this author believes merit attention. The reforms considered here are:

- a single economic forecast
- biennial budgeting
- balanced budget constitutional amendments
- enhanced rescission
- line-item veto
- a two stage budget process used to set revenue and expenditure targets

Each of the reforms will be discussed with special focus given to the last reform.

Possible but Unlikely Reforms

Single Economic Forecast. One suggested reform is to force the agencies that are supplying budget forecasts to agree on one set of projections. Budgeting is always based on economic forecasting. A problem in Washington is that Office of Management and Budget and the Congressional Budget Office often have widely different budget forecasts. Thus, the policy differences between the president and Congress get obscured by forecasting assumptions. This reform would help budget decisions on policy instead of arguments over economic assumptions. The *Bousher v. Synar* court decision vests power to estimate costs of legislation with OMB and this makes a consensus approach to forecasting impossible.

Biennial Budgeting. The federal government uses a one-year budget and appropriation process. Yet many states use a two-year budget. With this reform less time would be devoted to budget and appropriation matters. This reform has been tried at least partially in the defense area.

Balanced Budget Constitutional Amendment. This proposal has won a great deal of support among the state legislatures but little in Congress. There are different versions of the amendment. Generally, it requires Congress to pass a balanced budget except in times of national emergencies. A super majority vote would be required to override the balance requirement. Efforts to achieve this reform have failed, and renewed attempts are not likely.

Enhanced Rescission and Line-Item Veto. Both would give the president authority to reject very specific programs and are viewed by many in Congress as tipping the balance of power in the president's favor. President Bush has considered a Supreme Court test of presidential line-item authority, but the arguments for its legality appear to be weak.[7]

A Two-Stage Budget Process

First Stage. One reform might be to create a two-stage budget process. The first stage would be to pass a budget plan with targets for revenue raising and domestic and defense spending levels. This reform was attempted using a voluntary agreement between the White House and congressional leaders in FY 1988 and 1989. In 1989, the voluntary process failed with the announcement by Senate Majority Leader Mitchell that the Senate Democrats would not negotiate a 1990 budget plan with President Bush. Senator Mitchell felt that the president's insistence on lowering capital gains tax rates proved that the president was not serious about reducing the national yearly deficit.

If a law required the president and Congress to set budget target levels, this could be done by using a joint budget resolution to be signed by the president instead of the current concurring resolution. This proposal would continue to bar the appropriations committees from taking money earmarked in budget resolutions for defense and using it for domestic programs. This proposal is not popular with the powerful appropriations committees who wish to retain discretion in their decision making. It suffers also from the possibility that Congress and the president could not agree on ceilings. To be effective, some type of penalty would have to be imposed such as no pay for political congressional and executive leaders unless such a resolution were passed.

With this reform, the first stage would be to pass a joint budget resolution of Congress which sets revenue targets and expenditure ceilings. The targets would be addressed to each revenue source, but expenditure ceilings would be addressed only to totals for departments and independent agencies. The president would have the opportunity to veto the resolution. The resolution would be legally binding on the congressional committees in preparing their revised authorization language for entitlements and similar programs, money raising legislation, and appropriation bills. If the joint budget resolution was not passed in a timely manner, then each of those committees would use the prior year's targets and ceilings until the resolution passed. Executive branch agencies would be required to submit budget information to Congress consistent with the budget resolution.

Second Stage. At this stage Congress would pass detailed budget bills for the various departments and independent agencies. The bills would be placed in ten to fifteen separate groups as is currently done. Care would be taken to match revenue sources with expenditures so that each bill addresses a separate accounting fund. Thus, decisions on each bill will address trade-off decisions of revenue, entitlements, and appropriations. For example, transportation could be a separate bill with revenue sources like gasoline tax, landing fees, and so on. Commerce and education could be grouped together with corporate income tax and various fees being their revenue source.

Joint Budget Resolution. The detailed budget bills would have to be consistent with the joint budget resolution unless the bills resulted in greater revenue or less expenditures than the joint budget resolution. The exceptions would permit deficit-reducing outcomes. Projected revenue generated by committee action could be more than revenue targets. Projected expenditures resulting from committee decisions could be less than expenditure ceilings set by the joint budget resolution. When a detailed budget bill is brought to the House or Senate floor for debate, if budgeted revenues and expenditures violate the joint budget resolution target, then the Congressional Budget Office would notify the Congress of that incon-sistency. Any member of Congress could rise to a point of order that an inconsistency exists. If that occurs, then all expenditures in the bill would automatically be reduced proportionately so that the expenditures are consistent with the budget resolution ceiling. The Congressional Budget Office and OMB would be responsible for making the calculations and reporting the results to the Congress. Like other legislation, the president would have the power to veto the bill and the Congress would have the power to override that veto.

Each agency would be required to use only the legally appropriated funds, but any unanticipated additional revenues would remain in its fund unless a fund transfer is decided upon by Congress. The expenditures, obligations, and administrative reservations would be monitored carefully by the executive branch. If any overspending in entitlement and similar programs appears likely before the end of the fiscal year, Congress would be notified immediately by the Office of Management and Budget. Congress would have thirty days after notification to pass a supplemental budget consistent with any revised joint budget resolution. If such a bill is not passed, then the appropriated funds would be reduced proportionately to ensure that the expenditures in the fund for that fiscal year do not exceed the revenue. The Congressional Budget Office would make the calculations on how much the appropriated funds must be reduced to comply with the law.

Advantages of a Two-Stage Process. These advantages are as follows:

- Entitlements and other uncontrollables would not get preferential treatment because they would be treated equally with the controllable.
- Both the president and Congress would decide the overall budget policy first.
- This approach eliminates the current game of chicken in which one group forces the other to accept a budget provision or face the unrealistic prospects of having no appropriations at all.
- Individual authorization, finance, and appropriation committees would continue to have a great deal of policy discretion as long as they acted within the established budget framework.

With the two-stage process, both appropriation and authorizations committees making entitlement decisions are treated equally in the budget process. Each is given a budget target. In the case of authorization committees, they would be expected to adjust the law so that the outlays for the targeted fiscal year will fall within the targeted amount. Like all budgeting, forecasting is important and the Congressional Budget Office and OMB would be tasked with the responsibility of accurately forecasting likely outlays due to various entitlement policies considered by the authorization committee.

An important feature of this recommended budget process is the cooperation of the president and the Congress in setting the budget resolution. Under current law, the Congress alone sets the budget resolutions. Given the president's power of veto, especially of tax-raising bills, to not include the president in the formulation of the budget resolution is foolish. In FY 1988, international concerns over the U.S. deficit forced a joint presidential and congressional budget resolution. Included in framing the budget resolution targets, the president becomes part of the compromise. For him to later veto legislation inconsistent with the earlier budget resolution he signed is possible but not likely because he publicly committed himself to the budget resolution.

The president and members of Congress have often played a game of chicken in the budget process. The elements of the familiar game are to dare another party to say "no" to a smaller policy matter or suffer the potential loss of a much larger policy question, such as the passage of the entire budget. This gamesmanship strategy has led to larger than necessary budget deficits because the president found it difficult to veto large omnibus appropriation bills but much easier to veto the smaller revenue bills. The consequences were higher spending and less revenue. This type of gamesmanship is neutralized in the suggested reform. Individual appropriation and authorization committees would find it nearly impossible to submit bills over the established budget targets because of the use of the point of order.

Some concern exists in Congress that the budget committees of each chamber are beginning to use the budget resolutions to interfere with the legitimate decision-making activities of their committees. The recommended policy is to permit the budget resolution only to set overall targets for each authorization, finance, and appropriation committee. The difficult policy decisions of how to legislate within those targets should be left to the respective committee as is done in the current process. The enforcing point-of-order provision would apply only to violations of the overall committee budget resolution target and not to any advisory or more detailed matters included in the budget resolution.

Other Possible Reforms

Enforcing Tax Laws. The U.S. Internal Revenue Service Commissioner Fred T. Goldberg says that tens of billions of dollars go uncollected due to personnel problems at IRS. According to early Bush administration estimates, the fiscal year 1991 GRH deficit target is $64 billion and a properly functioning IRS could generate $40 billion or more in revenues for the Treasury. IRS's hiring and personnel practices are in shambles with newly hired professionals scoring on average at the bottom one-fifth of their standardized entry test. Turnover is high. IRS has the nation's largest data base, yet it uses a computer system designed in 1961. It uses keypunch operators to transfer data manually. The combination of significant tax changes, greater use of IRS for drug crackdowns, massive hiring freezes and staff cutbacks, little training money, the private sector paying more for professional talent, and veteran IRS staffers reaching retirement age results in an ineffective federal tax collection system with very loose enforcement standards.[8]

Using Capital Budget. Capital budgeting is commonly used in state and local governments. The budget is divided into operational and capital elements or even into separate operating and capital budgets. Capital budgets are used only for large capital acquisitions and are financed often by proceeds from long-term loans. In contrast, the federal government uses loan proceeds to finance over one-fifth of its yearly budget with no attempt to match the loan proceeds with the capital purchases.

The mandate of the federal government includes national defense and the common welfare. Woodrow Wilson once argued that a national capital budget should also be used for war costs as victory benefits future generations as much as those who fought. A similar argument can be made that anti-depression measures should also be financed by loan proceeds as a healthy economy also benefits future generations.

An immediate shift to using loan proceeds only for capital purchases or national emergencies would probably mean a sharp cut in the annual budget deficit. However, such large cuts would create economic and political hardships for several years. If such a policy were adopted, a transition period of five to ten years would be necessary to avoid drastic cuts in domestic and defense spending that would harm the economy. Also, capital-intensive programs, such as water and sewerage plants, transportation, and large weapons, could be more easily funded by loan proceeds than could programs that required intense use of labor. In the United States, there is a significant need for infrastructure funding; therefore, such a shift in funding policy might be opportune.

DEALING WITH LIABILITIES

Unfunded Liabilities

When a government or private company does not set aside money for its incurred liabilities, such as its retirement obligation to its employees, then it is merely engaging in another type of deficit financing. Future taxpayers will have to pay those liabilities just as they must pay debt service costs on bonds and notes. Private companies and state and local governments set aside funds out of each pay period to cover a substantial portion of the retirement liability. The balance of the liability should be earned by the retirement fund's prudent investment strategy. The federal government incurs significant pension fund liabilities each year, but it has no pensions fund. Instead, the assumption is made that the necessary monies will be appropriated each year, much like the debt service payment.

An alternative federal pension policy could not only fund that liability but also provide a major source of investment capital for the United States. The federal government could set aside for the employees an amount designed to cover most of the government's retirement liabilities. The funds could be invested with the proceeds and the original investments together covering the entire retirement liability. The pension funds could be used to invest in private sector activities designed to increase national productivity and competitiveness. An alternative is to use the funds for social programs such as low-income housing. Regardless of the investment policy adopted, care must be taken to insure that proper return on investment occurs.

There would be no increased risk to retirees. The federal government would continue to guarantee its liability to its former employees just as it does under present law. The only difference is that the employees would have the added protection of having specific investment funds to back up the words of the government.

Some critics of this proposal might argue that tremendous new sums of money would be necessary to fund the liability each year. This need not be the case if the money could be transferred from the portfolios of existing federal government loan programs and still accomplish the purposes of those programs.

Contingent Liabilities

The federal government guarantees many loans of individuals and groups. When this occurs, the interest charged for the loan is often lowered significantly. In a similar manner, the federal government guarantees savings in banks and savings and loan institutions as well as the pensions of private companies. In the case of bank failures, the government guarantees it will pay the deposited amount up to a maximum. Normally, the federal government creates a public corporation to watch over the guarantee groups. Small losses can be paid by the corporation's reserves, but large losses must be paid by the federal government. That contingent liability is large. For example, if all contingent liabilities had become real liabilities for the federal government in the FY 1987, the federal government's debt would have increased from $2,355 billion to $5,945 billion. That is a 152 percent increase. In 1990, OMB Director Richard G. Darman estimated the liability at $6 trillion.[9]

The use of the contingent liability approach by the federal government is not inherently wrong. Technically, the federal deficit is not increased just because there is a large set of federal guaranteed loans in existence. If those guaranteed loan programs were managed using prudent risk management policies, then the contingent liability risk would be very small. In properly organized programs, costs of the program are covered by user fees at the time of the loan or are built into the payment schedule. Essentially, a user fee is charged to cover program administration and a reserve is established to pay defaults much as is done by an insurance company.

There is a relationship between contingent liability and the federal deficit. The concern is that the contingent liability can become a true liability and thus increase the yearly deficit significantly. To prevent this from occurring, the federal government must make sure each contingent liability program has proper policies in place, is being managed correctly, and has accurate program risk assumptions. The tendency in such programs is (1) not to recognize that conditions have changed and previously valid risk management policy assumptions are no longer valid and (2) to succumb to case-by-case political pressure to overlook prudent risk management policies. Unfortunately, when problems do arise, Congress acts only when the situation reaches serious proportions and the amounts needed to resolve the financial problem are remarkably high.

Again the danger of contingent liability programs is the possible impact of a truly severe economic recession or depression. Under such conditions, many of the guarantee programs will exhaust their reserves and require federal appropriations at a time when federal revenues would be falling and when other programs such as food stamps would be automatically expanding at a rapid rate. The result in such a fiscal year would be huge increases in the already large yearly deficit. The U.S. Treasury Department might find it difficult to raise the needed sums. In addition, the current 15 percent of total revenue-to-debt service amount would grow significantly, making it difficult for the federal government to honor its contingent liability commitment without resorting to the highly inflationary policy of overprinting currency.

Having both high contingent liabilities and a large yearly federal deficit are not compatible policies. Until such time as the federal debt service level is lowered, contingent liabilities should not be increased significantly and possibly should be lessened so that possible economic emergencies could be met. The 1990 reforms do address contingent liabilities as explained earlier by requiring budget authority for sums estimated to be necessary to pay for liabilities by the Treasury in a given fiscal year. This reform permits a much more reasoned approach to budgeting for contingent liabilities.

GETTING MORE FOR LESS

The federal government has a tremendous opportunity to increase productivity given the remarkable technological advances that are occurring and the publicly recognized need to economize. This can be accomplished by (1) focusing more attention on enhancing government program productivity, (2) tying more programs to user fees and increasing the fees to meet costs, and (3) using an internal service fund concept to foster a more cost effective management.

Focusing on Program Productivity

For productivity to be achieved, information on program products and services must be gathered and used in connection with program resources data. Since the Hoover Commission, the federal government has been using performance measures in its budget process. Nevertheless, the focus in budgeting is placed on the price tag for each year's policy decisions.

With advances in technology, we have the potential of not only expanding services but also doing what we are accomplishing with less resources. More productive management will probably require different resource mixes and more sophisticated program administration. Creative management should be able to design more effective and efficient ways to accomplish the same end results. The challenge for policy makers and top administrators is to release the creativity in existing agencies and permit significant program redesign when necessary.

This can be done by knowing each program's impacts and its specific program products and services. Greater productivity is gained by increasing the ratio of program resources to program products and services. Given the need to lower the deficit, decision makers should focus primarily on productivity gains in which program inputs are lower.

Significant government productivity improvements can be accomplished only with strong White House and Office of Management and Budget support. This means there must be a strong White House political effort which is designed to enlist active congressional leadership support. Minds must be open to new administrative approaches and be willing to challenge vested political interests that are dysfunctional to increased productivity.

A task force using the nation's best managerial creative talent should be assembled and given both presidential and congressional mandates to recommend program changes. The task force should strive to gather opinions and information from those involved in lower level administration by focusing on their frustrations and barriers which are keeping them from being more productive.

A joint presidential/congressional commission rather than a presidential task force is likely to be more influential especially when the congressional and executive branches are controlled by different parties. In order to gain needed efficiencies, politically important groups may lose status or money. A joint task force with a national perspective and sufficient political strength is in a better position to achieve the necessary changes. Even with optimal support, political opposition must be minimized by dealing effectively with small but legitimate complaints about the efficiency improvements. For example, if military bases need to be closed, then efforts must be made to explain how the bases will be converted into viable community assets rather than being simply abandoned.

Tying Programs to User Fee Revenues

Many taxpayers may not wish to see their taxes increased, but they would be willing to pay fully for services rendered. Increasingly, voters are realizing that important government services require additional fees or charges. The use of trust funds has become increasingly popular for new congressional programs because Congresses have discovered significant funds can be raised without increasing income or other taxes. Arguments against this policy stress that all government programs should compete in the public policy arena on an equal basis.

By tying revenue streams to programs, the budget process becomes biased in favor of those programs that can find a user fee or some other form of dedicated revenue source such as the Social Security tax. The use of enterprise funds in local government budgeting illustrates that there is some validity in that argument. General fund agencies tend to be less well funded than enterprise activities. When user fees and other revenue streams are tied to specific programs, then administrative complexity, inflexibility, and unequal funding biases do occur. However, there are also important overriding advantages. Without those enterprise-generated user fees, useful and sometimes vital services such as water treatment would not be available to the public. Essentially, enterprise fund activities are treated like private businesses within a government that is providing a service to the public for a fee. Ideally, enterprise funds generate revenues that equal their outlays. If there are subsidies from other revenue streams such as income tax, those additional sums are clearly labeled as such.

The federal government could adopt a much greater use of the enterprise approach. Within the constraints of law, every attempt should be made to create broad enterprise trust funds. For example, there could be, and in some cases are, such funds for transportation, environmental improvements, postal service, commerce, housing, and Social Security. Many of the existing smaller trust funds could be merged into larger funds, giving greater administrative flexibility and lessening the unequal funding bias. Each enterprise trust fund would be balanced and have a corresponding capital budget. Cross subsidizations from one fund to another (e.g., general fund to postal service) could exist as long as the purpose of the funds is not violated.

The major advantage of this approach is that it encourages decision makers to balance revenues with expenditures within the funds. Decision makers would look to increasing fees or decreasing services. Currently, many such potential enterprise activities have inadequate user fees, and income tax revenue is being used to subsidize those programs.

The common argument made against user fees is that they are regressive and that the progressive income tax achieves greater economic equity. A closer examination of many user fee programs, such as the national parks and boat safety, show those programs are used by middle and upper economic groups and not the poor. If we wish to establish better economic equity for the poor in those programs, the solution is a subsidy targeted for them from the general fund and full user fee charges for the program's beneficiaries. The use of an enterprise fund approach forces policy makers and managers to adopt some of the same microeconomic reasoning so useful to the private sector without abandoning the overall public purpose of the program.

Internal Service Funds

The internal service fund activity is somewhat similar to the enterprise fund activity except the services are provided to other parts of the bureaucracy itself. Internal service fund activities charge for the services they render to other parts of government. Each charge need not equal the actual cost of the services rendered so long as the total charges equal the total cost of the services for the fund. The arguments against the internal service fund are that there are high bookkeeping costs associated with keeping track of all the charges and that it is difficult to set prices for services rendered.

Internal service funds do help identify inefficient overhead activities as well as their location. Potentially, significant productivity savings could be generated. Internal service funds also help create an incentive to manage more efficiently. Given modern computer technology, the increased bookkeeping cost is a less serious disadvantage than it was in the past. Opponents argue that this information can be gathered in a less expensive manner.

Another means to increase competitiveness and lower government costs is to break the monopoly of internal fund agencies. Often, other federal agencies are required to buy from them. An alternative policy is that those purchasing agencies must buy from internal service fund agencies unless they can document a better price from a private vendor. Some procedural provisions to deal with quality control and favoritism would also be necessary. This policy would force the internal service fund agency to be competitive with the private sector. If it fails that challenge, then it ceases to exist just like an inefficient private business. Thus, these agencies should be given administrative flexibility to operate as semiautonomous organizations.

CONCLUSIONS

In spite of the Darman–Byrd reforms, federal budget reform will remain an important policy subject. The 1990 reforms seem like magic that works by diverting the audience away from the true nature of the trick. The 1990 reform diverts the public's eye away from the high and growing deficit. Instead, the new focus is on federal spending levels that can be adjusted to exclude the major reasons for increased deficit spending: financing the loan guarantee, war preparation, and emergencies. Thus the president and Congress can declare they were winners when the nation's deficit situation is actually getting worse. This political ploy may be successful for awhile. But if the yearly amount to service the national debt climbs over 15 percent of tax receipts, the American people will again call for budget reform that successfully addresses the deficit problem.

The large budget deficit annually adds significant amounts to the national debt. Measured in terms of debt service, the national debt is similar to the one immediately after World War II. However, the United States is not at war and even the Cold War seems to be ending. Interest payments are high and getting higher. Paying the debt service has now become a significant financial commitment of the nation which is lessening future policy options. In addition, the yearly deficit and debt are having both short- and long-term negative impacts on the national trade deficit. The problem remains and demands attention.

Many budget reforms are being debated but few are likely to be passed. The key is achieving a bipartisan consensus between the executive and legislative branches on the reform package.[10] The reforms not requiring fundamental changes in Congress itself are the easiest to pass, but they are also not likely to be sufficient to resolve the deficit problem. More fundamental reforms require key members of Congress to change their congressional responsibilities and duties. Reforms of this character are possible only if a strong consensus emerges that supports such reform proposals. Reforms involving a realignment of power between the executive and legislative are normally the least likely to be adopted.

Federal budget reforms will occur only when the desire for reform of both the Congress and the president exceeds the concern for loss of their relative political power and the deficit grows. Reforms can be put in place that will not only improve the federal budget process, but over time will significantly help in achieving reductions in the federal debt and yearly interest payment. Some reforms that merit serious consideration are:

- a two-stage budget process to set targets and enforce the use of those targets
- more effective administrative practices in the Internal Revenue Service
- capital budgeting
- fully funded liabilities such as pension obligations
- prudent administrative practices in contingent liabilities programs
- congressional/executive supported productivity efforts
- user fees that are tied to government programs
- expanded use of internal service funds

The checks and balances nature of the federal constitution has served the country well for over two hundred years with only a few exceptions. One of those exceptions is the current federal budget process that has evolved into a contest between presidents and Congress. The resulting game of political chicken meant expenditures were not lowered to equal revenues because of congressional strength and revenues were not increased due to presidential strength. The 1990 reforms put this game aside, but did not address the fundamental deficit problem. Although not everyone will agree with this list of federal budget reforms, most will agree that some reforms could be adopted to improve the current process and possibly even to reduce the deficit.

The current failure of the federal budget process is due to a lack of willingness at the highest levels in our national leadership to address the problem squarely. Only when the deficit is alarmingly larger, and interest rates are growing into the double digit numbers, will there be some willingness to pay the political price necessary to reach a bipartisan workable reform package.

NOTES

Representative Timothy J. Penny was kind enough to review this manuscript from the perspective of a member of Congress interested in federal budgeting. All positions taken are solely those of the author.

1. Ellen Hume, "Americans See Deficits as a Disease, but They Balk at Proposed Cures," *Wall Street Journal*, Feb. 11, 1986, 1.

2. Allen Rosenstein and Phillip Burgess, "U.S. Competitiveness in Global Markets," *The Bureaucrat* (Fall 1989): 21–29.

3. Charles A. Bowsher, "The Deficit Crisis: Beyond the Numbers," *P.A. Times* 13, no. 2 (Feb. 1, 1990): 8.

4. Lawrence J. Haas, "Losing Its Punch," *National Journal* (Dec. 30, 1989): 3106.

5. Steve Mufson, "Missing the Broad Side of the Barn," *Washington Post National Weekly Edition*, May 28–June 3, 1990, 13.

6. Paul Blustein, "The Flap over Social Security," *Washington Post National Weekly Edition*, Jan. 22–28, 1990, 6.

7. Gerald F. Seib, "If Bush Tests Constitutionality of Line-Item Veto, Reverberations Could Transform Government," *Wall Street Journal*, Oct. 30, 1989, A12.

8. Hilary Stout, "The Real Loophole," *Wall Street Journal*, Jan. 2, 1990, 1; and R. A. Zalidivar, "IRS Owed $87 Billion in Back Taxes," *The Miami Herald*, Feb. 21, 1990, 7A.

9. Herbert Rowen, "What's a Few Trillion between Friends?" *Washington Post National Weekly Edition*, May 28–June 3, 1990, 5.

10. Bowsher, "The Deficit Crisis," 9.

SELECT BIBLIOGRAPHY

Blustein, Paul. "Playing a Game of Budgetary Chicken." *Washington Post National Weekly Edition*. No. 13–19, 1989, 14.

Boskin, Michael J. "Capital is a Useful Tool . . . " *Wall Street Journal*. July 4, 1987, 1712–17.

Bowsher, Charles A. "The Deficit Crisis: Beyond the Numbers." *P.A. Times* 13, no. 2 (Feb. 1, 1990): 8.

Carter, Stephen L. "You Have the Bombs, but We Have the Bucks." *Washington Post National Weekly Edition*. Nov. 26–Dec. 2, 1990, 24.

"Gramm–Rudman Blinksmanship." *Washington Post National Weekly Edition*. November 13–19, 1989, 29.

Green, Charles. "Mitchell: Bush Angered Congress in Budget Talks." *The Miami Herald*. Oct. 21, 1989, 28A.

———. "U.S. Seeks 3 Trillion Debt Limit." *The Miami Herald*. Oct. 30, 1989, 1.

Haas, Lawrence J. "If All Else Fails, Reform." *National Journal*. July 4, 1987, 1712–17.

———. "Paying as You Go." *National Journal* 20, no. 43 (Oct. 22, 1988): 2644–48.

———. "Losing Its Punch." *National Journal*. Dec. 30, 1989, 3106–09.

———. "New Rules of the Game." *National Journal*. Nov. 17, 1990, 2793–97.

Harriss, C. Lowell, ed. *Control of Federal Spending*. New York: Academy of Political Science, 1985.

Horowitz, Irving Louis, ed. "Controversies: Congressional Budgeting." *Society* 20, no. 4 (May/June 1983): 4–31.

Lynch, Thomas D. "Federal Budget Reform." *The Bureaucrat* 16, no. 4 (Winter 1987–88): 31–36.

———. "Confronting the Budget Deficit." *The Bureaucrat* 17, no. 1 (Spring 1989): 49–52.

Penner, Rudolph G., and Alan J. Abramson. *Broken Purse Strings: Congressional Budgeting 1974–88*. Washington, D.C.: Urban Institute, 1988.

Rostenkowski, Dan. "Cold Turkey: How We Can Eliminate the Deficit in Five Years." *Washington Post National Weekly Edition*. March 19–25, 1990, 23.

Rowe, James L., Jr. "How Do You Spell? Sequestration?" *Washington Post National Weekly Edition*. November 13–19, 1989, 33.

Seid, Gerald F. "If Bush Tests Constitutionality of Line-Item Veto, Reverberations Could Transform Government." *Wall Street Journal*. Oct. 30, 1989, A12.

Stout, Hilary. "The Real Loophole." *Wall Street Journal*. Jan. 2, 1990, 1.

Thai, Khi V. *Structural Budget Deficits in the Federal Government: Causes, Consequences, and Remedies*. Lanham, Md.: University Press of America, 1987.

Thelwell, Raphael. "Gramm–Rudman–Hollings Four Years Later: A Dangerous Illusion." *Public Administration Review* (March/April 1990): 190–98.

U.S. Advisory Commission on Intergovernmental Relations. *Significant Features of Fiscal Federalism 1987 Edition*. Washington, D.C., June 1987.

U.S. Congress. Budget Enforcement Act of 1990: Excerpts from Joint Explanatory Statement.

———. Preliminary Summary of the Budget Enforcement Act of 1990.

U.S. Congressional Budget Office. *Reducing the Deficit: Spending and Revenue Options*. Washington, D.C., 1986.

———. *The Federal Deficit: Does It Measure the Government's Effect on National Saving?* Washington, D.C., March 1990.

Wessel, David. "Congress Is Shifting More Power over Spending to the President." *Wall Street Journal*. Oct. 19, 1990, A6.

White, Joseph, and Aaron Wildvasky. *The Deficit and the Public Interest*. Berkeley, Calif.: University of California Press, 1989.

Yang, John E. "Ever-Growing Deficits Establish the Failure of Gramm–Rudman." *Wall Street Journal*. Oct. 3, 1989, A1.

———. "Gramm–Rudman–Hollings Rudux." *Washington Post*. Oct. 10, 1990.

5

FORECASTING AND THE FEDERAL BUDGET

JOHN FORRESTER

A multi-year view provides Congress with a better long-range perspective and can make an important contribution to restoring more effective control over the Federal budget.

—House Budget Committee, 1979[1]

Controlling and managing the federal budget is a continual challenge. Politicians and administrators are responsible for determining public policies and analyzing their impacts on the federal budget.[2] One means for analyzing the budget that has been tapped by both Congress and the executive in recent years is multiyear forecasting.

In this chapter, we will examine forecasting used by the federal government and the impact it has on the federal budgetary process.[3] Little research has been done on federal forecasting, even though Congress has promoted its use through legislative action,[4] and the Congressional Budget Office asserts that "reliable estimates of federal spending and revenues, and a clear understanding of their dynamics, are important to the federal budget process."[5]

The chapter begins with a brief overview of the history of budgetary forecasting which, like most analytical tools, has evolved over time.[6] Next, we will examine the context in which the agenda for forecasting is set. Then, the chapter will identify how the budgetary policies set forth by agendas are forecasted. Finally, we will reflect on the findings to identify ways of making forecasting more responsive to the needs of federal decision makers.

CONTEXT OF FORECASTING

What Is a Forecast?

There is more than one way to look at the financial future of government. What a forecast is and how it is forecasted depends upon budgetary priorities, prognosticating technology, and the organization's financial environment. Since political priorities are dynamic—broadening, narrowing and changing in mix[7]—forecasts, especially forecasts more than one year out, are more likely to "reflect long term goals for proposed economic policy" rather than to be actual predictions.[8] For instance, basing 1990s expenditure projections on expenditure patterns since 1980 would likely overestimate interest on the debt and underestimate payments to individuals.[9] And the impact of 1989 events in Eastern Europe may decrease American military spending to an extent unfathomable since the 1950s.

Similarly, the economic and social environment of the federal government has also changed in unforeseen ways which complicate historically based forecasting efforts. Radical change was especially evident in the topsy-turvy economy of the early 1980s when economic predictions of policy proposals were especially difficult to make.[10] Clearly, then, forecasts can not reasonably be budget recommendations nor predictions. Rather, estimates of the economy, revenues, expenditures, and deficits simply "provide a useful analytical base from which various budget alternatives may be evaluated."[11]

Congressional and Executive History of Forecasting

Pre–1970s. Forecasting grew out of the organizational and procedural budget reforms of the twentieth century. Critical organizational reform occurred with the Budget and Accounting Act of 1921. It established the Bureau of the Budget, which centralized executive budget preparation responsibilities and skills in one office. This concentration of budget power institutionalized executive budgetary preparation and control, setting the stage for procedural reforms.

Procedurally, the reports of both Hoover Commissions (1949 and 1955) pushed for management and planning as central budgetary objectives. The first commission argued that the federal budgetary process should be organized by programs and include information on costs, performance, and accomplishments.[12] Its efforts came to fruition very quickly; performance and program budgeting were statutorily implemented in the Department of Defense with amendments to the National Security Act in 1949 (63 Stat. 578), and more broadly by the Budgeting and Accounting Procedures Act of 1950 (64 Stat. 832). Establishing a need to collect and analyze budgetary data to evaluate the past, a key element of the reform, was necessary before planning for the future could be considered realistic.

The first direct call for multiyear forecasts came in the 1960s. In 1961, the Department of Defense (DOD) first experimented with the Program Planning Budgeting System (PPBS). Four years later, *Program Budgeting* was published. Its authors recommended long-term projections "should be available to the executive and congressional authorities who review the budget." They argued a program budget should be used so that decision makers would benefit from sharper "intuition and judgement."[13]

By October 1967, the President's Commission on Budget Concepts published a report in which its members pressed for five budgetary improvements, one of which was "more information on budget prospects beyond the immediate budget year."[14] Acknowledging the concerns of the Joint Economic Committee and the U.S. Chamber of Commerce Committee for Improving the Federal Budget, the commission said:

Many Government programs have larger future than current expenditure consequences which should be taken into account when they are initiated. . . . If major decisions of collective choice such as [military weapons, space and education] are to be made wisely, the public and the Congress need to have forward estimates, not only of the benefits and costs of the particular programs in question, but of the total budget of which these proposals are intended to become a part.[15]

The report asserted that most agencies already had to prepare five-year projections and submit them to the central budget office.

1970s and 1980s. Dabblings in forecasting became more serious in 1971. In that year, the presidential budget included projections of aggregate outlays and receipts four years out. Shortly afterwards, the Legislative Reorganization Act (Public Law 91–510, § 221 (a)) required that annual budgets include five-year budget authority (the legal right of an agency to obligate resources to result in immediate or future outlays) and outlay projections for the executive branch's legislative proposals for major new or expanded programs. By 1979, agency projections contained budget requests with a "planning period" extending three years beyond the request year.[16]

Congressional forecasting took root a little slower. Statutory guidelines to congressional forecasting, although general, were finally established by the Budget Act of 1974 and amended by Gramm–Rudman–Hollings (GRH) in 1985 and the Reaffirmation Act of 1987.[17] These statutes identified what was to be projected and the sources of data on which to base the projections. The projections were intended not as future decisions but as "attempts to direct budget priorities" and to "serve as guidelines for the consideration of [current] legislation with future spending impact."[18] The statutes did not specify forecast methods to be used.

While the legislation gave congressional forecasting direction, it also planted the seeds for future conflicts with the executive. By requiring the Congressional Budget Office (CBO) to forecast *outlays* (payments on obligations), Congress inadvertently sought more direct control over the execution phase of the budgetary process.

The House did not include projections in its budget resolutions until FY 1977, and the Senate did not begin to do so until FY 1978. However, up through FY 1980 both houses made much progress in their reporting and use of projections which addressed economic objectives and planning concerns.[19]

More recently, GRH and the Reaffirmation Act upset the continuity of the historical data base that forecasting depends upon by trying to make the federal budget more unified or rational. Specifically, the legislation moved previously off-budget entities to on-budget and the two Social Security trust funds off-budget:

As a result, there are trust intrafund payments from off-budget to on-budget accounts; interfund payments from on-budget Federal funds to off-budget trust funds; and interfund payments from off-budget trust funds to on-budget Federal funds.[20]

The effect was to change the format of reporting budgetary data. Thus, forecasters had to spend more time cleaning the data. While GRH may have made the federal budget more rational, it made projecting future expenditures and receipts more difficult.

Forecasting by the executive branch is further guided by OMB guidelines found in Circulars A–11 and A–34. As with the CBO's forecasting effort, the guidelines provide much flexibility for agencies and departments. Circular A–11 ("Preparation and Submission of Budget Estimates") designates the process for departments to follow in making multiyear planning estimates, current service estimates, and receipt estimates. Circular A–34 ("Instructions on Budget Execution") provides instructions for apportioning funds, thereby giving structural guidance for forecasting outlays.

Most recently, DOD and Congress agreed in the 1987 Defense Authorization Act to test "milestone budgeting." This method of funding would at least partially replace "the annual budget process for the research and development (R&D) and procurement of weapons systems." It would allow Congress to "approve up to five years program funding in advance," and review of program authorization would normally not be done "until the next milestone or until five years had elapsed." Both parties hope that the effort will cause defense program managers "to focus on longer-term issues and project management rather than each year's funding request."[21]

Together, executive and legislative budgetary reforms have laid the foundation for federal forecasting as it exists today. Forecasting has affected all departments for at least fifteen years. Historical data bases for forecasting now exist, but many have been affected by changes in legislation.

FORECASTING THE FEDERAL BUDGET: SETTING AN AGENDA

The impact of forecasting on budgetary policy will be determined in large part by three factors: institutions within government that determine budgetary policies (agenda setters); the internal support staff and independent external organizations responsible for generating economic and budget forecasts (forecast generators); and elements largely affected by current forecasts, which will in turn, eventually, affect present and future forecasts (external factors). In this section, we will direct our attention to agenda setters, since these budgetary actors most broadly determine the scope of what is to be forecasted.

The components of present and future budgets are determined by the president's priorities, congressional policies and reforms, as well as the Treasury Department's management of the public debt. Actions taken by these actors are not always predictable, but they are manageable and subject to change.

Presidential Priorities

By advocating changes in revenue, expenditure, and economic policies, a president can complicate executive and congressional forecasting efforts. This is particularly true when a new administration takes office and presses for change. However, even administrations that have been in power and have an established policy agenda make revenue and expenditure forecasting problematic. Also, the timing of publishing the projections of the president's budget office is important.

The president's budget request may be only marginally different from many past presidential policies overall, but a president is not necessarily restrained from being vague with or changing fiscal, economic, and other policy priorities.[22] Such ambiguities by the Reagan administration appear to be the major culprit leading to differences between projections made by the administration and the Congressional Budget Office.[23] Changes in the policy agenda of the first Reagan administration also hampered forecasting efforts. For instance, while the president supported federal general revenue sharing in his 1980 presidential campaign, only a few years later he strongly supported its elimination. Yet, as Penner argues,

It is important first to emphasize that a president's budget is not intended to provide the best possible forecast of final budget outcomes. It represents a series of recommendations to Congress . . . [and there may be] a high probability that Congress will reject those proposals.[24]

Generating policy-relevant forecasts may be especially difficult when a new administration with new policy objectives takes office. With a change in power, historically based assumptions may lose their relevance to current attempts at revenue and expenditure forecasting. Fortunately, as Penner points out, "up until the Reagan revolution, . . . those changes have been relatively minor."[25]

The president can affect budgetary forecasts by timing the release of the forecast report. If the economic forecasts are made early, then departments can begin forecasting their budgets early, but they are bound to be in error. If the executive forecasts are delayed too long and are not clear about the president's priorities, then the CBO may not have the information it needs to generate accurate budgetary forecasts or to compare its forecasts to those produced by OMB.

Congressional Policies and Reforms

Along with the president, Congress has historically affected forecasting, but has done so in conjunction with presidential efforts. Two methods Congress has relied on include expenditure and revenue legislation and budgetary reforms, both of which are very political in their nature. Unfortunately, the assumptions of congressional forecasts have also been politicized.

Expenditure and Revenue Legislation. Congress signals what is to be forecasted and how the forecasting is to be done through the expenditure and revenue legislation it passes. The former is governed by nearly all legislative actions that concern expenditures and revenues. The latter has been governed by budget reform efforts and by formulas included in authorizing legislation.

Forecasting expenditures is complicated by changing congressional priorities and emergent programs. The status of programs is especially unpredictable when their authorization and funding status are unclear. For example, in GRH many indexed retirement and disability programs were subject to the same sequestration policy as were other federal programs, only to be exempted from sequestration one year later by the Omnibus Budget Reconciliation Act of 1986.

Forecasting expenditures is also complicated when Congress supports policies that depart from the past. For instance, federal programs with little historical precedent that could or have complicated historically based forecasting include the social programs of the 1960s, the rise and fall of general revenue sharing, and fend-for-yourself federalism.[26] Expenditure forecasting is frustrated further when Congress decides to bypass normal routes of fiscal control. Recently, Congress has put the authorizations of new programs off-budget that in the past may have been put on-budget, most likely because of the deficit targets set by the Reaffirmation Act.

In addition to expenditures, Congress determines revenue raising policies for the federal government, in turn affecting revenue forecasting. According to testimony from a 1989 House appropriations committee hearing, "The revenue loss in 1989 due to the [rate reductions and indexation of the] 1981 [Economic Recovery] Tax Act will be $285.5 billion, or more than the entire estimated unified budget deficit."[27] The impact of major tax legislation[28] over the past six years has been just as strong to:

- reduce tax rates and increase investment incentives
- curb tax shelter abuse, limit unwarranted tax benefits, and increase taxpayer compliance
- increase payroll taxes as part of overall legislation to restore the solvency of the social security system
- increase gasoline taxes to fund infrastructure improvements[29]

An objective of tax reform in the early 1980s was to simplify the tax code and encourage investment and economic growth. Generally this has resulted in lowered levels of income taxation and higher levels of other, more regressive taxes and fees, and consequently a changing data base which complicates budgetary forecasting.

Budgetary Reforms. A second means Congress has for influencing forecasting is budget reform. The legacy of twentieth-century reforms is deep and a mixed picture of success and failure. The reforms that most directly affect forecasting try to integrate the planning (the future) with budgeting (the present), such as the Congressional Budget and Impoundment Control Act of 1974 (Budget Act or P.L. 93–344), the Balanced Budget and Emergency Deficit Control Act of 1985 (Gramm–Rudman–Hollings or P.L. 99–177), and the Reaffirmation Act of 1987 (P.L. 100–119).[30]

More specifically, procedural reforms that affect forecasting include the midsession review set up by the Budget Act and information found in reconciliation instructions. From midsession review estimates of the economy and policies come updated revenue, outlay, deficit, and budget authority projections.[31] Reconciliation instructions, one product of budget reform, provide the clearest explanation of congressional budgetary objectives. In them, the budget committees specify ceilings for outlays *and* budget authority for the current fiscal year and perhaps the next couple of fiscal years.[32] Statements by members of Congress also may affect forecasts insofar as they affect the economy.[33]

Congressional Forecast Assumptions. Finally, the forecasts generated by Congress' budget office are only as good as the assumptions on which they are based. Unfortunately, in the past these assumptions have been the target of political pressure and may even have been influenced by the political pressures. For example, the assumptions used by Congress in the early 1980s were more accurate than those of OMB, yet President Reagan tried to persuade the public that the congressional estimates were too big and "budget busting":

The budget committee made the crucial tactical error of basing its estimates on a less optimistic—but as things turned out, a more accurate—set of assumptions, and it appeared as though committee members wanted a higher spending total than the president. The latter was able to attack them as big spenders, and they were never able to explain successfully to the public that the difference was mainly one of assumptions.[34]

Thus Congress may be under pressure from the president to use optimistic assumptions as the basis for its forecasts.

Congress has also put pressure on forecasters by implicitly making assumptions about the growth and behavior of the economy and government by creating out-year targets for eliminating the deficit. The new criterion is to guide budget expansion using a regulatory approach whose measure is a fixed decremental scale that constricts traditional decision-making strategies. Consequently, if the economy does not behave as anticipated, Congress may have to meet the deficit targets by adopting budgetary policies that counter historical trends, in effect complicating historically based forecasting even more.

Treasury's Debt Management

Finally, the Treasury Department is responsible for (1) financing and managing the federal debt, and (2) forecasting revenue receipts. The cost of financing debt depends upon the financial behavior of the bond market. Forecasters must consider the total public and private outstanding debt, new debt, and interest rates demanded by the market.

Together, the president, Congress, and the Treasury Department are responsible for setting a political and administrative agenda within which forecasting will occur. As we will see, the responsibility for forecasting the budget lies, directly and indirectly, with various legislative, executive, and nongovernmental actors. Evidence suggests that budgetary forecasting is alive but it is not in the best of health.

Generating the Forecast: The Economy, Revenues, and Expenditures

Ultimately, the government is interested in forecasting the revenue it takes in and the expenditures incurred in providing services. Once the budget and forecast agenda has been set by the agenda setters, then CBO,

OMB, departmental budget offices, and other internal and external groups begin forecasting the budget and the consequent deficit. Specifically, budget reform acts and circulars direct or infer that the following be forecasted:

- the economy
- budget authority
- budget baseline estimates
- bill cost estimates
- deficits

Economic Forecasting

Because economic vitality and stability affect the federal budget, any robust forecast of the budget must be a function of expected trends in the economy. Indeed, the 1967 Commission on Budget Concepts recommended that long range projections be based on not only "estimates of the future costs of present decisions" but on "revenues which would be forthcoming from a specified set (or sets) of economic assumptions."[35] While critical, this step was limited in at least two ways: (1) The assumptions did not acknowledge any recursive relationship between budget decisions and the economy, and (2) the forecasts ignored the impact of the economy on expenditures, such as an increase in unemployment might have on the demand for various income security programs.

Accurately modeling the true relationship between the budget and the economy is practically impossible even using today's technology. The best projections (determined after the fact) are defined as those with the least amount of error and bias. Nevertheless, a forecast that is consistently biased might be a durable yardstick and predictor of future budgets. In those cases, the amount and direction of error could be estimated, making the forecast useful in budgetary and policy analysis.[36]

Short- and long-term projections of the economy are provided to the budget, appropriations, and other congressional committees by both governmental and nongovernmental sources. The output of various economic projections are used to forecast revenues and expenditures.[37] Economic forecasts for the executive branch are provided by the Office of Management and Budget (OMB), the Council of Economic Advisors (CEA), and the Office of Tax Analysis of the Treasury Department (OTA). The troika's projections are used by executive departments to forecast revenue receipts and expenditures found in the president's budget and in midyear estimates.[38]

Congressional estimates of the economy are provided by the Fiscal Analysis Division of the Congressional Budget Office. This division

analyzes the U.S. economy, prepares projections of future economic conditions, and studies how that future could be affected by different economic developments [production, income, international affairs, credit] or policies. The economic projections serve the two Budget Committees in developing the concurrent resolution on the budget and the entire Congress as it considers and passes a budget.[39]

The econometric models used by the CBO are generally developed with cooperation by external think tanks and an independent panel of experts.[40] External groups, such as Data Resources and the Brookings Institution, generate their own set of economic assumptions, models, and predictions. These provide CBO alternatives against which to compare its estimates and modify its models. In the end, CBO's revenue and expenditure forecasts reflect the direct and indirect input of external forecasters and its own specialists.

Nevertheless, while significant amounts of resources are devoted to projecting the future economy, economists and the government have little reason for depending on any one set of economic projections. In the early 1980s, this was due to the unpredictability of the course of the economy and the effects of policy changes.[41] More recently, Mr. Green of the House Appropriations Committee asked, "How can we improve economic forecasting so that it can be more useful to the executive and legislative branches in planning fiscal policy?"[42] The Council of Economic Advisors provided no answer or recommendation.[43] Nevertheless, recent evidence indicates that in the short term, the macroeconomic forecasts of the CBO, OMB, CEA, private firms, and the American Statistical Association/National Bureau of Economic Research are not statistically biased. However, long-term macroeconomic forecasts tend to be in error and optimistic.[44]

Revenue Forecasting

On the executive side, revenues are forecasted specifically by agencies, bureaus, departments, and OMB, and generally by the Treasury Department's Office of Tax Analysis (OTA).

Agencies, Bureaus, Departments, and OMB. A department is responsible for forecasting revenues (Treasury receipts) that fall under its responsibility. The data used to generate the forecast come from within the department and from the economic estimates provided by the troika (OMB, CEA and OTA).

While the forecasting process gives the department a framework for analyzing its revenue base, departments often encounter difficulties. For example, the Department of the Interior relies heavily upon proprietary receipts.[45] In projecting oil tract sale revenues, the department has to estimate or assume the worth of oil to oil companies years in the future (since it takes time for the oil to be found and processed), the changes in the economy, and the grades of oil likely to be found in various tracts. Timber sales are also difficult to predict; a timber contract is sold, but the department does not actually get the receipts until the timber is cut (as specified in the contract). However, if the market for timber is low, the contractor may decide not to cut the trees and pay a penalty to the government rather than suffer financial losses in the market.

Budget analysts in the Interior Department focus on forecasting accuracy rather than forecasting as a means for analyzing current and future policies. With the exception of FY 1990, in which OMB instructed the Interior and other departments to generate multiple sets of projections across-the-board (based on three different interest rate assumptions), the department has generated sensitivity analyses only at the request of OMB.

Treasury's Office of Tax Analysis (OTA). Where appropriate, OTA revenue forecasts also depend upon the troika's estimates. OTA also uses IRS income statistics, correspondence from the Social Security Administration, trust fund receipt data from the highway administration and various agencies, and information from the Bureau of Alcohol and Firearms. The OTA forecasts tax and nontax federal revenues over a five-year period. These forecasts are provided to OMB to be included in the president's budget. OTA generates the forecasts only twice a year, but it monitors receipts on an ongoing basis.

According to one OTA analyst, the department has no formal statement regarding receipt forecasting.[46] Receipt forecasting has "just evolved with time." Establishing policy guidelines for forecasting might be feasible, but they must not inhibit the ability of algorithms "to react to [changes in] the tax law." For instance, tax legislation of the early 1980s, such as the Economic Recovery Tax Act of 1981 (ERTA), the Tax Equity and Fiscal Responsibility Act of 1982 (TEFRA), and the Deficit Reduction Act of 1984 (DEFRA), has worked havoc upon revenue estimation.[47] More recently, GRH has given Congress and the president much flexibility in their attempts to balance the budget; expenditures may be cut and sequestered, and taxes may be raised. Unfortunately, these changes have severely hampered the comparability of revenue data used by OTA to forecast receipts since 1981.

Changes in tax laws generate an even more difficult problem for OTA. OTA must try to measure or factor into their models the estimated impact of new tax laws on consumer behavior, such as incentives to work and investment priorities. In addition, the ability of OTA to forecast revenues is impeded by limited understanding of the complex interactions between budgetary and economic factors (e.g., changing tax rates, work incentives, and inflation).

Congress. In Congress, revenues are forecasted by the Congressional Joint Committee on Taxation and the Tax Analysis Division of the Congressional Budget Office. This division

is responsible for estimating tax revenues, analyzing tax expenditures, and preparing related studies. The division analyzes the U.S. tax structure and proposes changes to that structure. Analysis focuses on the tax structure's effects on the economy and the budget, its relative efficiency, and the distributional implications of changes to the tax structure.[48]

The 1974 Budget Act requires that CBO report the annual projections for revenues for the five out-years.

Federal Reserve Board. Lastly, federal revenue forecasts (as well as forecasts of expenditures and the economy) are affected by the Federal Reserve Board (FRB). It governs the Federal Reserve System and formulates the monetary policy of the United States. It manages inflation by changing the discount rate and reserve requirements for member banks. In doing so, it also affects unemployment and the interest rate. FRB policies impact most directly federal tax revenues and social service programs. Consequently, the estimated impact of FRB policies on revenues and expenditures must be incorporated into the various forecasting models of the out-year estimates.

Expenditure Forecasting

Like revenue forecasting, estimating out-year expenditures is the responsibility of both Congress and the executive. Expenditures are forecasted at least four years out for Congress by the CBO's Budget Analysis Division. The executive branch relies on departments and the OMB. Expenditure forecasting is a two-fold challenge:

- Possibilities for error are manifold. Modeling an incremental decision must necessarily include an error component, stochastic and otherwise. Over time this error(s) grows at an exponential rate which subjects forecasts based on an incremental model to increasing amounts of error. A forecast model based on economic criterion is also likely to be in error due to unpredictable socioeconomic conditions and misspecification of the model.

- Unlike revenues, an "expenditure is not an expenditure." Forecasting expenditures is troublesome because there are multiple ways to classify expenditures, which include budget authority, baseline estimates, bill-cost estimates and credit.

Budget authority gives agencies the legal right to obligate resources to result in immediate or future outlays up to a level designated by appropriations. It may be one-year, multiyear or no-year. Forecasting budget authority is required by the Budget Act (see §30(e) and §307(c)) and is Congress' attempt at integrating planning with budget approval. Estimates of budget authority, as with various revenue and expenditure indicators, begin with baseline projections.

Budget Baseline Estimates. The starting point for estimating expenditures into the future is the present. Baselines are benchmark numbers against which Congress can measure proposed changes in taxing and spending policies.[49]

OMB and CBO generate baseline budget projections which "assume the continuation of taxing and spending policies in place at that time, including the carrying out of any future policy change [such as tax indexing] already enacted into law."[50] Entitlement program projections are based on a continuation of current laws, while projections of discretionary spending incorporate an inflationary factor. All baselines cover federal pay raises. The 1974 Budget Act requires that CBO's baseline projections be submitted to the budget committees by February 15 and they are usually updated in mid-August.

Baseline projections are used by the budget committees to construct budget resolutions which set forth appropriate levels for the fiscal year and planning levels for each of the two ensuing fiscal years for new budget authority, outlays, various loan obligations, revenues, surplus or deficit, and debt. They are also used to guide the development of reconciliation instructions (instructions given to congressional committees for adjusting revenue needs and expenditure requirements) (see §s 301, 301, and 303 of the 1974 Budget Act, revised). The instructions can be used to achieve a deficit target by identifying how much outlays must be cut.[51]

The budget committees may request two types of baselines, the most common of which is "current policy" or "current services". These identify "the level of spending or taxes that would occur if existing programs and policies were continued unchanged through the fiscal year and beyond."[52] The estimates adjust all programs for inflation and assume that existing levels of activity are maintained. The 1974 Budget Act requires that they be included as part of the president's budget request.

Current service estimates are methodologically simple and are computed in terms of receipts and outlays. Outlay estimates of OMB and CBO tend to be very similar. Plesko, in "Government Forecasts and Budget Projections," found less than a 1 percent difference between them.[53] He also found outlay estimates to be more accurate than receipt estimates, although the latter may be attributable to changes in laws governing tax receipts during the period of study.

In addition, Plesko found that both OMB and CBO tend to underestimate long-term outlays. Underestimates of out-year expenditure estimates most likely occur under three conditions:

- if the estimates do not include budget proposals likely to be adopted
- if major unforeseen policies are enacted (a new tax law)[54]
- if unforeseen events, such as natural disasters, occur. (The effects of these do get incorporated in updates during midyear review.)[55]

In the late 1980s, baseline estimates had become very important with the passage of GRH:

In estimating the budget baseline and baseline deficit for their sequestration reports, CBO and OMB use outlay rates [rates of outlays to new budgetary resources] for projecting levels of spending resulting from available budget authority. Under Gramm–Rudman–Hollings, OMB is required, for fiscal years 1989 to 1993, to use aggregate outlay rates for defense and nondefense programs that do not deviate by more than 0.5 percent from the aggregate outlay rates used in the previous year's sequestration report.[56]

OMB and CBO also generate estimates for revenue receipts based on current services. As with outlays, revenue projections are affected by the economy and new legislation. For example, forecasts of current service receipts for fiscal year 1982 were in error largely due to the economic malaise of 1981. Projections for receipts throughout the rest of the 1980s were also affected by changes in tax and revenue legislation, including the Economic Recovery Tax Act of 1981, the Tax Reform Act of 1986, the Tax Equity and Fiscal Responsibility Act of 1982, the Social Security Amendments of 1983, and the Deficit Reduction Act of 1984. Plesko attributes the optimistic bias of the distant out-year estimates of CBO's and OMB's forecasts to the new legislation, which made the old forecasts obsolete.[57]

The second type of baseline, used less frequently by Congress, is called a current law baseline, which "adjusts programs for inflation only where required by law."[58] An example is the deficit forecast used in the new budgetary process (due to GRH). This "is not the January current service estimate . . . but the fall current law forecast, which includes newly enacted legislation and the lapsing of expiring legislation."[59]

Bill-Cost Estimates and Credit. In addition to revenues and expenditures, the CBO is responsible for estimating bill costs and credit. Both are required by the 1974 Budget Act. Bill-cost estimates are prepared for public bills reported by committees, bill drafts, floor amendments, and conference committees. When appropriate, they should also show costs to state and local governments in meeting federal mandates over the next five years.[60] The methodology used to arrive at the estimate should accompany each estimate. Credit forecasts show the possible credit position of the government in the future.

DEFICIT FORECASTING

Who Forecasts?

Once the budgetary policies reflected in revenues and the outlays and off budget spending of the executive and Congress have been projected, CBO and OMB are responsible for estimating future deficits (and surpluses, if any) and interest payments.[61] Statutorily, required future deficit levels are spelled out in the Reaffirmation Act. In order to meet those levels, future deficits must be predicted accurately. If forecasts are pessimistic (whether or not they are in error), then the estimates become the basis for the president's initial sequester order:

- August 15—CBO and OMB independently estimate the deficit for the upcoming fiscal year.
- August 20—CBO reports its deficit estimate to OMB and the Congress:

    If CBO's estimated deficit exceeds the maximum deficit amount by at least $10 billion, then the CBO report will calculate spending reductions in nonexempt defense and nondefense programs to eliminate the entire deficit excess down to the maximum deficit amount.

- August 25—OMB will report to the president and the Congress its own deficit estimate. Any difference between this report and the one issued by CBO must be explained. Also, any appropriate sequestration calculations must be included in the report.[62]

To precisely estimate interest rate outlays on the debt, CBO and OMB factor in the debt and interest rate projections, which are based on past experience, since little basis exists for projecting the other means of financing beyond the current year. The estimate also is a function of the financing mix and seasonal borrowing patterns of the Treasury.

Methodological Quagmire

Arriving at the forecasted deficit is a methodological quagmire. On the one hand, economic cycles and periodic need patterns make Treasury borrowing (deficits) and future interest costs predictable.[63] However, even these are of limited value since the "interest rate [is] a major source of uncertainty in budget projections."[64]

On the other hand, three factors make forecasting deficits extremely difficult. First, the basis for determining outlays for many federal programs is not static but changes with revenue and spending policies. For instance, in just six months, new spending policies and changes in assumptions about the future cut baseline deficit projections in 1990 from $285 billion to $120 billion.[65] Also, social security and civil service retirement, which were not historically indexed to the economy (unemployment and inflation), are now tied to it directly, thereby decreasing the relevance of historical data. Second, programs such as Social Security, whose funding is based on the economy, are keyed to unpredictable factors. The economy has gone through many unforeseen swings in the past two decades, making forecasting a "perilous occupation."[66]

Third, and perhaps most methodologically crucial, is the way in which deficits are forecasted. GRH and the Reaffirmation Act tried to constrain budget expansion by establishing point values for future deficits, but not for revenues, outlays, or budget authority. However, unlike budget authority, outlays, and receipts, deficits are not forecasted per se but are the difference between projected receipts and outlays. As a result, a deficit forecast will be a function of the estimating errors of the two parent forecasts, thereby exacerbating its error. (Also, error is likely to increase as deficits comprise an increasing part of the budget and as the absolute size of the deficit increases.)[67] Consequently, Congress often puts little faith in deficit projections.

In spite of the limitations, CBO and OMB forecast federal deficits and debt service expenses. Recent legislation that establishes deficit targets, while of limited value, may effectively limit the growth of deficit financing, thus making deficit forecasting a little more predictable. One possible way to improve deficit forecasting is to estimate out-year deficits by moving average and econometric techniques. That may provide insight not gained by simply computing revenues minus expenditures. An alternative approach would be to set targets for the components of deficits.

SUMMARY AND CONCLUSION

In order for budgetary decisions to benefit from forecasting, the process and results must be credible. The following are some strategies to improve forecasting that would increase the credibility of budgeting and financial management.

First, there needs to be systematic experimentation with different policies and approaches to forecasting, and the results need to be disseminated to appropriate actors. OMB (and CBO) needs to work with departments, departments with their agencies, and departments with other departments. In addition, private sector specialists should be encouraged to forecast the budget and perhaps the deficit, not just the economy. The experimentation should incorporate various technologies, variables, and formats for presenting the forecasts. OMB could assume a coordinating role, but budget officers in departments and agencies could share their forecasting experiences as well. This is not currently being done.

The forecasting process used by OMB and executive departments can be improved. In 1989, this author interviewed budget officers in the Interior and Transportation Departments. They indicated that little progress has been made in forecasting. OMB, in cooperation with department directors and budget directors, could study various approaches to forecasting and determine the degree to which they are appropriate to departments and agencies. OMB does provide guidance to departments in their circulars and the economic data they generate. However, beyond that, OMB does little to help the departments improve their forecasting. Given that OMB has no statement on how to forecast revenues or expenditures, a lack of guidance by them to departments and agencies is not surprising.

Similarly, agency forecasters often receive little help from the departmental level. Their department counterparts hand down the information provided by OMB and other appropriate data. However, departments typically do not offer agencies procedural forecasting assistance. Again, this is not surprising since departments appear to have little if any policy or established procedures on forecasting.

Second, more research is needed to understand the recursive relationship between the budget and the economy. The current solution is to assume unrealistically a nonrecursive relationship and focus on the impact of the economy on the budget. Consequently, such a model is likely to be in error and the impact of federal policy on the economy remains unclear.

One area in particular in which recursive modeling is difficult to create is the relationship between citizen economic preferences and the budget. Modeling preferences is extremely difficult, because they change as the economy and social values change. Yet it is imperative since consumer confidence in the economy and government (as with the conference board's index of consumer confidence) and consumer attitudes towards current and prospective policies can affect future budgets. Without such modeling, these relationships cannot be understood. That means, for example, the degree to which reasonable sensitivity analysis can be done on revenue and expenditure policies is limited.

Third, if a key value of historically based forecasting is accuracy (as is indicated by the mandated out-year deficit targets), then the president and Congress need to consistently and clearly identify their budget policies. By changing the tax code nearly every year in the 1980s, the on-budget/off-budget status of various expenditures, and even the out-year deficit targets (through the Reaffirmation Act), the continuity between current and historical data has become less and less clear. The political nature of policy and decision making necessarily hinders the effectiveness of forecasting.

Fourth, with current methods of forecasting deficits, the law is too ambitious in specifying point expectations for out-years. Generating deficit projections based on revenue and expenditure estimates makes the projections subject to substantial amounts of error. Three feasible alternative approaches are:

• change the point figures to a range of acceptable deficit levels
• forecast the deficits by a technique whose main driving force is not revenue and expenditure estimates but whose algorithm necessarily includes such estimates (such as a moving average technique)
• simply set targets for the components of the deficit (revenues, budget outlays, and budget authority)

Finally, a possible appropriate response to the economic and budget uncertainties is for Congress and the president to request multiple scenarios of future budgets and economic performance, in short, to request a sensitivity analysis. The nature of the uncertainty—errors, fiscal and monetary policy, international policy—would provide the framework for conducting the analysis. Rudolf Penner argues that sensitivity analysis is impractical since it would require enormous staff resources and would be very complicated and confusing.[68] Nevertheless, this author believes some sensitivity analysis is quite practical. In fact, some is currently being used and more could be done.

Comparisons between various projections of the budget and the economy are made by numerous groups, although with limited success. For instance, CBO analyzes the budget projections made by OMB, but the explanations tend to be based as much on conjecture as on fact. While it may be difficult, CBO and OMB need to understand better the assumptions used by each other; without this understanding, any resultant analysis will be of questionable value.

Sensitivity analysis is also informally done longitudinally. Midyear estimates can be used by Congress to understand the impact of postbudget approval changes on the budget. While this procedure does not compare the impact of alternative assumptions on the budget at one time, it does show Congress the expected results of *recent* program and economic changes on future budgets.

Ultimately, the impact of forecasting on current and future budgets is limited by the value that departments, Congress and the president place on budgetary planning. The statutory requirement for forecasting in the Budget Act of 1974 is one indication that the participants value the future. Current forecasting practices, however, lack the direction needed for developing a coherent forecasted budget.

NOTES

1. U.S. House of Representatives, Committee on the Budget, *The Second Concurrent Resolution on the Fiscal Year 1980 Budget: A Multi-Year Perspective* (Washington, D.C.: USGPO, September 10, 1979), 4.

2. See Rudolf G. Penner, "Forecasting Budget Totals: Why Can't We Get It Right?" in *The Federal Budget: Economics and Politics*, edited by Aaron Wildavsky and Michael J. Boskin, 110 (San Francisco: Institute for Contemporary Studies, 1982); and Rudolf G. Penner, "Constitutional and Statutory Approaches," in *Reconstructing the Federal Budget: A Trillion Dollar Quandary*, edited by Albert T. Sommers, 231 (New York: Praeger, 1984).

3. The relationship between forecasting and municipal budgeting has been explored by John P. Forrester, "Municipal Forecasting: Possibilities for Budget Reform," a paper presented at the 1989 Southeastern Conference for Public Administration in Jackson, Mississippi, October 1989; and "Municipal Forecasting: Do Governments See Value in Reform?" a paper presented at the 1989 Conference for the ASPA Section on Budgeting and Financial Management in Washington, D.C., November 1989.

4. George A. Plesko, "Government Forecasts and Budget Projections: An Analysis of Recent History," U.S. Treasury Department, OTA Paper 58, October 1987.

5. U.S. Congress, Congressional Budget Office, *Federal Debt and Interest Costs: Special Study,* September 1984. Examples of CBO forecasts and plans include: U.S. Congress, Congressional Budget Office, *The Outlook for Farm Commodity Program Spending, Fiscal Years 1988–1993* (Washington, D.C., June 1988); U.S. Congress, Congressional Budget Office, *The NASA Program in the 1990s and Beyond* (Washington, D.C., May 1988); U.S. Congress, Congressional Budget Office, *The Army of the Nineties: How Much Will It Cost?* (Washington, D.C., December 1986); U.S. Congress, Congressional Budget Office, *Future Budget Requirements for the 600-Ship Navy* (Washington, D.C., September 1985); U.S. Congress, Congressional Budget Office, *The Federal Budget for Public Works Infrastructure* (Washington, D.C., July 1985); and U.S. Congress, Congressional Budget Office, *Prospects for Medicare's Hospital Insurance Trust Fund,* Senate Special Committee on Aging, 98–117, March 1983.

6. See Aaron Wildavsky, *Speaking Truth to Power: The Art and Craft of Policy Analysis* (Boston: Little, Brown, 1979).

7. U.S. Executive Office of the President, Office of Management and Budget, *Special Analyses: Budget of the United States Government: Fiscal Year 1989* (Washington, D.C.: USGPO, 1988), B–5, B–6.

8. Plesko, "Government Forecasts and Budget Projections," 1.

9. See U.S. Congress, House of Representatives, Committee on Appropriations, *The Federal Budget for 1989: Hearing,* 100th Cong., 2nd sess. (Washington, D.C., 1988), 9–10.

10. U.S. Congress, Senate, Committee on the Budget, Hearings before the Committee on the Budget, "President Reagan's Economic Program," 97th Cong., 1st sess. (Washington, D.C.: USGPO, February and March 1981), 178–80.

11. U.S. Congress, Congressional Budget Office, *Five-Year Budget Projections, Fiscal Years 1978–1982* (Washington, D.C.: USGPO, December 1976), 1.

12. See U.S. Executive Office of the President, Bureau of the Budget, *Work Measurement in Performance Budgeting and Management Improvement* (Washington, D.C., 1950); U.S. Commission on Organization of the Executive Branch of the Government, *Budgeting and Accounting: A Report to Congress* (Washington, D.C., 1955), 11–15, 17–27; and U.S. Commission on Organization of the Executive Branch of the Government, *Task Force Report on Budgeting and Accounting* (Washington, D.C., 1955).

13. *Program Budgeting: Program Analysis and the Federal Budget,* edited by David Novick, a Rand Corporation-Sponsored Research Study (Washington, D.C.: USGPO, 1965), 9, 39.

14. President's Commission on Budget Concepts, *Report of the President's Commission on Budget Concepts* (Washington, D.C.: USGPO, October 1967), 9, 73. The other reforms recommended by the commission included a unified budget concept, midyear updates of the budget estimates, a "breakdown of the aggregate budget estimates for the current and coming year," and streamlining and refining the budget appendix. The commission, however, argued against a federal capital budget as a means of budgeting and planning.

15. Ibid., 76.

16. U.S. General Accounting Office, *Budget Formulation: Many Approaches*

Work but Some Improvements are Needed, a report to the chairman, House Committee on Government Operations, U.S. Congress, by the Comptroller General of the United States (Washington, D.C., February 29, 1980), 33.

17. Sections 301 and 308 require that the report accompanying a concurrent resolution include the economic assumptions and objectives and five-year projections of (at least) estimated total budget outlays, total new budget authority, revenues (the major sources), surplus or deficit, and tax expenditures by major functional categories. Also, any concurrent resolution and accompanying conference report shall be based on a common set of economic and technical assumptions. A five fiscal-year forecast is to be presented "as soon as practicable after the beginning of each fiscal year," including not only the estimates above, but entitlement authority and credit authority as well.

Section 403 calls for the director of the CBO to estimate the costs over five fiscal years (current plus four) for "each bill or resolution of a public character reported by any committee" of the House or Senate, "and submit [the report] to such committee." The CBO is to specify the assumptions of the analysis, as well as compare its findings to estimates made by other committees or federal agencies. Title VI amends the Budget and Accounting Act of 1921, making it consistent the Budget Reform Act. Finally, Title VII gives the CBO room for experimentation with budget reforms. To date there is little evidence to suggest that much experimentation with forecasting in the federal government has been done, or how it should proceed.

18. U.S. Congress, Congressional Budget Office, *Advance Budgeting: A Report to the Congress* (Washington, D.C., March 1977), 26, 31.

19. Committee on the Budget, *The Second Concurrent Resolution on the Fiscal Year 1980 Budget*, 5, 6.

20. Office of Management and Budget, *Special Analyses: Budget of the United States Government: Fiscal Year 1989*, C–2.

21. U.S. Congress, Congressional Budget Office, *Assessing the Effectiveness of Milestone Budgeting: A Special Study*, July 1987, xii. Also, see the President's Commission on Defense Management (Packard Commission), Report of the Commission on Government Procurement (1972), Defense Resource Management Study (1979), Carlucci Initiatives (1981), and the Defense Authorization Act (1987).

22. Penner, "Forecasting Budget Totals."

23. See Committee on the Budget, "President Reagan's Economic Program," 192, 194.

24. Penner, "Forecasting Budget Totals," 90.

25. Ibid., 92.

26. Other examples include: the maritime subsidies proposal for FY 1987, which would "return to the industry responsibility for funding maritime R&D, and . . . eliminat[e] Federal funding after 1987"; the administration's proposal for FY 1987 to restrict "highway trust fund spending to annual user fee receipts, but not interest"; the Agricultural Act of 1984, which enacted new agricultural programs; the Federal Pay Comparability Act of 1970; the Paperwork Reduction Act; and changing the basis of outlays for Social Security and other programs to a function of cost-of-living. See, U.S. Executive Office of the President, Office of Management and Budget, *Major Policy Initiatives: Fiscal Year 1987* (Washington, D.C., 1987), 55, 56.

27. House of Representatives, Committee on Appropriations, *The Federal Budget for 1989*, 9.

28. Recent pieces of revenue legislation include the Tax Reduction Act of 1975, Tax Reform Act of 1976, Omnibus Reconciliation Act of 1980, Economic Recovery Tax Act of 1981, Omnibus Reconciliation Act of 1981, Omnibus Reconciliation Act of 1982, Tax Equity and Fiscal Responsibility Act of 1982, Highway Revenue Act of 1982, Social Security Amendments of 1983, Interest and Dividends Tax Compliance Act of 1983, Omnibus Reconciliation Act of 1983, Railroad Retirement Revenue Act of 1983, Deficit Reduction Act of 1984, Consolidated Omnibus Reconciliation Act of 1985, Federal Employees' Retirement System Act of 1986, Omnibus Reconciliation Act of 1986, Superfund Amendments and Reauthorization Act of 1986, Tax Reform Act of 1986, Continuing Resolution for 1987, and the Omnibus Reconciliation Act of 1987.

29. Office of Management and Budget, *Special Analyses: Fiscal Year 1989*, B–5.

30. Plesko, "Government Forecasts and Budget Projections," 1987.

31. See, Executive Office of the President, Office of Management and Budget, *Mid-Session Review of the Budget* (Washington, D.C., July 18, 1989).

32. An example for 1988:

The Senate Committee on Commerce, Science, and Transportation shall report (1) changes in laws within its jurisdiction which provide spending authority . . . sufficient to reduce budget authority and outlays [according to the Budget Act and (2) otherwise], or (3) and combination thereof, as follows: $394,000,000 in budget authority and $376,000,000 in outlays in fiscal year 1988 . . . , and $94,000,000 in budget authority and $93,000,000 in outlays in fiscal year 1990.

Found in Senate, Committee on the Budget, *The Congressional Budget Process*, Appendix V.

33. See a statement by Representative Bobbie Fiedler of the House Budget Committee: U.S. Congress, House of Representatives, Hearing before the Committee on the Budget, "Economic Outlook for the Second Budget Resolution," 97th Cong., 1st sess. (Washington, D.C., September 1981), 72.

34. Penner, "Forecasting Budget Totals," 99.

35. President's Commission on Budget Concepts, *Report*, 78.

36. See Arnold Zellner, "Biased Predictors, Rationality and the Evaluation of Forecasts," *Economic Letters*, no. 1 (1986): 45–48; and Jacob Mincer and Vistor Zarnowitz, "The Evaluation of Economic Forecasts," in *Economic Forecasts and Expectations*, edited by Jacob Mincer (New York: National Bureau of Economic Research and Columbia University Press, 1969).

37. See, Committee on the Budget, "President Reagan's Economic Program," 186–87; and U.S. Congress, Congressional Budget Office, *The Multipliers Project* (Washington, D.C., August 1977): a methodology for averaging the results of simulations with several major econometric models as developed by the CBO.

38. Forecasts produced by the CEA are published in *The Economic Report of the President*. These predictions "are released in late January or early February, well before any official economic data for the calendar year are reported." See, Michael T. Belongia, "Are Economic Forecasts by Government Agencies Biased? Accurate?" *Federal Reserve Bank of St. Louis*, November/December 1988.

39. U.S. Congress, Congressional Budget Office, *Responsibilities and Organization*, 1988–1989, 9–10.

40. These may include, but are not limited to, forecasts provided by the Brookings

Institution, the American Enterprise Institute for Public Policy Research, Data Resources Inc., the Federal Reserve System, and others. See Congressional Budget Office, *Responsibilities and Organization*, Appendix.

41. Committee on the Budget, "President Reagan's Economic Program," 183.

42. House Committee on Appropriations, *The Federal Budget for 1989*, 185.

43. The CEA simply stated that planned spending is affected more by changes in legislation than economic projections and that revenue projections are a function of both economic conditions and changes in the tax code.

44. Michael T. Belongia, "Are Economic Forecasts by Government Agencies Biased? Accurate?" Belongia also found that CBO and OMB tend to be optimistic, CEA estimates of GNP tend to be greater than CBOs predictions, and CEA estimates of unemployment tend to be less than CBO estimates. Also, ASA/NBER forecasts have a higher explanatory power than those of either CBO or OMB, and private sector forecasts are generally more accurate than those of CBO.

45. This discussion is based on an interview with an employee in the U.S. Department of the Interior, October 5, 1989.

46. This discussion is based on an interview with an employee in the U.S. Treasury Department, October 5, 1989.

47. See Plesko, "Government Forecasts and Budget Projections," 13.

48. Congressional Budget Office, *Responsibilities and Organization*, 10.

49. Congressional Budget Office, *Responsibilities and Organization*, 13.

50. Congressional Budget Office, *Federal Debt and Interest Costs*, notes. Also, see U.S. Congress, Congressional Budget Office, *Analysis of the President's Budgetary Proposals for Fiscal Year 1985* (Washington, D.C., February 1984); and U.S. Congress, Congressional Budget Office, *Baseline Budget Projections for Fiscal Years 1985–1989* (February 1984) for examples of baseline budget projections.

51. U.S. Congress, Senate, Committee on the Budget, *The Congressional Budget Process: An Explanation*, 100th Cong., 2nd sess. (Washington, D.C.: USGPO, 1988), 36.

52. Senate, Committee on the Budget, *The Congressional Budget Process*, 37.

53. Plesko, "Government Forecasts and Budget Projections," 15.

54. Ibid., 6, 15.

55. Penner, "Forecasting Budget Totals"; and Penner, "Constitutional and Statutory Approaches."

56. Senate, Committee on the Budget, *The Congressional Budget Process*, 39.

57. Plesko, "Government Forecasts and Budget Projections," 10, 13.

58. Senate, Committee on the Budget, *The Congressional Budget Process*, 15.

59. Plesko, "Government Forecasts and Budget Projections," 15.

60. Congressional Budget Office, *Responsibilities and Organization*, 3.

61. Congressional Budget Office, *Federal Debt and Interest Costs*, xx, 5.

62. Senate, Committee on the Budget, *The Congressional Budget Process*, 7.

63. Congressional Budget Office, *Federal Debt and Interest Cost*, xviii.

64. Congressional Budget Office, *Federal Debt and Interest Costs*, 1, 5, 21.

65. More specifically, CBO made the following baseline deficit projections (amounts in billions of dollars):

	1986	1987	1988	1989	1990
August 1985 Baseline Deficit	212	229	243	264	285
MAJOR CHANGES:					
Lower Defense Outlays	(9)	(26)	(48)	(71)	(96)
Lower Non-Defense Discretionary Spending	(10)	(19)	(20)	(21)	(22)
Changes in Other Noninterest Outlays	6	(4)	(4)	(8)	(12)
Lower Net Interest Costs	nill	(7)	(16)	(31)	(51)
Lower Revenues	9	9	10	11	16
February 1986 Baseline Deficit	208	181	165	144	120

U.S. Congress, Congressional Budget Office, *Reducing the Deficit: Spending and Revenue Options: A Report to the Senate and House Committees on the Budget— Part II*, 1986 Annual Report (Washington, D.C., March 1986), Table I–2.

66. Fremont J. Lyden and Marc Lindenberg, *Public Budgeting in Theory and Practice* (New York: Longman, 1982), chap. 3, p. 39.

67. Plesko, "Government Forecasts and Budget Projections," 19; and Penner, "Forecasting Budget Totals," 92.

68. Penner, "Forecasting Budget Totals," 102.

6

RECENT DEVELOPMENTS IN FEDERAL ACCOUNTING AND FINANCIAL MANAGEMENT

RONALD POINTS

The federal government of the United States is the country's single largest employer and consumer. It dwarfs the major multinational corporations in terms of revenue, expenditures, and assets. For example, the federal government owns one-third of the total U.S. land mass, employs over 5 million civilian and military personnel, and accounts for more than $2 trillion in cash flow annually.

To understand the magnitude of the dollars involved, a comparison of the amounts as a percent of the U.S. gross national product (GNP) might be helpful. Over the past decade federal revenues as a share of GNP increased from 18.1 percent to 20.2 percent. During the same period federal expenditures rose from 17.6 percent to 23.9 percent.[1] In short, the federal government is big business.

BRIEF HISTORY

Federal government accounting and financial management have their origins in the U.S. constitution and in an act of Congress in 1789. Article I, Section 9 of the Constitution provides that: "No money shall be drawn from the Treasury, but in consequence of appropriations made by law; and a regular statement and account of receipts and expenditures of all public money shall be published from time to time."[2] The Treasury Act of 1789 provided for the first auditor and comptroller in the Department of Treasury.

The current financial management structure in the federal government has its genesis in the period following World War I when the government became more visible to the citizens as a result of the enactment of the federal income tax and the dramatic increase in federal expenditures due to the war. Therefore, the cost of government operation and the management of public finances became a major concern of citizens as well as of Congress.

Budget and Accounting Act of 1921

The landmark financial management legislation was the Budget and Accounting Act of 1921. This act created the Bureau of the Budget within the Department of the Treasury and required the president to submit an annual budget to Congress for approval. It also created the General Accounting Office (GAO) in the legislative branch and moved the comptroller general from the Treasury Department to the newly created position in GAO. The new GAO was to act as the congressional independent auditor over executive branch expenditures.

Budgeting and Accounting Procedures Act of 1950

The second major legislative effort that addressed financial management was the Budgeting and Accounting Procedures Act of 1950. The more significant provisions of that act include:

- preparation of the budget on a performance basis, with financial information provided in terms of the functions and activities of the government
- promulgation of accounting principles, standards, and related requirements by the GAO, to be observed by the executive agencies
- establishment and maintenance by heads of executive agencies of systems of accounting and internal control, in conformity with the standards prescribed by the GAO
- cooperation by the GAO with the agencies in the development of their accounting systems
- review and approval by the GAO of agency accounting systems[3]

The Bureau of the Budget was transferred in 1939 from the Treasury Department to the Executive Office of the president. In 1970, the Bureau of the Budget was reorganized into the Office of Management and Budget (OMB). The new office not only absorbed the budgeting responsibilities but also included a number of management responsibilities:

- improvement of government organization, information, and management systems
- development of new information systems to provide the president with needed performance and other data

- improvement of governmental budgeting and accounting and financial reporting
- improvement of governmental budgeting and accounting methods and procedures[4]

Congressional Budget Act of 1974

Subsequent to the creation of the OMB, Congress enacted a major piece of legislation to change the congressional budget process. In 1974 the Congressional Budget and Impoundment Control Act was passed with the following significant provisions:

- established the congressional budget process
- created the Congressional Budget Office
- changed the federal fiscal year from July 1 through June 30 to October 1 through September 30 in order to allow sufficient time for the new congressional budget process[5]

Other Legislative Initiatives

During the late 1970s and early 1980s, numerous initiatives have been aimed at improving financial management in the federal government. A brief discussion of those initiatives follows:

- The Inspectors General Act of 1978 created Offices of Inspectors General in major departments and agencies to coordinate the previously separate audit and investigation activities.
- The Federal Managers' Financial Integrity Act of 1982 requires heads of departments and agencies to perform annual evaluation of their internal control systems and report the results to the president and Congress. In addition, they must report annually to the president and Congress on whether their accounting systems conform to the principles, standards, and requirements prescribed by the GAO.
- The Debt Collection Act of 1982, as amended, requires that a comprehensive credit management program shall be established by each department and agency to assure collection of all amounts due the federal government, to enable management to evaluate credit policies, to provide efficient and effective account servicing, and to improve the accuracy and timeliness of financial reports related to debt collection.
- The Prompt Payment Act of 1982, as amended, requires the federal government to pay its contractors within thirty days after receipt of an invoice or according to prevailing industry practices, or to pay interest.

Because senior financial managers within the federal government do not aggressively develop good financial management policies and practices, Congress tends to pass specific legislation concerning financial management as indicated by the above recent initiatives.

FINANCIAL MANAGEMENT ROLES AND RESPONSIBILITIES

When the U.S. government was established, financial management was viewed as a shared function between the legislative and executive branches. The Constitution gives Congress the power to allocate the government's resources through the budget process. The executive branch was charged with administering the activities of the government and reporting on its stewardship to the Congress as well as to the citizens. The individual and shared financial management roles and responsibilities within the federal government are illustrated in Figure 6.1. These roles and responsibilities are discussed in the following paragraphs.

Office of Management and Budget (OMB)

As an agency within the Executive Office of the President, OMB's primary functions are to:

- assist the president in the preparation of the budget and the formulation of the fiscal program
- supervise and control the administration of the budget
- review the organizational structures and management procedures of the executive branch to assure that they are capable of producing the intended results
- evaluate the performance of federal programs and serve as a catalyst for improving interagency and intergovernment cooperation and coordination
- keep the president advised of the progress of activities by departments and agencies with respect to those proposed, initiated, and completed

Critics of financial management within the federal government point to OMB's preoccupation with budgeting, to the detriment of the other functions. However, during the 1980s there has been effort by OMB to recognize the management aspects of its mission as illustrated by its recent financial management reform initiatives.

Treasury Department

The Department of the Treasury serves both as the government's accountant and its banker. Its major functions include

- providing services in support of the management of the public debt
- maintaining a system of central accounting and reporting for the government as a whole
- acting as the government's banker for the collection and disbursement of funds

Figure 6.1
Federal Government Central Financial Management Functions Organization Chart

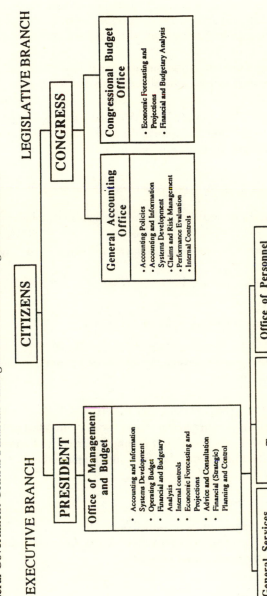

EXECUTIVE BRANCH

LEGISLATIVE BRANCH

CITIZENS

PRESIDENT

CONGRESS

Office of Management and Budget
- Accounting and Information Systems Development
- Operating Budget
- Financial and Budgetary Analysis
- Internal controls
- Economic Forecasting and Projections
- Advice and Consultation
- Financial (Strategic) Planning and Control

General Accounting Office
- Accounting Policies
- Accounting and Information Systems Development
- Claims and Risk Management
- Performance Evaluation
- Internal Controls

Congressional Budget Office
- Economic Forecasting and Projections
- Financial and Budgetary Analysis

General Services Administration
- Inventory Management
- Real Property Management
- Data Processing and Communication Systems

Treasury
- Credit Management
- Banking
- Banking Relations
- Debt/Equity Management
- Investor Relations
- Cash Management
- Investment Portfolio Management
- Foreign Currency Management
- Accounting Policies
- Collections and Disbursements
- Maintenance of Accounting Records
- Financial Reporting
- Economic Forecasting and Projections

Office of Personnel Management
- Compensation and Employee Benefits

- being responsible for cash management policies and procedures
- investing of federal government trust funds
- determining the reporting requirements necessary to gather financial management data, working with departments and agencies to ensure the integrity of financial data reported, and establishing central accounting and reporting policy for the federal government
- providing departments and agencies with regulations relating to central accounting and reporting, payroll, disbursing, and the federal depository system

The Treasury's accounting focus is generally limited to that which will enable departments and agencies to provide the information Treasury requires in order to meet its central financial reporting mandate.

General Services Administration (GSA)

The major functions for the General Services Administration include:

- managing the federal government inventory and property including construction and operation of buildings
- establishing policy and procedures for records management
- procuring and distributing supplies
- establishing policy and procedures for transportation and travel
- managing the government-wide information management resource program
- preparing annual reports of real property owned by the federal government based on departments and agencies reporting

A basic problem with the GSA property records function is that it is not integrated with other financial reporting systems and the accumulated property costs included in the GSA's reports are not reconciled to other financial reports prepared by the departments and the Treasury Department.

Office of Personnel Management

The Office of Personnel Management is responsible for determining policy and procedures related to employee compensation, including pay, leave, retirement insurance, and other personnel benefits.

General Accounting Office (GAO)

The GAO assists Congress in overseeing the executive branch carry out programs. It audits and evaluates programs, activities, and financial operations of federal departments and agencies as well as their contractors and grantees, and makes recommendations for improving efficiency and effectiveness. GAO's primary financial management functions include:

- prescribing accounting principles, standards, and related requirements for executive branch departments and agencies
- cooperating in the development and improvement of agency accounting and financial management systems
- reviewing and approving departments' and agencies' accounting systems
- auditing the programs, activities, and financial records of the federal government and reporting the audit of the federal government and its results to the Congress and the departments and agencies

Congressional Budget Office (CBO)

The Congressional Budget Office was created to provide Congress with information regarding budget and related issues. Its specific duties include:

- economic forecasting and analysis of fiscal policy
- cost estimates of proposed legislation
- an annual report on the budget
- special budget-related studies as requested by the congressional committees

The Missing Link

When one reviews the overall federal financial management structure, a most glaring problem emerges. No single organization bears responsibility for directing or carrying out the federal government's financial management functions. This missing link has resulted in fragmentation and overlap of agencies' jurisdiction over accounting, reporting, and financial management activities.[6] This serious flaw will be discussed later.

FEDERAL GOVERNMENT FINANCIAL MANAGEMENT STRUCTURE

The federal government has a series of systems and subsystems which tracks its budgetary and financial operations in both the individual departments and agencies and in the government as a whole. The appropriation is generally considered the primary accounting entity, with the department or agency considered the secondary accounting entity. The broad objectives of government management are set forth in legislation. They are:

- full disclosure of the financial results of department and agency activities
- production of adequate financial information needed for department and agency management purposes

- effective control over and accountability for all funds, property, and other assets for which each department and agency is responsible
- reliable accounting reports to serve as the basis for preparation and support of department and agency budget requests, for controlling the execution of the budget, and for providing financial information required by OMB
- suitable integration of department and agency accounting with the central accounting and reporting operations of the Treasury Department[7]

To achieve the above objectives and also develop a much needed modern, effective, and reliable federal financial management structure, sustained coordinated leadership from both the Congress and executive branch is needed.[8]

Standard General Ledger

The government has recently adopted a standard general ledger of accounts. This is an initial step towards standardization of its accounting structure. A dual track general ledger will provide for both "expense" and "expenditure" type accounting and reporting. In other words, it allows both budgetary and proprietary accounting within the same accounting structure. Figure 6.2 illustrates this concept.

Accrual Accounting

Federal departments and agencies are required by law to maintain their accounting systems on the accrual basis. In addition, their accounting systems must provide information on obligations incurred and liquidated in order to assist in expenditure control and disbursement planning, and for reporting on the status of appropriations. This is best illustrated when

- an order is placed and an *obligation* is recorded
- the materials ordered are delivered and an *expenditure* is recorded
- the materials are used, and an *expense* is recorded
- payment is made, and a *disbursement* is recorded

Therefore, federal government accounting systems must include data on obligations, expenditures, expenses, and cash disbursements—not one basis of accounting over another.

Although there are statutory requirements for the government accounting systems to adopt accrual accounting, there has been a high degree of noncompliance. This is because of the overemphasis on the budget process within the government's financial management structure.

Over the years, OMB and GAO have not been able to agree on the benefits

Figure 6.2
Federal Government Standard General Ledger

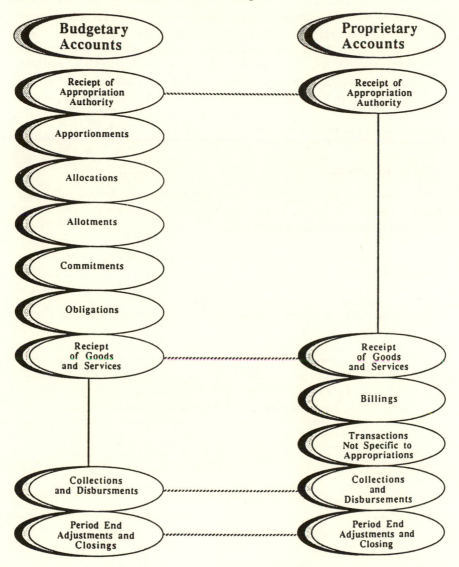

of accrual accounting data. Since OMB does not adopt accrual accounting in the budgeting process and because department and agency managers focus on the status of their budgetary resources, there has been no demonstrated need for accrual accounting data in the current financial management structure. Congress has consistently agreed with OMB on the lack of usefulness of accrual data.

However, GAO reports that major commitments of federal resources are only partially recognized in accounting and management reports since accrual accounting has not been fully implemented by departments and agencies. The GAO can only report the noncompliance since they lack the authority to mandate accrual accounting. Until the Congress, OMB, and department and agency managers find accrual data useful in the decision-making process, full implementation of accrual accounting in the federal government will proceed at a slow pace.

Fund Accounting

The reporting entity is generally the appropriation or the federal department or agency. However, fund accounting is also practiced. Two main types of funds are used in federal accounting:

- Funds derived from general taxing and revenue powers and from business operations. These include:
    - —*General Fund*. There is only one general fund in the federal government which has a centralized cash account under control of the Treasury Department. Each department and agency general appropriation is treated as a subdivision of the general fund with its own self-balancing group accounts.
    - —*Special Funds*. Receipt and expenditure accounts established to account for receipts which are earmarked by law for a specific purpose.
    - —*Revolving Funds*. A revolving fund is credited with collections that are earmarked by law to carry out business-type operations in which the government is the owner.
    - —*Management Funds*. These are funds in which monies from two or more appropriations are merged in order to conduct a common purpose or project, but not involving a cycle of operations.
- Funds held by the government in the capacity of custodian or trustee. These fall into two categories:
    - —*Trust Funds*. Trust funds are established to account for receipts which are held in trust in accordance with agreement or statute.
    - —*Deposit Fund*. Receipts and expenditure accounts are established to account for receipts held temporarily and later refunded or paid to some other fund.[9]

The Federal Budget Process

The four stages of the government's budget process are illustrated in Figure 6.3:

Figure 6.3
Federal Budget Process

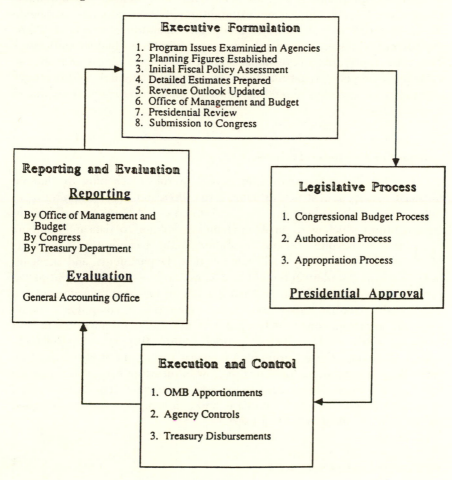

- formulation of the executive branch budget
- congressional action
- execution of the approved budget
- budgetary reporting and evaluation

As required by law, the president is to submit the executive branch budget to Congress each January. Then Congress considers the impact of the president's budget on the national economy and establishes federal fiscal policy for the coming year. In order to accomplish this task, Congress has developed a three-step process. First, Congress establishes federal tax laws and creates federal programs to respond to national needs. The second step is the enactment of appropriations for each department and agency. Appropriations are not based directly on current expenditures, but on authority to obligate the government to make disbursements for expenditures incurred. Thus, department and agency appropriations are really their "budget authority." The third step is the congressional budget process. Congress annually establishes fiscal policy regarding the amount of total spending and revenues and how total spending should be allocated among the major programs of government.[10]

Impact of Computer Technology

Computers have also played an important role in shaping the federal financial management structure. During the 1960s and 1970s computer technology carried the federal government into an era of large powerful mainframe systems which were capable of handling volumes of data and numbers of transactions beyond previous capability. Without computers many parts of the government simply could not function. Departments' and agencies' data processing underwent rapid and continuous expansion. Centralized organizations became the most feasible mode of financial management because of the data-handling power of that generation of computers. Today, there are approximately 19,000 computers in the federal government, but many are outdated. The 1990s offer opportunities through computer technology to change the government's financial management structure. The technology of computers continues to grow in quantum leaps and is moving the financial management area from large centralized hardware-oriented systems to widely decentralized micro- and minicomputer systems designed to meet the needs of individual users.[11]

FINANCIAL REPORTING

Federal managers must have the information and resources necessary to manage the affairs of government. In addition, they must also demonstrate their financial responsibilities through the reporting process. Government managers generally lack the following types of information used for analysis and decision-making purposes:

- cost information
- periodic summary performance reports of budgeted versus actual expenditures
- periodic financial statements for each department and agency and the executive branch as a whole
- key statistics needed for analysis purposes

The current financial reporting process does not adequately provide reliable, timely, consistent information for policy formulation and management control. There are no performance reports of budgeted versus actual expenditures because of the lack of integration between the budget formulation process and the accounting/budget execution process. The budget is prepared at the program or activity level whereas department and agency accounting systems generally collect information at the organization/appropriation level.

Therefore, there can be no reporting of budgeted versus actual amounts since the data is accumulated at different levels. Until the budget formulation process is integrated with the accounting/budget execution process and until data are captured at the same level, this situation will continue to exist. With the advancement of computer technology and a desire on the part of management and the Congress, there is no reason why this integration cannot occur in the near future.

The issue that the financial reporting process does not produce reliable and timely data can be attributed mainly to the antiquated and fragmented financial management systems employed by the departments and agencies. This is important since most departments and agencies are very large, often with worldwide operations.

Also there is not a strong centralized financial management function in most departments and agencies. This results from a lack of coordination as well as a lack of strong leadership to ensure reliable and timely financial reports. A possible solution could be a program to modernize and upgrade the federal financial management systems. Another could be passage of legislation to create a chief financial officer for the federal government.

Financial reporting within the government generally revolves around central agencies, such as OMB or Treasury, reporting requirements which focus on obligations, cash receipts, and disbursement data. Although department and agency managers determine their own internal reporting needs, that information generally relates to their status of funds or appropriation balances.

Key financial reports of the federal government include:

OMB Requirement

• *Report on Budget Execution*. This is a monthly report submitted by departments and agencies to OMB reporting on the status of budgetary resources by appropriation.

Treasury Requirements

• *Statement of Transactions*. This is a monthly report submitted by departments and agencies to Treasury reporting on their monthly cash transactions by appropriations.

- *Year-end Closing Statement.* This is an annual report submitted by departments and agencies that reflects the official financial results of appropriation balances in terms of available budgetary authority. Managers are required to certify the information on this report. This report serves as input to the president's budget document as well as to the annual report submitted by the Secretary of Treasury to Congress.
- *Business-Type Financial Reports.* These reports are generally prepared annually by departments and agencies. The focus of these reports is on the department or agency rather than the appropriation level. They are prepared on an accrual basis. The reports include:

     —Report on Financial Position and related schedules
     —Report on Operations
     —Report on Cash Flow
     —Report on Reconciliation

Treasury also has financial reporting responsibility on the operations of the federal government as a whole. The principal reports include:

- the daily statement of the U.S. Treasury
- the monthly statement of receipts, expenditures, and balance of the U.S. Government. The input for this report is from the Statement of Transactions monthly report submitted by departments and agencies.
- combined statements of receipts, expenditures, and balances of the U.S. Government. This is the Secretary of Treasury's annual report to the Congress as required by law.
- consolidated financial statements of the U.S. Government. The input for these financial statements is the business-type financial reports submitted by departments and agencies which are prepared on the accrual basis.

GAO Requirements

The accounting principals and standards issued by GAO require four basic financial statements to be prepared annually. They are:

- Statement of Financial Position
- Statement of Operations
- Statement of Changes in Financial Position
- Statement of Reconciliation to Budget Reports

Department and agency compliance with the GAO reporting requirements is extremely low. Agencies are more concerned with complying with the central agencies' requirements. The reason is that information provided to the central agencies is used for analysis and decision-making relating to the federal government as a whole, whereas the GAO reports are prepared generally for financial audit purposes which do not occur in most departments and agencies.

MAJOR PROBLEMS WITH CURRENT FINANCIAL MANAGEMENT STRUCTURE

One of the most pervasive problems of the federal government today is its continuing stream of inadequate, unreliable, and untimely financial information. There is universal agreement among government financial leaders, professional accounting organizations, and others that the government's financial management structure needs strengthening.

There is a wealth of data from various studies which is not being used simply because the federal government generally lacks the will and capacity to agree on and implement the needed reform. Recent reform efforts highlight the fundamental fact that the government suffers from the failure to implement real change. Rarely do political leaders have the experience and motivation to spend part of their precious time dealing with the problems of the current financial management structure.[12]

This is not to say that Congress and the president have been idle in confronting significant financial management problems. On the contrary, the list of their various initiatives is very impressive, but it is only a beginning.

Identified Problems

Major problem areas with the government's financial management structure are listed below:

- *The federal budget process creates management disincentives.* The federal budget process is unrealistic, inflexible, and unnecessarily burdensome. The budget process is forced to become an allocation of scarce resources which in turn heightens political conflict and places greater strain on the process itself.[13] The annual budget cycle forces managers to focus on short term goals rather than long term initiatives. This has led to poor management policies and practices. The real world is certainly not a one-year world.[14] The budgeting process is a formalized, stand-alone process that often ignores decisions or crowds out activities in other areas of financial management

- *Primary emphasis on fund control.* The historical and continuing emphasis on fund control has hindered the integration of budgeting and accounting and has led to inadequate attention to other areas of financial management. Because these systems are not integrated, budgets are generally developed without reliable accounting data

- *Poor quality of financial management information.* Today's financial reports provide a flood of information which is usually inconsistent, incomplete, unreliable, and untimely

- *Inadequate attention paid to monitoring and comparing budget activity with actual results.* Because budget formulation and execution systems are not fully integrated, the budget's usefulness as a management tool is reduced. It is difficult to compare budget authority granted by Congress with actual results

• *Inadequate disclosure of assets, costs, and liabilities.* Major commitments of federal resources are only partially recognized in accounting and budget reports

• *Antiquated and fragmented financial management systems.* The old financial management systems of the federal government cannot support the new demands being placed upon them. Many systems employ outdated technology and equipment and are not designed to provide the information needed by management today.[15]

Overemphasis on Budget Process

The problem areas that contribute significantly to the decline of the federal government financial management structure are the first two areas listed above. These deal with the budget process. The overemphasis that has been placed on the budget process over the years has created a financial management structural problem. Also, the lack of discipline within the financial management systems, highlighted by the large deficits, contributes to this problem. Some people believe that a constitutional amendment to require balanced budgets would provide the discipline. However, with our democratic form of government, it is healthier when budgeting decisions can be made through open legislative debate and action rather than mandated by legislation.[16] The concept of biennial budgeting could be a start toward streamlining both the budget formulation and the execution process.

Chief Financial Officer

Another reform proposed is the creation of a Chief Financial Officer of the United States. No major corporation should be without a strong centralized financial management function. An independent chief financial officer would provide the government with the needed focus and coordination. Without a single authoritative source for federal management policy, the critical gap or missing link would still exist in the financial management structure. A single organization would be responsible for managing the government's financial functions, instead of the current structure in which the responsibility is shared by the central agencies.

CONCLUSION

The Comptroller General of the United States, Charles A. Bowsher, has summarized the problem. He stated that for reform to be successful, an integrated approach must be taken for developing comprehensive financial management structure. The changes should be government-wide, serving the needs of both Congress and the president, and ensuring that consistent financial data are available across department and agency boundaries. Implementing this new structure will require new systems incorporating proven financial management concepts and the latest in technology.[17] The time has come for the federal government to demonstrate that it has the will and capacity to agree on and implement the needed financial management reform.

NOTES

1. This chapter was written in late 1989. U.S. Office of Management and Budget, *Special Analysis Budget of the United States Government*, Fiscal Year 1988, B–7, B–8.

2. U.S. General Accounting Office for the Committee on Government Operations, U.S. Senate, *Financial Management in the Federal Government*, vol. II (Washington, D.C.: U.S. Government Printing Office, 1971), 125–26.

3. Gerald Murphy, "Federal Financial Management—Will We Get Our Act Together?" *Government Accountants Journal* 34 (Spring 1985): 12–13.

4. Ibid.

5. Committee on the Budget, U.S. Senate, *The Congressional Budget Process* (Washington, D.C.: U.S. Government Printing Office, March 1988), 2.

6. Joseph E. Connor, "Federal Financial Management: A Vote of No Confidence," *Journal of the Institute for Socioeconomic Studies* 8 (Winter 1983–1984): 36.

7. Edward S. Lynn and Robert J. Freeman, *Fund Accounting: Theory and Practice* (Englewood Cliffs, N.J.: Prentice-Hall, 1983), 663–78.

8. John R. Cherbini, "Federal Financial Management Systems-Core Requirements," *Government Accountants Journal* 23 (Spring 1988): 45.

9. Leon E. Hay, *Accounting for Governmental and Nonprofit Entities* (Homewood, Ill.: Richard D. Irwin, 1985), 683–90.

10. *The Congressional Budget Process*, 1.

11. National Academy of Public Administration, *Revitalizing Federal Management: Managers and Their Overburdened Systems* (Nov. 1983), 49–53.

12. Ibid., 9.

13. Ibid., 17.

14. Chester A. Newland, "Federal Government Management Trends," *The Bureaucrat* 12 (Winter 1983–1984): 4–6.

15. U.S. General Accounting Office, *Managing the Cost of Government: Building an Effective Financial Management Structure*, Washington, D.C. (Feb. 1985), 1.

16. Statement of Charles A. Bowsher, Comptroller General, "Federal Budget and the Budget Process," before the Subcommittee on Legislation and National Security Committee on Government Operation, U.S. House of Representative, Washington, D.C. (April 2, 1987).

17. Charles A. Bowsher, "Government Finances: A New Structure Needed," *Government Accountants Journal* 35 (Fall 1986): 7.

7

FEDERAL FINANCIAL MANAGEMENT

W. BARTLEY HILDRETH

As the largest financial operation in the world, the United States government employs an army of managers to control an enormous base of financial and physical assets for addressing diverse policy goals. There seems to be an emerging concensus among policymakers that good financial management enhances the delivery of services in a competitive budget environment. The challenge is enormous:

The government's financial systems are in poor condition. They are incompatible and costly to operate and maintain. Systems fail to produce the complete, timely, reliable financial data needed for policy-making and day-to-day operations. This situation is further compounded by weak internal controls. (General Accounting Office 1988c, 19)

Responding to the need for fundamental reform in financial management, the 101st Congress passed in its closing hours and President George Bush signed into law the Chief Financial Officers Act of 1990 (Public Law 101–576). The CFO act is sure to rank as one of the most significant steps taken by the U.S. government to focus attention on general management and financial management practices. Fundamentally, it gives a statutory basis to many recent administrative directives while establishing the infrastructure to effectuate more fundamental reform. It established in OMB a deputy director for management who shall be, according to the law, "the chief official responsible for financial management in the U.S. Government" (not quite a CFO by statutory title but close enough). This deputy director has responsibility over a new Office of Federal Financial Management, headed by the new position of controller, created to assist the deputy director in fulfilling the functions specified in the CFO act. Both the deputy director and the controller shall be presidential appointees with Senate confirmation. OMB can now be expected to devote the attention to general management and financial management that has long been held hostage to OMB's budget responsibilities.

The 1990 CFO act states that OMB's deputy director for management is to provide overall direction and leadership by establishing governmentwide financial management and general management policies for executive agencies, subject to the direction and approval of the OMB director. While the focus here is on financial management, the deputy director also will supervise OMB functions related to regulatory affairs, privatization, performance measurement, procurement, and property management, to name just a few. To keep the government moving on the path of improvement, the law requires preparation, maintenance, and yearly submission of:

- a financial management status report, summarizing the financial statements and internal control reports from federal agencies and government corporations; and
- a five-year financial management plan (with estimated costs), updated yearly, to improve federal financial management systems, including equipment acquisitions.

To strengthen the government's new emphasis on financial management, the deputy director for management (with the controller) has the responsibility to:

- review agency budgets for implications to financial management practices, systems, and plans;
- monitor budget execution;
- oversee, review, and make recommendations regarding agency administrative structures pertaining to financial management activities;
- develop qualifications for agency CFOs and advise agencies on their selection; and,
- assess overall professional qualifications of financial management staffs throughout the government.

By the new law, each cabinet level department and the Environmental Protection Agency and NASA will create the positions of chief financial officer and deputy CFO. While each CFO will be a presidential appointee confirmed by the Senate, each deputy CFO must be a career reserved Senior Executive Service member appointed by the agency head.

The major responsibilities for the agency CFO/deputy CFO are to:

- report to the head of the agency regarding financial management matters;
- oversee all financial management activities relating to the programs and operations of the agency;
- develop and maintain an integrated accounting and financial management system, including financial reporting, performance measurement, cost and internal controls;
- direct, manage, and provide policy guidance and oversight of agency financial management personnel, activities, and operations;
- monitor the financial execution of the budget of the agency in relation to actual expenditures, and prepare and submit timely performance reports;
- implement the five-year financial management systems plan prepared by OMB; and,
- review, on a biennial basis, the fees, royalties, rents, and other charges imposed by the agency for services and things of value it provides and recommend revisions to these charges to reflect costs incurred.

Each department must submit a reorganization plan to OMB for approval. The plan must consolidate financial management activities under the CFO. Accountability is enhanced by this step.

The OMB deputy director for management will chair a Chief Financial Officers Council basically comprised of agency CFOs. While set up initially by executive action, a statutory council should give an added impetus to governmentwide improvements.

Positive changes had already touched nearly every area of financial management prior to the 1990 CFO Act. With billions of dollars at stake, the government had started managing its cash more prudently, accelerating the use of electronic funds transfer mechanisms, for example. Different agency accounting systems were yielding to some standardization and governmentwide integration. The cost-of-service concept was being used. The entire area of controls on financial transactions to enhance integrity was being applied. And, agency financial statements and audits were discussed seriously, but the 1990 act will greatly accelerate the pace of reform.

Commensurate with its size and scope of operations, the national government still has much to do, but it has made tremendous strides during the Carter, Reagan, and Bush administrations. This chapter surveys the current status of federal financial management, highlighting changes and pointing out areas deserving more attention.[1]

Financial management refers to the translation of fiscal matters into meaningful and relevant information for management and policy leaders. This chapter focuses on financial management elements for implementing financial strategy (Hildreth 1989). Clearly, strategic decisions are dependent upon the quality of transaction-level information—the incurring of a specific obligation, the authorization to disburse a payroll, or the receipt of a taxpayer's income tax payment, to name just a few (General Accounting Office 1985).

Therefore, we examine the status of federal financial management by focusing on the extent of efforts to:

• account for funds
• assess the cost of operations
• manage cash
• collect money due the government

Management initiatives to control funds, cost, cash, and collections are dynamic; thus many of the examples cited in the chapter have been or are in the process of being changed.

FUNDS CONTROL

Financial matters begin with the day-to-day accounting and reporting of the value (in dollars) of individual transactions. Fund control consists of managing the obligation authority (a budgeted fixed amount authorized by Congress), of managing outlay authority, and of reporting on the use of those funds. First we examine the issues related to general accounting systems, followed by appropriation and expenditure monitoring procedures. Later the focus turns to internal controls and, finally, to the generation and auditing of financial statements.

General Accounting

An accounting system is the total structure of methods and procedures used to record, classify, report, and interpret information on the financial affairs of the government or any of its funds or organizational components. How complex is the government's accounting responsibility? The 1991 budget reveals a yearly responsibility to collect nearly $1 trillion in revenue, manage a $2.5 trillion cash flow, process nearly $750 million in payments to employees, and procure over $200 billion in goods and services involving over 20 million transactions (Office of Management and Budget 1990). So, the size and complexity of the government's affairs are enormous. Unfortunately, decentralized financial controls at the agency level permitted redundant and incompatible accounting and administrative systems to spread throughout the government (General Accounting Office 1985).

One way to ensure proper development and use of an accounting system is to centralize operations, whereby all transactions are processed through one system. The federal government has not adopted a centralized system, however. In fact, the General Accounting Office (GAO) (1988b) recommends against such a system because it would be difficult to accommodate the varying internal management needs of diverse agencies; plus, it would be difficult to maintain security and reliability for one system.

The basic legal framework is in place for a decentralized, yet standardized system. The Accounting and Auditing Act of 1950 gives the comptroller general of the United States (the head of the GAO), in consultation with the director of the Office of Management and Budget (OMB) and the secretary of the treasury, the responsibility for prescribing the principles, standards, and related requirements for accounting systems. Furthermore, the GAO must approve each agency's accounting systems. Strengthening this authority is the Federal Managers' Financial Integrity Act of 1982 mandate for the head of each agency to report annually whether that agency's accounting system conforms to the principles, standards, and requirements prescribed by the comptroller general. Where areas of nonconformity exist, the annual report must include a schedule of corrective action (Joint Financial Management Improvement Program 1984). More recently, OMB directives require agencies to establish and maintain a modern, single, integrated financial management system.

The goal is to achieve a governmentwide integrated financial management system while permitting agencies to have some flexibility to meet unique accounting and control needs. Much progress has been made. Standards have evolved to ensure consistency of data. Agencies are adopting a single primary financial system to aggregate budget and accounting information within the agency. Redundant systems are yielding to cross-servicing arrangements. And, the use of commercial off-the-shelf software is being pursued as a means to minimize development costs and time.

An overall system architecture is based upon a governmentwide standard general ledger supplemented with agency and subsidiary systems meeting core financial systems requirements. The starting point is for all financial transactions and subsidiary financial systems to conform to the U.S. Standard General Ledger comprising a standard chart of general ledger accounts. Most agencies have already implemented the standard general ledger, with the rest set to come into compliance soon.

The Treasury's Financial Management Service (FMS) serves as the lead agency to minimize the number of accounting systems throughout the government (Murphy 1989). An implementation schedule has been agreed upon to accomplish these goals. As a result subsidiary systems are quickly fading to a manageable number. For example, unlike in the past when numerous payroll systems were found in each agency, most agencies now are allowed only one payroll system.

Smaller agencies are encouraged to use cross-servicing arrangements where agencies with proven systems provide financial services to others. Cross-servicing helps eliminate redundant, obsolete systems while achieving better service at reduced costs. All major administrative processing services are candidates for cross-servicing, including personnel, payroll, accounting, and contractual payments. An alternative to building and maintaining an agency specific system, cross-servicing is offered to agencies on a reimbursable or pay-for-service basis. The largest host agency for payroll/personnel services is the Department of Agriculture's National Finance Center located in New Orleans.

Appropriation and Expenditure Monitoring

Congress authorizes and appropriates funds for specific programs administered by agencies. Once the president signs the legislation, the Treasury Department prepares an appropriations warrant authorizing the amounts to be entered into accounting records. The OMB then divides the agency's appropriations into specific amounts for portions of the fiscal year, a process termed apportionment. After receiving an apportionment, an agency can enter into obligations against that amount. The primary control focus is on obligations (when an item or service is ordered) and outlays (when the bill is paid). Basically, obligation transactions reveal the extent to which agencies are making commitments for future payments. In the recent past, politicians and agencies were more interested in the use of obligation authority than in the timing of outlays. But, with the introduction of Gramm–Rudman deficit controls, outlay management has become a part of each agency's appropriation management process.

Agencies are held responsible for using congressionally appropriated funds for authorized purposes within the amounts authorized and available and in the time period specified by the law. Plus, funds must be used in an economic and efficient manner. To ensure that such efforts are achieved, extensive laws, policies, and procedures are in force (General Accounting Office 1985).

In spending over $1 trillion a year, federal agencies generally meet spending restrictions, although problems surface from time to time (General Accounting Office 1988b, 7). The military's recent history is just one case in point. The Army, as a result of losing track of how much foreign military sales obligation authority it had in 1978, ended up obligating more than it was allowed. In 1981, the Air Force obligated funds before congressional appropriations were made. And, then in 1984, the military services obligated funds after the obligation period had expired. Not only the military services have had problems, however. In 1985, for example, the General Services Administration incurred obligations in excess of available funds. In another example, the Child Nutrition Program illegally paid for meals one year out of the following year's funding. So, various agencies have run afoul of appropriate obligation and expenditure controls.

Agency heads are responsible for establishing procedures to ensure that spending does not exceed approved levels. The Antideficiency Act requires that administrative systems be designed to:

- restrict obligations or expenditures to the amount appropriated and apportioned
- fix responsibility for the creation of obligations, incurring of expenditures, or making disbursements

These procedures must gain OMB approval. Under the law, violations of the Antideficiency Act must be reported immediately through the OMB to the president and the Congress. Individuals responsible for such violations face possible criminal prosecution.

Agencies must also review their unliquidated obligations—obligations for which payment has not been made. The year-end and periodic obligation review seeks to determine the continuing validity of each recorded obligation. A report by the GAO (1989) shows, for example, that many of the Veterans Administration medical centers around the country neglected such year-end reviews, masking the true status of liabilities and the amount of funds committed to specific programs. Needless to say, Congress is especially interested in knowing which obligations are still valid since this information can influence future budget plans. It is clear then that departments and agencies should improve their expenditure reporting systems to enhance accountability over public funds. Taking a significant step, the new CFO act assigns responsibility both to agency CFOs and the new OMB deputy director to monitor budget execution practices and to submit timely performance reports.

Internal Controls

Internal controls are those management actions that provide reasonable assurance that government resources are protected against fraud, theft, and other diversions or misuse. Program as well as financial and administrative areas fall within the scope of internal controls. The Federal Managers' Financial Integrity Act of 1982 establishes stringent requirements regarding control systems and their periodic evaluation. It mandates five-year management control plans with periodic status reports, especially on progress in correcting material weaknesses. Material weaknesses are those of sufficient importance to warrant the attention of the president and Congress. The focus is on anticipating problems and preventing their occurrence.

Agencies are required to identify their internal control problems, but their reports do not always provide an accurate, clear assessment of the overall status of their control systems. Continuing weaknesses in agency internal control and accounting systems, many of which are long-standing, have a profound effect on government programs and operations. For example, agencies have disclosed weaknesses that resulted in overpricing of procured parts, increased vulnerability to failure and fraud in income payment programs, failure to monitor delinquent debts, and inadequate accountability for property. Many agencies, however, state that they had reasonable assurance their internal control systems, taken as a whole, were adequate—despite the seriousness of the problems highlighted in their annual reports. The administration and Congress need to give priority to correcting known, long-standing internal control problems. Plus, agency leaders must be held accountable for making the necessary improvements (General Accounting Office 1988c). A step in the right direction is the CFO act with its provisions for agency CFOs to assume leadership in their agencies regarding internal control policies and procedures.

Presidents have campaigned on preventing waste, fraud, and abuse. Agencies have found themselves vulnerable to the charges. Presidentially appointed inspector generals are now in place in departments to ferret out the mundane as well as the sensational internal control problems and to help fix them. Management and policy interests watch this area with renewed vigor. The stakes are high. Good management expects nothing less.

Financial Statements and Audits

The preparation and audit of financial statements help improve financial management by promoting discipline and accountability. By disclosing the cumulative financial effect of decisions on the nation's resources, financial statements provide early warning signals on emerging financial risks to policy makers and taxpayers. Financial statement audits ensure that the financial statements present fairly the financial operations in accordance with generally accepted principles. The federal government, however, lacks the type of audited financial statements common to business and, increasingly, state and local governments.

At the agency level, financial statements have received little attention and have a history of weakness, although this is changing. The Veterans Administration (VA), for example, was one of the first federal agencies to prepare consolidated financial statements for the federal government, in accordance with generally accepted accounting principles, and to have them audited. The GAO has reported on several weaknesses, however. Most noteworthy, the financial statement consolidated process was not integrated with the underlying accounting systems. For fiscal year 1986, VA manually prepared its consolidated financial statements primarily with financial information produced by 42 different financial management systems. For 1987, the VA used a microcomputer spreadsheet to improve consolidation of material. As the new governmentwide accounting standards are implemented, the VA's consolidated financial statements are expected to be more accurate and timely (General Accounting Office 1989).

In addition to a cash/budget basis report derived mainly from its own records, the Treasury publishes a consolidated financial statement on a modified accrual basis dependent upon less reliable program agency data. The consolidated statement is not based on a governmentwide accounting system; thus data are subject to manual entry at several levels of aggregation. Treasury uses accrual accounting concepts not equally practiced by all agencies. Plus, the report's consolidated format aggregates data for all funds; it does not present fund categories (Moraglio & Kerrigan 1986). One benefit from the government moving to a governmentwide integrated accounting system is that the consolidated report should more accurately reflect the government's financial affairs.

The form and content of a financial statement for a sovereign government presents problems unlike any other financial enterprise. A joint project undertaken by the comptroller general of the United States and the auditor general of Canada was to design a comprehensive annual financial report for a federal form of government (General Accounting Office 1986). The joint project resulted in illustrative annual financial reports for each country. To produce the U.S. report, however, several technical issues were not totally resolved:

- How should fixed assets be defined, valued, and depreciated?
- Should the financial statements of all government majority-owned corporations as well as the central banking system be consolidated with those of the federal government?
- How should social security be reported?
- How should tax expenditures be reported?

Despite these unsolved issues, the comptroller general's work demonstrates the extent to which sovereign governments with federal forms of government can produce annual reports to foster comparative analysis.

In summary, each department and agency should prepare and have audited annual financial statements. The CFO Act of 1990 mandates audited financial statements for trust, revolving, and commercial activity funds by 1994. The inspectors general within those agencies will determine how the audits will be accomplished. The U.S. government should also issue an annual report, including audited financial statements. Taken together, these steps would foster accountability in public finance.

COST CONTROL

Informed resource allocation decisions depend upon knowing the cost of operations or the total resources consumed in carrying out a specific operation. This allows for full disclosure of a program's costs, thereby facilitating a comparison with program benefits. The federal government's budgetary system places an emphasis on the acquisition of new obligation authority, not on program costs. This section highlights the need for an emphasis on program costs and project reporting along with renewed attention to performance analysis and program audits.

Program Costs

Basically, to produce a service or program, inputs are transformed into outputs. The purpose of a program cost orientation is to compare outputs to the costs involved in input acquisition and service delivery. Costs arise from factors of production—equipment, capital, materials, personnel, and time. Transforming these factors into the legally required set of services or outputs is the crux of management and the justification for taxation. Congress, the executive branch, and interested taxpayers deserve reliable operational and cost data so that they can more meaningfully judge program efficiency, evaluate policy decisions, and assess management performance.

The government provides a wide range of services or programs and should know the true cost of each. With a few notable exceptions—commercial federal enterprises like the Tennessee Valley Authority, Naval Weapons Plants, and government sponsored enterprises—cost-based systems are lacking in the government. Despite the flood of information on programs and the cash-based approach to budgeting, many costs are either estimated incorrectly or just ignored. For example, the cost of each medical procedure at a VA hospital and the total cost of a weapons system are determined in woefully inadequate manner at this time. Major cost measurement problems arise when dealing with loans, loan guarantees, and retirement benefits for civilian federal workers. Finally, the continuing myopic attention of policymakers to the manipulation of planned year-end outlay levels in order to meet arbitrary deficit reduction targets overshadows serious attempts to make budget decisions on a total cost basis.

Cost information requires the inclusion of fixed assets in reported assets and the treatment of their allocated cost or value as an expense when consumed (General Accounting Office 1985). The total value of the government's assets, both real and other, is not known with precision. For example, what is the replacement cost or market value of a B–52, a stealth bomber, or the Grand Canyon National Park? Until these asset valuation questions are resolved, program cost determination will be problematic.

Recent initiatives to contract-out or sell-off certain public assets are dependent upon adequate cost-level information. How can the government determine if VA medical services should be contracted-out in part or sold-off in whole? In another example, when the Forest Service sells timber from national forests, it has done so without basic data upon which to judge the economic merits of sales, monitor the extent of below-cost sales, determine why losses occur, or make timely cost reductions. Recently, the GAO has taken steps to rectify agency slighting of cost systems (General Accounting Office 1988a). Plus, the 1990 CFO act gives agency CFOs the responsibility to develop and maintain systems that provide cost information.

Project Reporting

The federal budget generally provides a yearly restocking of spending authority. Projects begun in one fiscal year often continue into succeeding ones, thus making it easy to mask total resource costs and even budget control. An integrated budget and accounting system could be expanded to track projects across budget years with information on planned and actual cost. Such an approach would shed light on the development of major weapons systems and the construction of capital assets. While the Defense Department uses acquisition reports to summarize cost information, they are not fully integrated with the core accounting system; plus the information lacks comparable and consistent results over time. A proposed project reporting system by the GAO (1985) incorporates:

- defined project phases
- estimated resource requirements to completion
- estimated cost of those resources for each phase
- expected milestone dates for each phase
- identified funding sources

The key to the project reporting system is the linkage of planned, actual, and completion costs to appropriations and obligations, thus bringing into one report all relevant information. To foster accountability, we recommend the preparation and disclosure of project reports.

Performance Analysis

Those in charge of a program should meet performance guidelines. Federal program managers are responsible for the effective use of an enormous base of financial and physical assets as well as personnel. Administering a program according to the law is a given, but managers must operate a production system to achieve programmatic and financial goals. A cost accounting system permits the assignment of costs which managers must use to assess performance. Yet career managers must contend with some laws and political agendas which thwart effective management performance. For example, the protection of an nonessential military base or the location of a new federal research center may help maximize the electoral advantage of an incumbent but may fail any other cost-benefit test.

The call for performance measurement of federal programs goes back many decades. While this is not the place for details, suffice it to say that a more effective performance measurement system would help not only program managers but also executive and legislative officials as well as the taxpaying public. The goal would be to assess the economy, efficiency, and effectiveness of government operations. This should enlighten those involved in the budget process. The GAO (1986) recommends against including such information in the U.S. government's proposed annual financial report due to the confusion and clutter that might be caused by the additional data. Nevertheless, there is little, if any, debate that the data would be useful. As in other areas, the CFO Act of 1990 directly addresses this need by specifying that the OMB's new deputy director has responsibility over the systematic measurement of performance and that agency CFOs must make sure that systems accommodate performance measurement reporting needs.

Program Audits

An expanded scope of audit encompasses not only financial results but operational results as well. In this matter, success is measured against program goals and performance criteria. Cost-level information is required for effective program audits. The GAO has utilized program audit guidelines for many years and in the process achieved a high level of recognition and acceptance for impartial evaluations of programs. Agencies should conduct more internal program audits utilizing GAO audit guidelines. Development of the office of the inspector general (IG) within each major agency is a start. To date, much of the IG's time has been spent on internal controls, however. A new emphasis is in order. Plus, audit recommendations must be acted upon.

CASH CONTROL

The federal government must manage a two trillion dollar annual cash flow.[2] Managing cash represents the steps taken to accelerate receipts (the expeditious billing, collection, and depositing of receipts); disburse payments in a timely manner (the scheduling of payments on due dates, not early or late); and invest any temporary excess cash balances. In recent years, extensive executive and legislative attention has focused on improving the government's knowledge of its cash position and its disbursement practices.

Cash Position

An entity's cash position represents its liquidity or the ability to pay current bills. This requires tracking, projecting, and monitoring every cash flow in every agency. While all aggregate cash flows were tracked, individual categories of cash flows were less well known. That is changing now that the Treasury Department's Financial Management Service (FMS) has taken the lead and worked with each agency to identify and improve each agency's cash flow (Murphy 1989).

Cash position projections are central to deficit calculations, with enormous implications under the Gramm–Rudman–Hollings deficit control law. Furthermore, cash shortages result in borrowing, thus increasing outstanding debt and pressing the statutory debt ceiling (Murphy 1989).

In terms of cash monitoring, one recurring problem is similar to that in personal finance when the checkbook does not reconcile to the bank balance.

Frankly, some federal agencies have not routinely reconciled agency financial records (their "checkbook") with those maintained by the Treasury Department (their "bank"). For example, the General Services Administration, to meet the Treasury's recorded 1986 balance, had to reduce its cash balance by $36 million for unaccounted-for differences. Part of the problem was that prior year differences had not been resolved, thus making prospective reconciliation captive to past problems. In another case, the Federal Financing Bank's records for one month in fiscal year 1985 reflected a $2.5 billion balance while the Treasury's record showed a balance of only $8 million— quite a discrepancy (General Accounting Office 1988a).

Movement to a governmentwide integrated accounting system should help resolve the reconciliation problems. Furthermore, the Treasury's FMS reports that a recent redesign permits it to reconcile each check paid against payment information for that check (Murphy 1989). In the end, the goal is to have accurate and timely cash balance statements. This should be achieved as soon as possible.

Cash Disbursements

Disbursements represent the outflow of cash from the U.S. Treasury in the form of checks issued and cash payments made. Cash disbursements are controlled through timely payment of approved invoices. Disbursements are generally authorized by an agency and then sent to the Treasury where payments are made by check. Historically, the Treasury prepared and mailed checks in the order received, irrespective of the due date. More recently, agencies assign a payment date on each voucher to allow the Treasury to pay on the due date.

The basic principles of cash disbursement are the same for business and government. The principles include:

- pay when due, not before
- prepare paperwork (invoices, vouchers, accounting controls) beforehand to maximize efficiency and to ensure the check is issued on the proper day
- monitor the mail float to have the check arrive on the due date, not earlier
- use electronic funds transfers if feasible and cost-effective

Several innovative programs indicate new attention to these principles, including more reliance on electronic funds transfer, direct deposit, and timely vendor payments.

Electronic funds transfer (EFT) enables funds to be automatically transferred from one account to another without using checks. This avoids the vagaries of the mail, thus permitting disbursement of funds exactly when they are due. Over 250 million EFT payments now flow from the government, amounting to over a half trillion dollars annually, with reliability (defined as an effective delivery rate to recipients) of 99.99 percent. Plus, the government saves money since an EFT payment costs about four cents compared to thirty cents for a check (Murphy 1989).

More and more government programs are moving to direct deposit of funds into a recipient's bank account. The Treasury's FMS reports that "80 percent of Federal salary and allotments, 60 percent of recurring benefit payments like Social Security and veterans benefits, and 60 percent of vendor payments" are made by direct deposit (Murphy 1989, 36). The direct deposit rate for recipients of Social Security's supplemental security income program is markedly lower, however, because so many participants do not have personal bank accounts. To get around this hurdle, the government has tested delivery of benefits via plastic access cards and automated teller machines (ATMs).

The timely payment of vendors by the government has garnered much attention. A program termed Vendor Express allows the government to save money by electronically transfering payments. A further enhancement gaining momentum is Electronic Data Interchange which permits agencies to reduce paperwork by electronically transmitting information to and from vendors as well as to automatically generate, certify, and transmit payment requests to the FMS, which in turn will disburse the funds electronically. Starting in 1990, all companies doing business with the government were required to be able to receive payments electronically (Joint Financial Management Improvement Program 1988; Murphy 1989).

The Prompt Payment Act of 1982 requires federal agencies to pay their bills on time, to pay interest penalties when payments are late, and to take discounts only when payments are made within the discount period. Amendments in 1988 further restricted agency payment delays; plus they extended the law to cover construction contracts and the timely payment by prime contractors to subcontractors with interest penalties imposed for late payments.

Under the Prompt Payment Act, agencies must provide compliance reports to the OMB with an annual report to Congress. Recent reports submitted by the agencies reveal long payment delays. As a result, agencies have had to pay interest penalties, with some penalties due but not paid. During a recent fiscal year the Army paid over $2 million in interest penalties for failing to meet the payment deadlines (Jeffcoat 1989). In summary, the pace of innovations in this area has accelerated but agencies still have a way to go to get their disbursement practices in top shape.

COLLECTIONS CONTROL

Collections represent money due to the government. The goal is to minimize the lapse between the time money is due to be received by the government and the time the money is available for disbursement. To illustrate the types of collection controls required, we examine receivables monitoring and debt collection.

Receivables Monitoring

The key to receivables monitoring is to know what is due (or assessed) and when and then to process the receivables quickly. Several items deserve mention. A recent trend is for agencies to accept credit cards for purchases or payments. This allows, in some cases, next day credit for such sales. By accepting credit cards, agencies increase funds availability, reduce delinquencies and bad checks, and improve the information on what is due.

The government has used the lockbox system to expedite the receipt and processing of payments. A lockbox is an arrangement where receipts are mailed directly from payers to a post office box that is serviced by a designated bank. When a check is received in the lockbox, the bank processes the checks and wire transfers that amount into the agency's account.

Another effective tool is the automated cash concentration system. During the 1980s, the system linked commercial depositories where agencies made their deposits through five concentrator banks to the Treasury's account. Treasury generally received funds on the next business day. A new system eliminates the concentrator banks, allowing funds to move directly into Treasury's account at the Federal Reserve. The benefit by having on-line, immediate access to all deposit information is that it enhances the cash reconciliation process (Murphy 1989; Joint Financial Management Improvement Program 1988).

Efforts to expedite payments from corporate and individual income tax payers also enhance collections. Renewed attention has been given to the mechanism whereby employers withhold from employees' paychecks income tax and social security taxes and remit those funds to the Treasury. The Federal Tax Deposit (FTD) system used by corporations represents about 80 percent of all tax collections. Efforts are underway to convert the system from paper-based to electronic, thereby effecting many economies (Murphy 1989). Plus, policy makers keep accelerating the frequency by which the remittances must be made. All this adds to quicker collections.

Debt Collection

Debt collection involves the proper accounting for receivables and prompt, aggressive collection action. The Debt Collection Act of 1982 gives federal agencies an assortment of options regarding debt collection, including the referral of delinquent debt to consumer reporting agencies; the use of salary offsets, where applicable, for recovering delinquent debts; the ability to assess interest penalties and administrative costs on delinquent debts; and the authority to use private contractors to service and collect government debts (Joint Financial Management Improvement Program 1984). Finally, a new tax refund offset program is proving very effective in resolving debts owed to the government (Murphy 1989).

Since the government asserts its right to allocate credit to certain borrowers and sectors of the economy, government loan programs require special attention. The process consists of establishing loan program objectives and credit policies, reviewing loan applications, disbursing funds, monitoring payments, and following up when delinquencies occur.

Credit extension and debt collection are linked in theory as well as in normal business practice but too often are neglected in public policy discussions. A wide range of individuals, including farmers, students, military veterans, property owners in flood-prone areas, and struggling business owners enjoy the largess of government credit programs. Problems associated with this program are exacerbated by the fact that many of the beneficiaries of such credit are marginal credit risks, unlikely to get credit without Uncle Sam's help.

Credit advocates have an incentive to keep the cost of each credit program under wraps. Recent initiatives seek to disclose the full cost of credit, including the subsidy created by longer terms and lower rates than those found in private credit markets. One approach is to require an appropriation for the subsidy costs of each loan program. The purpose of such an effort is to place the spending inherent in credit programs on a comparable basis with federal spending for grants, transfers, and purchases.

Once credit is extended, the government must collect the debt. The size, much less the value, of the government's portfolio of all outstanding loans has been hard to determine due to inadequate record-keeping over the years. To reduce the loan portfolio in a cost-effective manner, the government has allowed some borrowers to repay on favorable terms rather than wait for a lump sum payment. Some loan portfolios have been sold to the private sector at amounts less than face value of the loans. Agencies even sell the servicing rights to some loan programs for an up-front fee, based on the calculations that the cost of in-house portfolio servicing over the loan's expected life will exceed the net present value of selling servicing rights (Office of Management and Budget 1989).

Not all agencies agree on how to define delinquencies. Different standards have been used on what constitutes a delinquency and when loans should be considered uncollectible. Varying definitions allow distortions to arise in assessing individual program performance. As a result, the quality of a loan portfolio can deteriorate. The VA, for example, assessed delinquent debtors only one-half of the legally required interest rate and neglected to bill patients for services received in excess of eligible amounts (General Accounting Office 1988a). A recent innovation allows lender agencies to check with one another to help determine the applicant's credit standing. The Justice Department has instituted a centralized debt collection office to track and resolve cases referred to it by agencies. Agencies can report to private credit bureaus on both current and delinquent commercial accounts (Office of Management and Budget 1989).

Methods to get funds from delinquents are expanding. The Department of Education is examining the use of a preauthorized monthly charge against a delinquent debtor's credit card. Even the Internal Revenue Service has sought changes which would enhance its ability to deal with delinquents. It wants the ability to accept taxes by means other than check or money order. An experimental preauthorized debit system allows taxpayers to voluntarily agree to have their bank accounts debited for set amounts over a given time period until the amounts due the government are paid off (Office of Management and Budget 1989).

Recent revisions in OMB guidelines to agencies (Circular A–129) focus on managing credit. The guidelines state that agencies must limit the federal risk to 8 percent of the outstanding loan limits, must require banks to document billings and collections and to report problems promptly, and must fix the loan term equal to the life of the collateral or security for the loan. Further, agencies must use state-certified appraisers to foster accountability for credit programs (Office of Management and Budget 1989).

In summary, accounting for receivables continues to be inadequate. Problems include underestimating the amount of delinquent debt, neglecting to establish allowances for loan losses, and failing to promptly record amounts due. As in other areas reviewed, much has been done but much remains to be done.

CONCLUSION

Managing government finances is a challenge due to their amount and complexity. That is no excuse, however, for weak controls. In fact, it justifies the need for laws, policies, and procedures which clarify the public's expectations regarding the management of public assets.

This chapter has illustrated the nature of the changes occurring in federal financial management, especially in terms of funds, costs, cash, and collections. The results are striking. The financial giant is making progress but more work is required.

The need for strong financial leadership has finally been recognized. In the closing days of the 101st Congress, the Chief Financial Officer (CFO) law was passed and then signed into law by the president. The legislation creates a chief management officer in the OMB, as well as establishing CFOs in executive departments and agencies. Agency CFOs have responsibility over all financial management activities within their agencies and are charged with developing systems to provide accurate and timely reporting of financial information, and implementing a five-year financial management plan to be updated yearly. The 1990s open with major legislation giving clearer long-term direction and oversight to the army of public managers who have been striving for some time to improve their own agency financial management systems.

NOTES

1. Much of the material in this chapter is based on the work of the General Accounting Office. It is supplemented by the work of the Joint Financial Management Improvement Program, the Treasury Department's Financial Management Service, Reform 88, the Office of Management and Budget, and the president's Private Sector Survey on Cost Control. I want to thank these observers of and participants in federal financial management for producing public documents of superior quality. Furthermore, I want to thank Marcus W. Page and Clyde E. Jeffcoat for commenting on an earlier draft. Of course, they are not responsible for any remaining problems.

2. This section relies on reports by the Treasury Department's Financial Management Service. See Murphy (1989).

SELECT BIBLIOGRAPHY

Hildreth, W. Bartley. 1989. "Financing Strategy." In *Handbook of Strategic Management*, edited by Jack Rabin, Gerald J. Miller, and W. Bartley Hildreth, 279–300. New York: Marcel Dekker.

Jeffcoat, Clyde E. 1989. "Improving Army's Financial Management." *Government Accountants Journal* 38, no. 3 (Fall): 37–40.

Joint Financial Management Improvement Program. 1984. *Financial Handbook For Federal Executives and Managers*. Washington, D.C.

———. 1988. *1988 Report on Financial Management Improvements*. Washington, D.C.

Long, Donald C. 1988–1989. "Reagan's Financial Management Legacy." *The Bureaucrat*, 25–28.

Moraglio, Joseph F., and Harry D. Kerrigan. 1986. *The Federal Budget and Financial Systems: A Management Perspective*. New York: Quorum Books.

Murphy, Gerald. 1989. "A Status Report on the Fiscal Operations of the Government." *Government Accountants Journal* 38, no. 1 (Spring): 35–42.

U.S. General Accounting Office. 1985. *Managing the Cost of Government: Building an Effective Financial Management Structure, Volume II Conceptual Framework*. Washington, D.C.

———. 1986. *Illustrative Annual Financial Report of the Government of the United States, 1984*. Washington, D.C.

———. 1988a. *Financial Management: Example of Weaknesses*. Washington, D.C.

———. 1988b. *Financial Management: Responses to 17 Questions*. Washington, D.C.

———. 1988c. *Financial Management Issues*. Washington, D.C.

———. 1989. *Financial Management: Opportunities for Improving VA's Internal Accounting Controls and Procedures*. Washington, D.C.

U.S. Office of Management and Budget. 1989. *Management of the United States*

Government, Fiscal Year 1990. Washington, D.C.: U.S. Government Printing Office.

————. 1990. *Budget of the U.S. Government, Fiscal Year 1991.* Washington, D.C.: U.S. Government Printing Office.

8

DATA PROCESSING IN FEDERAL BUDGETING AND FINANCIAL MANAGEMENT

STANLEY B. BOTNER

HISTORICAL DEVELOPMENT

The Bureau of the Census in 1951 acquired the first large-scale, fully automatic data processing system utilized by a federal agency.[1] During the following eight years more than 175 systems were installed by federal agencies with annual rental costs of about $50 million.[2] Scholars were prompt to sense the implications of the new technology. Writing in 1964, Ronayne declared:

It is safe to conclude ADP is here to stay in public administration—at *all* levels of government. More than ever, knowledge of ADP is vital to the governmental administration for it provides the power to enhance *performance* while balancing the force of technology with the treatment of human beings.[3]

Reilly, in 1962, suggested that the principal significance of ADP was to be found in a concept, and not in speed or economy:

But when the historians look back upon this first decade, I think they will note as our greatest achievement the development of the systems concept; the realization that no problem is an "island unto itself," but that most activities are related to one or more programs in a particular agency, in a particular substantive field within the government, or even within a society.[4]

The evolution of the computer environment accelerated during the following three decades, during which federal departments and agencies moved rapidly to develop and employ data processing systems to support budgeting and financial management functions.

Today, the United States is the single largest user of information technology (computers and communications) in the world. More than 118,000 federal workers manage some 18,000 medium and large-scale computers. In addition, some 600,000 microcomputers are in use, compared to only 2,000 in 1980.[5] The growth in federal expenditures for data processing and other information technology activities since 1982 is shown by Figure 8.1. At the same time, the number of employees engaged in information technology has gradually increased as a percentage of the total federal workforce since 1983 and is expected to level off at about three percent.[6]

During the 1960s, the federal government was the leader in the application of modern computers and telecommunications. By the late 1970s, however, it had fallen behind. Its systems were outdated and not cost-effective. Efforts by the agencies to upgrade systems lacked planning for future needs and were often economically infeasible or technically obsolete when installed.

Today, the government is engaged in a far-reaching effort to modernize and upgrade its computer and data processing systems. Advance planning for ADP needs was mandated by the Paperwork Reduction Act of 1980. Under this act, the Office of Management and Budget (OMB) is required to develop and revise annually, in consultation with the administrator of General Services, a five-year plan for meeting the automatic data processing equipment and other information technology needs of the federal government.[7]

In the early 1980s, President Reagan launched a comprehensive program called Reform '88 to improve the management systems of the federal government. One of the objectives of the Reform '88 program was more effective management of the federal government's information resources.[8] In 1982, the Federal Managers' Financial Integrity Act required establishment of governmentwide standards for both financial systems and information.[9] Standards developed by the General Accounting Office (GAO) in cooperation with OMB were implemented by agencies pursuant to OMB Circular No. A–127, "Financial Management Systems," issued December 19, 1984.[10] OMB Circular No. A–127 requires agencies to "establish and maintain a single, integrated financial management system, which may be supplemented by subsidiary systems." In addition, support for budgets is provided by a requirement that financial management data be recorded, stored, and reported to facilitate budget preparation, analysis, and execution.[11]

This was followed in 1985 by OMB Circular No. A–130, "Management of Federal Information Resources," which among other things requires agencies to "acquire off-the-shelf software from commercial sources, unless the cost-effectiveness of developing custom software is clear and has been doc-

Figure 8.1
Information Technology Budget in Current and Constant (1982) Dollars

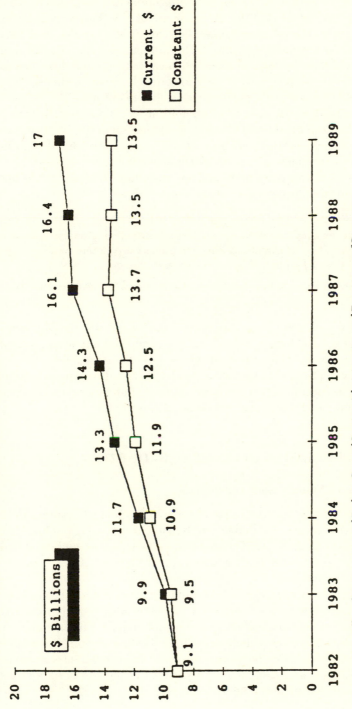

Source: U.S. Office of Management and Budget, General Services Administration, and Department of Commerce, *A Five-Year Plan for Meeting the Automatic Data Processing and Telecommunications Needs of the Federal Government,* vol. I, June 1988.

umented."[12] Finally, a memorandum of understanding signed in February 1987 by the OMB and the Department of the Treasury designated the Treasury's Financial Management Service (FMS) as the lead agency for financial management systems.[13] The administration's original target was implementation by 1988 of a consolidated governmentwide financial management information system operating in all major agencies. While that timetable was not met, "good progress" has been made.[14]

To coordinate the execution of Reform '88, President Reagan in 1984 established the President's Council on Management (PCM). It was made up of key management officials in large agencies and charged with not only leading the implementation of management improvements but also identifying possible future problems and opportunities. With respect to budgeting and financial management, the objectives are to:

- improve financial management systems by installing a single, governmentwide financial system, electronically linked to primary accounting systems in each major agency that are supported by subsidiary and program systems
- integrate the linkage between budget systems and financial systems data bases[15]

Key steps toward achieving those goals were the development of the standard general ledger in 1986 and the establishment administratively of a governmentwide chief financial officer (CFO) in the OMB in 1987. The former was designed to provide a standard accounting structure for financial information accumulation and processing, to enhance financial control, and to support budget and external financial reporting.[16]

DATA PROCESSING IN FEDERAL BUDGETING

Office of Management and Budget

At the present time two aged, incompatible budget systems are used by the OMB to prepare the budget and transmit it to Congress. One, the Budget Preparation System (BPS), is used to collect agency budget submissions. The other, the Central Budget Management System (CBMS), produces management information.

Plans for improving the federal budget system call for the replacement of the budget systems presently used by OMB with a single modern system based on current technology policies and federal information processing standards. Objectives include smoothing the flow of budget data in support of the budget process; providing improved information access for agencies, the president, and Congress; and permitting increased responsiveness to changes in policymakers' information requirements.[17]

Department of Transportation

The methodology used by individual departments and agencies to provide data processing support for budgeting and financial management varies considerably. As an example, the Department of Transportation (DOT) currently uses microcomputers extensively to prepare, analyze, and present budget requests. Spreadsheet and word processing programs are among the software used in the department's budget formulation. In addition, the financial management data used in budget execution resides in accounting systems reliant upon mainframe and minicomputer systems. More detailed analyses of budget execution data also involves the use of microcomputers.[18]

DOT budget formulation and execution data is transmitted to the OMB by using the Budget Preparation System of the latter. This process involves the inputing of budget data from DOT agencies into a microcomputer located in the office of the secretary, and transmitting it from there to the BPS. Finally, DOT is in the process of implementing the Departmental Accounting and Financial Information System (DAFIS) throughout the department. As of 1989, some 59 percent of DOT's accounting transactions were processed by DAFIS.[19]

As in the case of DOT, most departments and agencies transmit budgetary numeric data to the OMB by entering the information via online terminals (PCs) into the BPS. Some, however, such as the Department of Education, transmit their budget submissions to the OMB in hard copy format.[20]

The BPS operates on a mainframe computer in the executive office of the president. While this system does not presently permit file uploading via telecommunications, the General Services Administration is testing an alternative that will permit personal computers to be used to simulate uploading to OMB's hardware.[21] The Department of Transportation, on the other hand, plans to eliminate data entry involvement by the Office of Budget by expanding use of the BPS in the office of the secretary of DOT. Once the Office of the Secretary has approved the budget data of the department's Operating Administrations, those units will enter the data into their own microcomputers and transmit the information to the OMB.[22]

Department of the Interior

All bureaus and offices within the Department of the Interior use personal computers in some capacity, primarily for word processing, spread sheets, and graphics, to develop and present their budget requests. "The use of computers," according to one official, "has enabled us to present a variety of complex and voluminous material to a variety of audiences (ranging from high level policy officials in the department to the press and special interest groups) more effectively than had previously been possible."[23]

Department of Housing and Urban Development

Officials of the Department of Housing and Urban Development stress the importance of treating information as a valuable resource. Managers are encouraged to view information resource management not as a separate activity, but as an integral part of ongoing efforts to improve overall program management. HUD, like many other departments, has developed a strategic ADP long-range plan (LRP) for information management for the period 1988–1992. The LRP, done in accordance with OMB Circular No. A–130, "Management of Federal Information Resources," estimates future ADP requirements along mission/program lines and projects plans for the acquisition and use of ADP equipment resources to meet these estimated requirements.[24]

Department of Commerce

The Department of Commerce is in the process of developing a Financial and Management Information System (FMIS). A departmentwide, single, integrated financial system mandated by A–127 FMIS is scheduled to be implemented by October 1993.

FMIS will include a single, departmental primary accounting system; standard financial management data structures and codes; and a uniform, Commerce-wide management information structure. A–127 improvement initiatives centered on budgeting will also be pursued. For example, a departmental budget execution data base will be established and linked directly to the departmental accounting system. Finally, a departmental budget formulation data base will be implemented which will be linked to the budget execution data base.[25]

Environmental Protection Agency

The U.S. Environmental Protection Agency is considered to be one of the federal agencies at the cutting edge in the development of new management information systems technology. In keeping with OMB Circular A–127, issued in December 1984, EPA conducted a study of its existing financial and budget systems which led to a determination that far-reaching modifications were required. After alternative solutions were considered, EPA settled on procuring commercially available, off-the-shelf software to comply with basic A–127 requirements. Such software was procured and utilized in the development of EPAs Integrated Financial Management System (IFMS).[26]

Phase 1 of IFMS, the objective of which was to install core systems, was implemented in February 1989. Under Phase 1, the most significant improvement occurred in the Office of the Comptroller operations. After the usual start-up problems, the budget process was automated, and interface points with the financial systems were fully integrated. Agency financial management improved substantially in functions, such as receivables and payables.

The off-the-shelf software package entitled "Federal Financial System" utilized by EPA has been employed by a number of other federal agencies to fill their budgeting and accounting requirements. They include the Internal Revenue Service, the Departments of State, Veterans Affairs, and Interior, as well as the General Accounting Office.[27]

The use of off-the-shelf software from outside suppliers reflects a growing trend. More than 100 state and municipal government agencies in the United States use such software, as do several of the main departments of the Canadian federal administration—including Defense.

DATA PROCESSING REFORMS ABROAD: KUWAIT AND DENMARK

Federal agencies in the United States, in their efforts to improve the utilization of data processing in budgeting and financial management, might well draw upon the experiences of other countries in this area. For example, utilization of commercial software reflects only one of several options with respect to installation of new information systems. Other options include modifying the existing system to meet current needs, borrowing another department's already-operating system, and developing and installing a customized system.[28]

The governmental administration of Kuwait, in considering how to install a new information system, decided to refashion its existing system and customize the software to its needs. To insure that the system dovetailed with user needs, future users were involved in the installation of the system from the beginning. The Kuwaiti Integrated Financial Information System (IFIS) is a highly structured model with some sixteen information subsystems, including ones in budget accounting and financial information. An important component of IFIS is a twenty-two-character account number system, including a classification by function, subfunction, program, activity, and subactivity, the last two being cost centers.[29]

Federal officials in the United States might also profit by studying the program of Financial Management Reform initiated by the government of Denmark in 1984. A key objective of the effort was to establish an information system for management control in the agencies and to provide documentation of performance and efficiency measures to departments and top management. Modernization of computer systems ensued, based on "open architecture and a tripartition of the data capacity." Data required by individuals are located in PCs, data needed by groups are placed in local minicomputers, and data required by central authorities are located in data centers. These and other modernization initiatives are designed to "bring about a management system which is similar to the systems used in large private corporations, but adapted to the specific circumstances of the public sector."[30]

DATA PROCESSING IN STATE AND LOCAL GOVERNMENTS

Federal officials involved in improving the use of data processing in budgeting and financial management might draw also on processes and techniques developed by state and local governments in the United States. For example, Kansas City, Missouri, has computerized the entire budgetary process and offers "on-line access to all budgetary and financial data."[31]

As another example, the State of Colorado has developed a system for submission of agency budgets to the governor on disks, while Kentucky and Louisiana are planning to transfer budget requests electronically.[32]

Political Impact of ADP

Data processing has been extensively employed to support budgetary and financial management functions in federal departments and agencies. However, comparatively little is known as to what impact ADP systems have had politically, in terms of who gains and who loses power. Seeking answers to this question, the author conducted a survey of the use and impact of data processing techniques in budgeting and financial management in seventeen federal departments and agencies.[33] Federal officials were queried as to the impact of computerization in terms of who gains and who loses power. While some have contended that computing has shifted power to the technocrats, fourteen federal officials did not agree. Only one official agreed, and two were uncertain. It has also been suggested that interest groups have been strengthened by the availability of computers and other technological tools. Federal officials narrowly accepted this proposition. Seven agreed, five disagreed, and five were uncertain.

Finally, the proposition has been advanced that computing provides the current power elite with the tools to perpetuate and increase their power, and therefore preserves the status quo. King and Kraemer have written that "recent empirical research suggests that the latter is the most common outcome of computing."[34] However, federal officials have a different view. Twelve federal respondents disagreed, four were uncertain, and only one agreed.

In summary, then, while the phenomenal increase in the use of data processing techniques has greatly facilitated the performance of the budgeting and financial management processes and contributed to more in-depth analyses, the impact politically has not been great, in the opinion of federal department and agency officials.

Overall Efficiency and Effectiveness

Department and agency officials were asked to assess the "degree of overall efficiency and effectiveness" of their computerized budgeting and financial management systems. One assessed its systems as "very efficient and effective," while twelve graded their systems as "efficient and effective." One system was characterized "inefficient and ineffective" and another as reflecting "no change." One department did not respond to this question.

Department and agency officials were also requested to indicate the most serious deficiencies of their data processing financial management systems. The most frequent deficiency cited was lack of systems integration. Others included difficulty in keeping up with technology changes, especially in software; lack of knowledgeable staff; and poor maintenance arrangements.

Technological Advances and Trends

As great as has been the impact of data processing to date, federal officials predict further dramatic changes as more advanced automation tools and streamlined processes are introduced. Enormous gains in throughput per dollar are resulting from expanded computer power and decreasing hardware costs. Officials of the Department of Housing and Urban Development cite the microprocessor revolution, sophistication and usefulness of prepackaged software, and telecommunication networks as trend areas which will play an important part in influencing and meeting HUD's ADP goals during the next five years.[35]

Other significant trends and developments in data processing include:

- Mainframe computer equipment has become more modular, allowing for easy expansion. In addition, memory access times have decreased, the cost/performance ratio is decreasing, and a smaller amount of space is now needed for equipment.

- The end user now benefits from equipment offering more computing power, including a desktop general computer with the power of one MIPS (millions of instructions per second), and a microcomputer which fits under a desk with the power of five MIPS.

- The development of fourth-generation languages (4GLs) offers much potential in terms of user friendliness and software development productivity. These highly sophisticated software packages permit users to express their requests in English-like phrases which are then translated into a database query.

- Expert systems, commonly referred to as Artificial Intelligence (AI) systems, are expected to become a routine part of office work by 1995. AI systems are designed to store and process information of a logical nature. "In this type of system, the logical decision sequences performed by a human being are stored in the AI computer and then invoked by the AI operator, who responds to a logical progression of decision sequences which the expert system presents to the user.[36]

As to the future, one official offered this comment:

Nine years ago the only automation my office had was an IBM Selectric typewriter.
... What will the future bring and how soon will it get here? We have no idea. We
only know that it will come three times as fast as automation did nine years ago.[37]

CONCLUSIONS AND RECOMMENDATIONS

While federal agencies in the United States have made progress in recent
years toward improving their computer and data processing systems, much
remains to be done. The development of the standard general ledger in 1986
and the establishment of a governmentwide chief financial officer (CFO) in
1986 were key steps toward development of a single, governmentwide financial system with electronic linkages to agency accounting systems. However, while good progress has been made toward implementation of such a
system, completion still lies ahead.

As a result of the failure to move more quickly to integrate the flow of
information between the OMB and the departments and agencies, two aged,
incompatible budget systems are used by the OMB to prepare the budget
and transmit it to Congress. Further, agency officials still complain of lack
of systems integration, inflexibility, obsolete equipment and technology, too
many manual processes, and lack of availability of data to operating managers.

In November 1988, the U.S. General Accounting Office released a "transition series" of reports addressing major policy, management, and program
issues facing the new administration. Included in the series were reports on
"Information Technology Issues" and "Financial Management Issues." The
GAO cited some major deficiencies in the information technology environment in the federal government:

- Some of the major systems development projects "have had costs escalate by
  hundreds of millions of dollars and schedules slip by years. In many cases the new
  systems do not work as planned or meet user needs, and wasted millions of dollars."[38]
- Although strategic planning for computers is critical, "in too many instances agencies do not complete strategic plans or develop plans that are not effective." As a
  result, "millions are spent on computer systems that do not meet agency needs,
  do not perform as desired, are not cost-effective, and are not compatible with
  existing and future agency systems."[39]
- Finally, a governmentwide shortage of technical staff "has resulted in many federal
  agencies not being able to meet crucial objectives."[40]

A related problem is the poor condition of the government's financial
systems. These systems, reported the GAO, "are incompatible and costly
to operate and maintain. Systems fail to produce the complete, timely,

reliable financial data needed for policy-making and day-to-day operations."[41] In addition, internal controls are weak.

The technology now exists to correct such deficiencies and restore the federal government as the leader in the application of modern computers and telecommunications. Application of such technology coupled with achievement of the remaining objectives of the Reform '88 program would go far toward attaining this goal.

NOTES

1. Geoffrey Y. Cornog, "Automatic Data Processing—Dr. Jekyll or Mr. Hyde?" *Public Administration Review* 21 (Spring 1961): 105. This chapter will be limited for the most part to a treatment of electronic data processing. However, data processing is only a portion of office automation.

2. Ibid. Computer usage was especially widespread in the Department of Defense.

3. Maurice F. Ronayne, " 'Leads' to Pertinent ADP Literature for the Public Administrator," *Public Administration Review* 24 (June 1964): 125.

4. Frank W. Reilly, "Policy Decisions and EDP Systems in the Federal Government," *Public Administration Review* 22 (September 1962): 131.

5. Office of Management and Budget, *Management of the United States, Government, Fiscal Year 1988* (Washington, D.C.: Government Printing Office, 1988), 47. Also U.S. Office of Management and Budget, *Management of the United States Government, Fiscal Year 1989* (Washington, D.C.: Government Printing Office, 1989), 72.

6. Office of Management and Budget, U.S. General Services Administration, and U.S. Department of Commerce, *A Five-Year Plan for Meeting the Automatic Data Processing and Telecommunications Needs of the Federal Government*, vol. I, June 1988 (Washington, D.C.: Government Printing Office, 1988), 3.

7. U.S. Office of Management and Budget, U.S. General Services Administration, and U.S. Department of Commerce, *A Five-Year Plan for Meeting the Automatic Data Processing and Telecommunications Needs of the Federal Government* (Washington, D.C.: Government Printing Office, 1987), iv.

8. Office of Management and Budget, *Management of the United States Government, Fiscal Year 1987*, 3.

9. Office of Management and Budget, *Management of the United States Government, Fiscal Year 1988*, 26.

10. Ibid., 28.

11. Office of Management and Budget, Circular No. A–127, "Financial Management Systems" (December 19, 1984), 2.

12. Office of Management and Budget, Circular No. A–130, "Management of Federal Information Resources" (December 12, 1985), 6.

13. Joint Financial Management Improvement Program, *1988 Report on Financial Management Improvement*, 13.

14. Jimmie Brown, Chief, Financial Systems and Policy Branch, OMB, letter to author, August 17, 1989.

15. Office of Management and Budget, *Management of the United States Government, Fiscal Year 1990*, 3–17.

16. *U.S. Government Standard General Ledger*, ii.

17. Office of Management and Budget, *Management of the United States Government, Fiscal Year 1990*, 3–27.

18. Joyce D. Shelton, Director of Financial Management, U.S. Department of Transportation, letter to author, September 14, 1989.

19. Ibid.

20. Carlos Rice, Director, Office of Information Resources Management, U.S. Department of Education, letter to author, October 16, 1989.

21. William B. Early, Jr., Deputy Controller for Budget, U.S. General Services Administration, letter to author, August 25, 1989.

22. Shelton to author, September 14, 1989.

23. Anthony L. Ittelag, Director of Budget, U.S. Department of the Interior, letter to author, September 26, 1989.

24. Office of Administration and Office of Information Policies and Systems, U.S. Department of Housing and Urban Development, *ADP Long-Range Plan Fiscal Years 1988–92*, i, 6.

25. Richard E. Shute, Director, Management and Information Systems, U.S. Department of Commerce, letter to author, November 28, 1989. Also U.S. Department of Commerce, *Five-Year Financial Management Systems Plan for the 1991 Budget*, 1–2.

26. Vincette L. Goerl and Paul Wohlleben, "Financial Systems Reform at the U.S. Environmental Protection Agency." Paper submitted to the Working Group on the Modernization of Budgetary Techniques and Financial Control sponsored by the International Institute of Administrative Sciences and the Commission of the European Communities, March 18, 1988.

27. Paul Wohlleben, U.S. Environmental Protection Agency, telephone conversation with author, February 2, 1990.

28. Christian De Visscher, "The Modernization of Budgetary Techniques and Financial Control," *International Review of Administrative Sciences* 55, no. 3 (September 1989): 337.

29. Mohamed Mowafi H. Farid, Financial Adviser to the Minister of Finance (Kuwait), "The Kuwaiti Case." Paper submitted to the Working Group on the Modernization of Budgetary Techniques and Financial Control, 1988.

30. Ministry of Finance, Copenhagen, Denmark, "Budget Reform and Financial Management Reform in Denmark." Paper submitted to the Working Group on the Modernization of Budgetary Techniques and Financial Control, October 1987.

31. Verlyn J. Leiker, Budget Officer, City of Kansas City, Missouri, survey response, June 28, 1988.

32. Diane Halpern, Principal Policy/Budget Analyst, State of Colorado, survey response, June 21, 1987; Andrew J. Douds, Associate Director, Department of Information Systems, Commonwealth of Kentucky, survey response, July 3, 1986; Budget Section, Division of Administration, State of Louisiana, survey response, May 15, 1986.

33. A full account of the results of this study can be found in an article by the author on "Data-Processing Techniques in Federal and State Budgeting and Finance," *Social Science Computer Review* 7, no. 1 (Spring 1989): 57–60.

34. Kenneth L. Kraemer and John Leslie King, "Computing and Public Organizations," *Public Administration Review* 46 (November 1986): 492.

35. U.S. Department of Housing and Urban Development, *ADP Long-Range Plan Fiscal Years 1988–92,* 7.

36. Ibid., 7–9.

37. William B. Early, Jr., Deputy Comptroller for Budget, U.S. General Services Administration, letter to author, August 25, 1989.

38. U.S. General Accounting Office, *Transition Series, Information Technology Issues* (November 1988), 12.

39. Ibid., 9.

40. Ibid., 18.

41. U.S. General Accounting Office, *Transition Series, Financial Management Issues* (November 1988), 19.

9

PRIVATIZATION AND FEDERAL BUDGET REFORM

LAWRENCE L. MARTIN

This chapter explores the use of privatization as one approach to federal budget reform and to the reduction of the budget deficit. The argument is made that the privatization perspective provides insights into questions about the provision, production, and financing of government programs and services—questions seldom raised during the budget process and thus seldom answered.

The chapter begins with a discussion of the nature of privatization and its alternative conceptualizations. Next, a cross section of the federal programs and services most frequently mentioned as privatization candidates is identified. The scope and breadth of the activities discussed suggests the richness of privatization as a concept and its ability to cast federal programs and services in a new budgetary light. The technical feasibility of privatizing the identified federal programs and services is addressed as well as the potential impact of each on the budget process and the deficit. Finally, a recommendation is made that the federal government should consider more programs and services as potential candidates for privatization.

THE CONCEPT OF PRIVATIZATION

Perhaps no other recent addition to the government lexicon has demonstrated such a remarkable ability to generate optional meanings as has the term "privatization." Consequently, when dealing with the topic of privatization and federal budget reform, it is necessary to make the term's meaning explicit.

Lester Salamon and his colleagues at the National Academy of Public Administration state that the term "privatization" can be construed either narrowly or broadly.[1] The narrow construction views privatization as the task of transferring responsibilities and assets from the public to the private sector.[2] Thus, privatization involves load shedding, or denationalization, and sale of government assets. Using a provision/production decision framework, Kolderie calls this approach the privatization of the *provision* decision.[3] Should government provide this program or service to its citizens? When the answer is no, government declines to continue providing some program or service and turns the responsibility over to the private sector. Privatizing the provision decision through load shedding and the sale of government assets is the principal privatization approach used in Great Britain under Margaret Thatcher and in most other Western industrialized nations that have active privatization programs.

In its broader conceptualization, privatization is said to deal with both *provision* and *production* decisions. In Kolderie's schema, the *production* decision is analogous to a "make or buy," or implementation, decision. Having decided to provide, or to continue providing, some program or service to its citizens, government must next decide how the activity should be produced. Should the program or service be directly delivered by government or purchased from the private sector? In this sense, privatization refers not only to load shedding and the sale of government assets, but also to administrative techniques government can use to enlist the private sector in the delivery of government programs and services. Hatry has catalogued a number of these so-called "alternative service delivery" approaches, including grants-in-aid, contracting out, vouchers, franchises, the use of volunteers, public-private partnerships, and joint public-private ventures.[4] Privatizing the production decision, or alternative service delivery, is the form of privatization used most frequently by state and local governments.[5]

Another dimension of privatization that is equally important, but which receives less attention, is the financing decision.[6] After government decides to do something (the provision decision) and has settled upon an implementation strategy (the production decision), there is still a financing decision to be made. Should government pay for this activity or should the financing be partially or totally privatized? The privatization of the funding decision usually takes one of two major forms: a direct tax or a user fee. Examples of federal programs and services that have had at least part of their financing privatized through direct taxation include Social Security, Medicare, and unemployment insurance. User fees imposed by the federal government include the entrance fees charged at national parks and copyright and patent registration fees.

In the ensuing discussion of federal budget reform, the term privatization will be used in its broadest sense encompassing provision, production, and financing decisions. The three approaches are not mutually exclusive. For example, the privatization of the provision decision always implies the privatization of the financing decision. Likewise, the privatization of the production decision will frequently, but not always, also entail privatizing the financing decision.

Where possible, an estimate is provided of the potential savings to the federal treasury for each of the programs and services suggested for privatization. Where multiple cost estimates are available, the more conservative estimate is used in an attempt not to overstate the case for privatization.

Steve Hanke suggests that there are two general approaches to the identification and selection of potential government programs and services for privatization: the political approach and the technical approach.[7] The federal programs and services suggested for privatization in this chapter are selected on the basis of their technical feasibility and potential impact on the federal budget and the deficit. Political feasibility is not addressed. Some criticism may be leveled for separating technical from political feasibility. In defense of this approach, the point is simply made that political feasibility tends to be transient in nature. What may be perceived as politically infeasible one day can suddenly become feasible the next. The validity of this is aptly demonstrated by the sweeping political changes in the Soviet Union and Eastern Europe.

FEDERAL PRIVATIZATION PROSPECTS

The following federal programs and services are among those most frequently mentioned as prospective privatization candidates. Some are large activities involving billions of dollars in revenues and expenditures; others are considerably smaller and involve less significant sums. All, however, are said to represent opportunities for the privatization of the provision, production, or financing decisions.

U.S. Postal Service

At the head of most lists of federal program and services that could and perhaps should be privatized stands the U.S. Postal Service. Despite a work force of some 750,000 persons and the massive infusion of modern technology and automation, the productivity and reliability of the Postal Service continues to decrease while costs continue to increase. The Postal Service anticipates a net operating loss in fiscal year 1990 of $1.6 billion.[8]

Postal Service workers are paid premium wages (averaging $29,000 annually—a figure some 40 percent above the national average), yet 9 percent of third-class mail never reaches its destination and 80 percent of second-class mail arrives late.[9] The Postal Service openly admits that mail delivery is erratic and has suggested as the solution a cutback in service to every other day delivery.

Major options for privatizing the U.S. Postal Service include privatizing the provision decision through load shedding or privatizing the production decision through contracting out. In both cases the financing decision would also be privatized by ending federal subsidies and by the imposition of full cost user fees. In the load shedding scenario, the Postal Service's monopoly on first-class mail would be ended. Additionally, the Postal Service system would be subdivided into geographical regions, and private businesses like Federal Express, United Parcel Service, and others would be invited to compete for multiyear franchises. The franchisees would recover their costs and profit margin through the sale of stamps and the imposition of other user fees.

New Zealand, in totally privatizing its postal service through load shedding, attests to the technical feasibility of this approach. New Zealand Post, a corporation formed in 1987, has improved service and made a profit for its investors, while also paying income taxes to the national government.[10]

In the contracting scenario, the Postal Service would accelerate its current contracting activities. Nationally, some 5000 postal routes have already been privatized via contracting out, and the Postal Service itself has suggested that all rural routes should eventually be handled similarly. Contracting out the operation of postal windows could also generate significant cost savings to the Postal Service. The President's Private Sector Survey on Cost Control, more commonly called the Grace Commission, estimated that it costs the Postal Service twenty-four cents per revenue dollar to operate a postal window. In a 1981 study of twenty-four contracted postal windows in Tucson, Arizona, the reported operating costs were only three cents per revenue dollar.[11]

The true cost of operating the Postal Service is difficult to determine, but a good estimate is around $40 billion a year.[12] In the load shedding scenario, the federal treasury could save at least $2 billion annually by privatizing the entire Postal Service. This $2 billion figure represents over $1 billion in federal subsidies per annum plus the federal government's assumption of the Postal Service's unfunded pension and health care liabilities estimated to cost an additional $1 billion per year.[13]

The estimated cost savings of contracting out all rural postal routes is $6 billion annually.[14] Even this minor privatization approach might be sufficient in itself to enable the federal government to end its annual $1 billion subsidy as well as preclude the necessity of postal rate increases for several years. Additional potential cost savings from contracting out include an estimated $165 million per annum from contracting the operation of small post offices and $1 billion per annum from contracting mail processing and presorting activities.[15]

Amtrak

When it comes to the National Railroad Passenger Corporation (Amtrak), privatizing the provision decision through load shedding and the sale of government assets would end significant annual federal subsidies while generating revenues through the sale of Amtrak assets.

Amtrak was created in 1970 to insure the continuation of intercity passenger rail service. Between 1971 when it commenced operations and 1977, the federal government granted Amtrak $1.6 billion in operating subsidies, $500 million in loan guarantees, and $229 million in capital grants for acquisition and improvements.[16] By 1981, total annual federal assistance had reached the $1 billion level which represented 60 percent of Amtrak's total revenues.[17] Dramatic passenger and revenue increases during the 1980s have resulted in Amtrak significantly increasing its nonfederal revenues. Nevertheless, Amtrak still wants $684 million from the federal treasury for fiscal year 1991.[18]

In addition, Amtrak is also plagued by two other chronic problems. Amtrak's routes and schedules must be determined in consultation with Congress. Amtrak thus is forced into the catch–22 position of attempting to operate an efficient railroad over a politicized route structure. Amtrak is also faced with the dilemma of rising passenger demand, but inadequate capital to expand service. Given all the other budgetary problems confronting the federal government, additional funding for Amtrak is problematic. Privatizing Amtrak via load shedding would take decisions on routes, service levels, and fare structures out of the political arena and allow them to be made on the basis of sound business practice. Privatization would also allow Amtrak to raise capital for expansion.

From the perspective of federal budgetary impact, the privatization of Amtrak could save the federal treasury an estimated $800 million a year.[19] The privatization of Amtrak through a direct sale or public stock offering would also net the federal treasury at least $1 billion in revenues based upon the similar sale of Conrail in 1987. Finally, the privatization of Amtrak would place a major business activity with sizable revenues back on the federal corporate income tax rolls.

Military Commissaries

The U.S. armed forces operate a number of commissaries both domestically and overseas. The original idea of the military commissary was to make U.S.-made products available to U.S. service personnel stationed in remote American bases and overseas. Over time, however, the commissary system has taken on a life of its own, growing far beyond its original concept. Today, virtually every military base in the world has a commissary, even bases located in major American metropolitan areas. For example, there are six military commissaries in the Washington, D.C., area alone. The total commissary system employs over 22,000 people and has annual sales of some $5 billion.[20]

The commissary system is considered extremely inefficient even by Department of Defense standards. One estimate suggests that the inefficient commissary system actually represents a subsidy of about $250 for every service person, retiree, and dependent who uses the system.[21]

A strong case can be made for the privatization of the commissary system when one considers just who benefits from its operation. By the Pentagon's own estimate, over six million of the ten million individuals who use the commissary system annually are military retirees living near American military facilities.[22] One commissary, at the El Segundo Base in Los Angeles, California, was established for the principal purpose of serving retired military personnel.

The commissary system was established to serve active duty military personnel, not retirees. Yet, the importance of the commissary system to active duty military personnel is highly questionable. A General Accounting Office survey of active duty military personnel reported that only 13 percent stated the commissary system was a factor in their enlistment.[23]

A plausible privatization strategy for the commissary system would be a combination of privatizing the provision decision through partial load shedding and privatizing the production decision of what remains through contracting out. In terms of load shedding, military retirees could simply be weaned from the commissary system. All military retirees could be given a one-time pension increase of $250 as compensation for having their commissary privileges revoked. Privatizing the fringe benefits of military retirees and dependents is not an unprecedented action. The Department of Defense has already partially privatized health care benefits for military dependents and retirees under its CHAMPUS program.

Taking retirees out of the commissary system would reduce the demand for commissary services by over half. The remaining demand could easily be met by contracting out the operation of the entire commissary system. Contractors would be required to recover their operating costs and a negotiated profit margin through the prices they charge. Based upon studies of contracting out in other areas, the Office of Management and Budget estimates that the military operated commissary system is 40 percent more expensive than a similar private operation would be.[24]

Buying out military retirees from the commissary system would cost $1.5 billion. The Grace Commission, however, estimated that the privatization of the entire commissary system would save the federal treasury $750 million per year in indirect costs.[25] Thus, the total privatization of the commissary system would break even after two years and generate significant cost savings thereafter.

Power Marketing Authorities

The federal government operates six regional electrical power marketing authorities (PMAs). The biggest of these are the Tennessee Valley Authority, located in the area whose name it bears, and the Bonneville Power Administration in the Pacific Northwest. Together these six PMAs operate 174 hydroelectric plants generating 10 percent of the nation's total electrical production.[26]

For the most part, these PMAs were not set up to provide electricity, but to solve such problems as flooding in the Tennessee Valley and the irrigation needs of western states. The production of electricity was a byproduct. Today, the real problems which created the PMAs have been solved, but they continue to operate providing taxpayer-subsidized, low-cost electricity to such areas as Las Vegas, Nevada.

The continued sale of electrical power at below market rates constitutes a federal subsidy with tremendous cost implications for the federal treasury. For example, the Bonneville Power Administration was created in 1936 and is supposed to be self-supporting today—but it isn't. As recently as 1985, the Bonneville Power Administration borrowed $400 million from the federal treasury, while continuing to sell electricity at below market rates.

By privatizing the provision decision via load shedding and the sale of government assets, the federal government would be removed from the power marketing business, the need for future grants and loans would be precluded, market rates could be established for the sale of electricity, and the federal treasury would generate between $70 billion and $100 billion in revenues.[27]

Air Traffic Control System

The air traffic control system is administered by the U.S. Department of Transportation. The annual budget is some $4 billion derived almost exclusively from airline user fees and ticket taxes.[28] The air traffic control system is badly in need of modernization and expansion. At the same time, over fifty airports nationally continue to be provided with air traffic control services even though these airports fall below minimum activity levels specified by the Federal Aviation Administration. Proposed increases in landing fees to cover modernization and expansion in metro areas, as well as efforts to discontinue services at marginal airports are continually—and successfully— opposed by the political clout of small plane owners, whose lower fees and continued service constitutes a federal subsidy.

Privatizing the air traffic control system would take the program out of the political arena and permit the charging of market-based fees and the discontinuance of service at marginal airfields. The combination of cost savings and increased revenues could then be used to modernize and expand the air traffic control system where needed.

Numerous precedents can be cited for privately operated air traffic control systems. The first air traffic control system in the United States was a private operation created in 1935 to serve the cities of Newark, Cleveland, and Chicago. Air traffic control services are totally privatized in Switzerland and Saudi Arabia. The U.S. military has successfully used private air traffic controllers in Vietnam. In the aftermath of the federal air traffic controllers strike in 1981, over sixty small communities hired private firms to operate their systems.[29]

Considerable support for the privatization of air traffic control services exists among the parties that would be most affected, with the exception of small aircraft owners. Both the Air Transport Association, which represents the major airlines, and the U.S. Air Traffic Controllers Organization have formally gone on record as supporting some form of privatization of the air traffic control system.[30]

The major benefits to the federal treasury of privatizing the air traffic control system would come in the form of future avoided costs for modernization and expansion of the system as well as the avoidance of unfunded liabilities in the form of pension and health care benefits for controllers. No exact estimate of the unfunded liability costs exists, but the Grace Commission did estimate that consolidation of the system and discontinuation of air traffic control services at marginal airports could save the federal treasury at least $100 million per year.[31]

U.S. Coast Guard

Many of the activities performed by the Coast Guard are inherently non-military and perhaps not even governmental in nature. Such activities targeted for privatization by the Grace Commission are non-life-threatening search and rescue, short-range navigation aids, and commercial vessel safety.

One of the largest Coast Guard programs is search and rescue. Of the 80,000 calls responded to annually by the Coast Guard, nearly 75 percent are classified as non-life-threatening convenience calls that involve recreational vessels and occur within three miles from land.[32] Having the Coast Guard responding to stranded pleasure boaters is analogous to having the U.S. Army providing emergency road service on the nation's highways.

The Coast Guard's short-range navigation aids program involves the maintenance of buoys, day-markers, fog signals, and other devices along inland waterways and coastlines. As its name implies, this is a strictly maintenance program that does not necessarily require the use of military personnel. The third program targeted for privatization is commercial vessel safety. This program involves the safety inspection of vessels, primarily pleasure craft; the conduct of boat safety classes; and the issuance of citations to boaters for noncompliance with safety regulations such as the failure to have sufficient numbers of life preservers on board. Again, this activity does not necessarily require the use of military personnel.

By privatizing the production decision of these three Coast Guard programs through contracting out, the federal treasury could save an estimated $50 to $75 million per year.[33]

Social Security

The current operation of the Social Security system is under question. As a result of planned changes made in the early 1980s, Social Security payroll taxes now raise more revenue than is currently needed to meet retiree payments. By 1993 the surplus is estimated to reach $100 billion.[34] This surplus is supposed to accrue in a trust fund to be used to pay the retirement benefits of the baby boom generation when it begins reaching retirement age in 2010. Social Security, however, does not maintain a true trust fund.

For some time now, the federal government has been borrowing from the Social Security surplus, leaving an IOU. The funds are then used to meet current general government operating expenses. This practice has been criticized for several reasons. First, beginning around the year 2010, either workers and employers will have to begin paying significantly higher Social Security payroll taxes, or income taxes will have to be significantly increased in order to pay the retirement benefits of the large number of projected retirees. The use of either of these approaches raises questions of intergenerational equity: one generation spending and the other paying. Second, the federal government's practice of borrowing the Social Security surplus artificially understates the annual federal budget deficit—by an estimated $75 billion in 1990.[35] This accounting sleight of hand comes about because the federal government treats the Social Security surplus as a revenue, but does not recognize the corresponding and offsetting pension liability which is unfunded. Third, Social Security taxes are generally considered more regressive than the personal income tax. In 1990, for example, Social Security taxes will be applied only to the first $51,000 of earned income. Regarding the borrowing of Social Security reserves to fund general government operations, the argument is made that the regressive Social Security tax is used to supplant the more progressive personal income tax.

The privatization of Social Security through partial load shedding would resolve much of the current criticism by returning the trust fund to solvency and placing the surplus revenues out of the reach of Congress and the president. Privatizing Social Security is technically feasible and could be a relatively simple process. One of the many proposed privatization scenarios envisions a separate federally chartered corporation which would be independently managed but backed by the full faith and credit of the United States. This action would make Social Security revenues untouchable by

Congress and the president. This approach would also make Social Security an off-budget item which would preclude the use of surplus revenues to artificially reduce the size of the federal deficit.

The new Social Security corporation would manage a real trust fund. However, the type of investments the corporation could make would be circumscribed to avoid financial risk. For example, in addition to investing in U.S. Treasury bills—the current practice—the corporation might also be permitted to invest in state and local government bonds and high-grade corporate bonds.

Another feature of some Social Security privatization scenarios is the super individual retirement accounts (Super IRAs) option. The Super IRA concept would provide employees the option of having a percentage of their Social Security taxes, as well as a percentage of their employers' contributions, paid directly into an individual retirement account managed by a federally approved financial institution.[36] At retirement, employees selecting the Super IRA option would have their Social Security benefits reduced proportionately. This aspect of the privatization of Social Security is designed to broaden the retirement base by making fewer retirees exclusively dependent upon Social Security for their retirement.

As a byproduct, the privatization of Social Security would automatically balloon the annual federal budget deficit by at least an additional $75 billion. The net effect would be that either Congress would have to raise income taxes or possibly the Gramm–Rudman–Hollings legislation would require across-the-board cuts in federal spending. In either case, the privatization of Social Security would not only return the trust fund to solvency, but it would also reduce the federal budget deficit by at least $75 billion annually. An additional significant benefit of privatizing Social Security is that a large capital pool would be created for state and local government and private sector borrowing.

The Sale of Federal Lands and Buildings

The federal government is the largest land owner in the nation with over 27,000 separate properties comprising some 700 million acres. A great many of the federal government's land holdings, excluding national parks and wilderness areas, are not being used productively. The federal government continues unnecessarily to hold title to real estate that serves little, if any, public purpose while being costly to maintain.

The American Association of Appraisers has suggested that perhaps as many as 5,000 federal properties, with an assessed valuation in excess of $100 billion, could be considered surplus.[37] This surplus real estate could be leased or sold and the revenues used to pay down the federal deficit or accomplish some other public policy objective. The addition of this real estate to the public tax rolls would also be of benefit to state and local governments, particularly in the West where a great deal of the land is owned by the federal government. The following sample of federal properties illustrates the revenue potential of privatizing the provision decision with respect to public lands and buildings through the sale of government assets.

Military Bases. The United States military maintains about 4,000 domestic bases comprising nearly 24 million acres with an estimated total value of $150 billion.[38] Only 312 of these bases have been identified as "significant" by the Department of Defense.[39] The implication is that many—if not most— of the remaining 3,692 bases could be considered surplus. Some of these surplus bases and their revenue potential are:

- Ft. DeRussy, Hawaii, which consists of a 416-room luxury hotel and seventeen acres of beachfront property, is located next to Waikiki Beach. The hotel and beach are used exclusively by military personnel and retirees. Estimated value: $221 million.[40]
- Camp Bullis, San Antonio, Texas, consisting of 26,000 acres, is considered surplus because it sits at the end of an airport runway. Estimated value: $200 million.[41]
- The Presidio, a U.S. Army base, consists of 1,440 acres, all located within the city limits of San Francisco, California, with a 149-acre golf course and a panoramic view of the Golden Gate Bridge. Estimated value: priceless.[42]

In addition to generating revenue for the federal treasury, the sale of surplus military bases has the potential to significantly decrease the operations costs of the military base system. If only the 2 million acres with the highest market value were to be sold, the resulting base closures would generate an estimated annual operating cost savings to the federal treasury of at least $35 billion.[43]

Other Federal Assets. The military is not the only agency of the federal government sitting on expensive, underutilized, or surplus land and property. The federal government manages 142 million acres of national forests in 40 states which contain sufficient timber to qualify as commercial forests. The estimated value of this timber is $100 billion.[44]

The federal government also manages 170 million acres of range land in eleven western states whose only useful purpose is the open grazing of cattle and sheep. Rather than disposing of this land, the federal government has decided to spend $5.00 per acre per year in maintenance costs while generating only $1.00 per acre in revenues per annum.[45]

By privatizing the financing decision and the aggressive imposition of full cost user fees for firewood cutting and open range grazing, the Grace Commission estimated that the savings to the federal treasury would approximate between $75 and $100 million per year.[46]

In addition to undeveloped land holdings, the federal government also maintains one of the largest property management portfolios in the nation even when military bases are excluded. Frequently this property portfolio is not managed to the maximum benefit of the federal treasury or the federal budget, or even to the federal program or service activity the property supports.

The Veterans Administration is a case in point. The Veterans Administration (VA) owns and operates the largest health-care system in the nation. Among the VA's holdings are 172 hospitals, 93 nursing homes, and 50 satellite clinics. Many of these facilities were built decades ago and now occupy land that is extremely valuable. For example, the Veterans Administration operates an aging medical facility on 442 prime acres fronting Wilshire Boulevard in Los Angeles, California. The nearly empty facility is said to serve primarily as an overflow parking lot for students attending UCLA located just down the road. The estimated value of the land is somewhere between $1.2 and $2.4 billion.[47]

The Wilshire Boulevard facility illustrates how, by privatizing the sale of government land, the federal government can also privatize a future financing decision. The sale of the Wilshire Boulevard facility would generate revenues to permit the Veterans Administration to construct a new facility elsewhere in the city with significant revenues left over. The surplus revenues could be used to augment the Veterans Administration budget or could be placed in a trust fund for future capital needs.

AVOIDING FUTURE FEDERAL INFRASTRUCTURE COSTS

The costs of maintaining the nation's infrastructure (highways, bridges, waterways, tunnels) over the next decade will be enormous. The privatization of infrastructure provision, production, and financing decisions could help the federal government, as well as state and local governments, avoid billions in future expenditures.

The nation's investment in its infrastructure has been steadily declining since the early 1960s. During the government belt-tightening decade of the 1980s, the nation's infrastructure needs were simply deferred. Current annual federal, state, and local government infrastructure expenditure levels are not keeping pace with existing need—to say nothing of making amends for past neglect. Estimates of the annual underfunding of the nation's infrastructure needs run between $45 and $100 billion.[48] Privatization may be a partial answer to the infrastructure problem. As has been demonstrated with other federal programs and services, one can find considerable precedence for the privatization of infrastructure.

Roads and Highways

The privatization of roads and highways is technically feasible. The construction and operation of turnpikes and toll roads are well-known approaches. A new approach for the United States, however, would be to have private businesses construct, maintain, and operate roads and highways on a franchise basis recovering their investments, operating costs, and profit margins through user fees. The private construction and maintenance of roads and highways is a quite common practice in Europe. In Italy, for example, most of the limited access intercity highways are built and operated by the private businesses under long-term, twenty-five to thirty year leases or franchises.[49]

In the United States today some thirty existing toll roads have already been privatized.[50] The most noteworthy privatization of a highway is currently under way in Virginia. Toll Road Corporation of Virginia has been granted the right to construct and operate a toll road from Dulles International Airport to Leesburg. The anticipated cost of the project is $140 million.[51] Similar private toll expressways are being considered in Colorado, Illinois, California, and several other states. In California, Caltrans, the state department of transportation, recently issued a call for conceptual proposals for the construction and operation of four demonstration toll roads in the state.[52]

Bridges and Tunnels

Precedent also exists for the privatization of bridges and tunnels. The $11 billion rail tunnel under the English Channel connecting England and France is a privatized operation being built and financed by a company called Eurotunnel. The best known example of a private bridge in the United States is the Ambassador Bridge that connects Detroit, Michigan, with Ontario, Canada.

Federal law currently precludes the charging of tolls on federally supported highways. The federal government also has not looked favorably on privatized bridges and tunnels. The federal government's reluctance to consider infrastructure privatization options affects not only its own budget but also the budgets of state and local governments. The alternative to infrastructure privatization for the federal government is increased pressures on the underfunded Highway Users Trust Fund which is not even meeting current needs.

SUMMARY AND CONCLUSION

In this chapter, I have suggested privatization as a reform with significant potential for reducing the federal budget deficit. The nature of federal programs and services is determined by the responses to three separate—yet related—decisions: the provision decision, the production decision, and the financing decision. As part of the federal budget process, each federal program and service can, and should, be analyzed in terms of these three decisions. If the federal budget process was changed to require each federal program and service to give consideration to the provision, production, and financing decisions, then the Congress, the president, and the various federal departments and agencies might discover new policy, administrative, and fiscal options.

Privatization is no panacea; alone, it will resolve neither the federal budgetary problem nor the federal budget deficit. In conjunction with other federal budget reform and reduction plans, however, privatization can make a meaningful contribution. To borrow a phrase from the late Senator Everett Dirksen, privatization has the potential to save the federal government a billion here and a billion there. Pretty soon, it could add up to real money.

NOTES

1. Lester Salamon et al., *Privatization: The Challenge To Public Management* (Washington, D.C.: Academy of Public Administration, 1989), 7–23.

2. Steve H. Hanke, "Privatization versus Nationalization," in *Prospects for Privatization*, edited by Steve H. Hanke (New York: Academy of Political Science, 1987), 2; Salamon, *Privatization: The Challenge*, 7.

3. Ted Kolderie, "Two Different Concepts of Privatization," *Public Administration Review* 46 (July/August 1986): 285–91.

4. Harry Hatry, *A Review of Private Approaches for Delivery of Public Services* (Washington, D.C.: Urban Institute Press, 1983), 5–8.

5. *Privatization in America* (New York: Touche Ross & Company, 1987); Elaine Morley, "Patterns in the Use of Alternative Service Delivery Approaches," *The Municipal Year Book—1989* (Washington, D.C.: International City Management Association, 1989), 33–44.

6. Dennis J. Palumbo and James Maupin, "The Political Side of Privatization," *Journal of Management Science and Policy Analysis* 6 (Winter 1989): 25–40; Gerald S. Leighton, "Privatization: A Rich Concept," *The Bureaucrat* 17 (Fall 1988): 39–41.

7. Steve H. Hanke, "Privatization: Theory, Evidence, and Implementation," in *Control of Federal Spending*, edited by C. Lowell Harris (New York: Academy of Political Science, 1985), 111.

8. "The Post Office Wants Everyone to Pay for Its Mistakes," *Business Week* (March 5, 1990): 28.

9. John Naisbitt and Patricia Aburdene, *Megatrends 2000* (New York: William Morrow and Co., 1990), 164–66.

10. "In New Zealand Free Enterprise Delivers the Mail," *Wall Street Journal* (March 8, 1990): A14.

11. Hanke, *Privatization: Theory, Evidence*, 108.

12. Francis P. Clark. "Privatization in the United States," *Indiana University School of Public and Environmental Affairs Review* 10 (Spring 1989): 74–87.

13. Stewart M. Butler, *Privatizing Federal Spending: A Strategy to Eliminate the Deficit* (New York: Universal Books, 1985), 122–27.

14. Randall Fitzgerald, *When Government Goes Private: Successful Alternatives to Public Services* (New York: Universe Books, 1988), 243.

15. Ibid., 243; William R. Kennedy, Jr., and Robert W. Lee, *A Taxpayer Survey of the Grace Commission Report* (Ottawa, Ill.: Jameson Books, 1984), 29.

16. Lloyd Musolf, *Uncle Sam's Private Profitseeking Corporations* (Lexington, Mass.: Lexington Books, 1983), 53.

17. Butler, *Privatizing Federal Spending*, 77–78.

18. "Greyhound Striking, Tolls Are Rising, There's Fear of Flying. The Solution? All Aboard!" *The Miami Herald* (March 28, 1990): 1D–2D.

19. The $750 million figure is computed using 1988 passenger data (21.5 million riders) multiplied by the Congressional Budget Office's 1982 estimate of the per person federal subsidy of $37 per rider.

20. Clark, *Privatization in the United States*, 80.

21. Fitzgerald, *When Government Goes*, 230.

22. Ibid., 230.

23. Ibid., 231.

24. Clark, *Privatization in the United States*, 80–31; Kennedy and Lee, *A Taxpayer Survey*, 63.

25. Kennedy and Lee, *A Taxpayer Survey*, 122.

26. Fitzgerald, *When Government Goes*, 133.

27. Ibid., 246.

28. Butler, *Privatizing Federal Spending*, 133.

29. Fitzgerald, *When Government Goes*, 251.

30. Ibid., 251; Butler, *Privatizing Federal Spending*, 134.

31. Kennedy and Lee, *A Taxpayer Survey*, 15.

32. E. S. Savas, *Privatization: The Key To Better Government* (Catham, N.J.: Catham House, 1987), 145–46.

33. Ibid., 146.

34. Paul C. Roberts, "It's High Time We Retired the Social Security Tax Surplus," *Business Week* (January 15, 1990): 13.

35. Ibid.

36. Peter J. Ferrara, "Social Security and Super IRAs," in *The Privatization Option—A Strategy to Shrink the Size of Government*, edited by Stuart M. Butler (New York: Heritage Foundation, 1985), 76.

37. Fitzgerald, *When Government Goes*, 183–84.

38. Fred Thompson, "Why America's Military Base Structure Cannot Be Reduced," *Public Administration Review* 48 (January/February 1988): 557–63.

39. Kennedy and Lee, *A Taxpayer Survey*, 60.

40. Fitzgerald, *Privatizing Federal Spending*, 187.

41. Ibid., 185.

42. "The Peace Economy," *Business Week* (December 11, 1989): 54–55.

43. Thompson, "Why America's Military," 557.

44. Fitzgerald, *Privatizing Federal Spending*, 198–202.

45. Ibid., 202.

46. Kennedy and Lee, *A Taxpayer Survey*, 100–01.

47. Thompson, "Why America's Military," 559.

48. "Infrastructure: An Emerging Issue Needs Long-Term Solutions," *The Public's Capital* 1 (July 1989): 1–3.

49. Robert W. Poole, Jr. and Philip E. Fixler, Jr., "Privatization of Public-Sector

Services in Practice: Experience and Potential," *Journal of Policy Analysis and Management* 6 (1987): 612–25.

50. Fitzgerald, *Privatizing Federal Spending*, 168.

51. "Fifteen Miles—That'll Be $1.50," *Business Week* (August 14, 1989): 54.

52. "Santa Ana Promotes Highway Extension for Privatization," *Privatization Report* 5 (March 1990): 7.

Conclusion: Addressing the Problem

Thomas D. Lynch

In addressing the American people at the height of the Great Depression, President Franklin D. Roosevelt said that the only thing we have to fear is fear itself. FDR felt solutions could be found if the nation would only address fear—the real problem that was immobilizing government action. In the current economic crisis, the federal deficit, we are again confronted with an apparent inability of national leadership to address the real problem. Political budget deadlock cannot be allowed to continue even if the ultimate resolution involves a fundamental redistribution of political power between the legislative and executive branches. Essential budget decisions must be more intelligently made if the nation is to prosper and move effectively into the next century.

In almost everyone's view, the current federal budget process has created dysfunctional delayed budget decisions and crippling deficits and national debt. The major actors in the budget process continually try to place the failure on others, including the electorate.

DEFINING THE PROBLEM

The main failure is the budget process, but federal financial management is also a problem that needs addressing. The United States used to lead the world in applying computer technology to financial management. Today, most of the best examples of computer applications in financial management can be found in other countries, in state governments, and even in local governments. Professionalism in budgeting involves forecasting, and the federal government could do much better in that highly technical area. Federal financial management can be significantly improved across its full range of activities.

All the failures, missed opportunities, poor management, and related problems can be remedied. Solutions are not beyond our grasp. Our failure is due almost entirely to a lack of political will to face the problems and to make the political power adjustments necessary to solve the problems. Until there is a bipartisan mandate to reform the budget process to address both the deficit issue and the related federal financial management system, these failures, missed opportunities, poor management, and other problems will continue.

How can the necessary bipartisan political will be created? One significant step in the correct direction would be continuous exposure of the problems by the academic community and national press. Unfortunately these problems do not make interesting news stories, but their significance runs to the heart of our nation's future well-being. Continuous public discussion will inspire political action, but getting the media to address the topic will be the real challenge. A second step is to help our national leaders realize that their political dueling in the budget process is not only insane and unacceptable behavior but also must be stopped. In the past century, dueling as a means to settle disputes ceased only when social pressure demanded an end to it. We must expose the leaders that play the macho game of political dueling and demand they act responsibly. A third step is to reform the federal budget process as suggested in this book. A final step is for top officials to move the subject of federal financial management reform from low to high priority. The federal government should not only manage its over two trillion dollar cash flow correctly but the management should serve as a model to the rest of the world.

Creating the necessary political and social environment so that reform is likely will require commitment by the intellectual community. Such commitment can be and must be accomplished for the betterment of us all.

SOME RECOMMENDATIONS

In preparing this book, I deliberately asked the authors to include recommendations based on their research and professional expertise. I was surprised that there was so much agreement since I selected authors with varied perspectives. Certainly, not every author, including this editor, will agree with all recommendations found in this book. However, the harmony of views is striking. In this chapter, I merely summarize various recommendations that can be found in the previous chapters. My purpose is to highlight the policy reforms addressed in this book.

The Budget Process

1. Both the president and the Congress should use a multiyear budget.

2. Budgets should reflect the full cost of programs so that life-cycle costs can be understood when budget decisions are made.

3. Budget political dueling, especially between the president and Congress, needs to stop. "Truth in budgeting" needs to be a criterion used in developing and debating the budget so that people can have confidence in government.

4. The federal government should use a capital budget. This could be combined with a biennial operating budget, which could be passed in the first year of a new Congress, and a capital budget passed in the second year.

5. The budget structure needs to be revised so that the budget is easier to understand.

6. The tension between the executive and Congress as it relates to the budget process needs to be reduced. Incentives for political dueling need to be lessened, and incentives for high professional conduct need to be strengthened.

7. A two stage presidential/congressional budget process needs to be created in which the president and Congress first set the overall revenue and expenditure levels and then make the specific revenue and expenditure policy decisions.

8. The IRS should be funded at sufficient levels so that it can perform its legal responsibilities of collecting tax revenues.

9. A coordinated congressional/executive economic forecasting process should be established.

10. All currently unfunded liabilities, including pension obligations, should be budgeted fully, and necessary reserves should be created for those liabilities, as in the private sector.

11. Prudent administrative practices in the management of contingent liability programs should be followed without political interference, and those programs should be funded adequately so that managers can perform their duties correctly.

12. Top congressional and executive leaders need to support improving federal government productivity.

13. User fee income should reflect the cost of running federal programs they support.

14. Greater use needs to be made of internal service funds to create a private sector mentality for the financing of internal service activities.

15. Systematic experimentation with different policies and approaches to forecasting needs to be undertaken across the whole federal government.

16. Research is needed to understand the recursive relationship between the budget and the economy.

17. More care needs to be taken by political leaders in both the congressional and executive branches to identify consistently and clearly their budget policies or alternative policies so that forecasters can be more effective in their forecasting.

18. The current means used to generate deficit projections needs to be revised in order to improve the accuracy of forecasts.

19. Political leaders should experiment with using sensitivity analysis in reviewing multiple future budget and economic performance scenarios.

Public Financial Management

20. Financial information that needs to be upgraded includes cost information, periodic performance reports, periodic financial statements, and key statistics. The current process does not provide adequately reliable, timely, and consistent information for policy formulation and management control.
21. An up-to-date computerized federal budget and financial management information system should be created. Current problems needing solutions include lack of systems integration, inflexibility, obsolete equipment and technology, overuse of manual processes, and a lack of data for operating managers.
22. A federal governmentwide integrated financial management system should be established.
23. Reporting involving the Antideficiency Act and unliquidated obligations should be improved so that accountability over public funds can be achieved.
24. Reports on internal control practices should be improved so that there is an accurate, clear assessment of the overall status of their control systems.
25. Financial statements, especially at the agency level, need to be improved, and the statements should be uniform across the government. The U.S. federal government should issue an annual audited financial report.
26. Financial information at the program levels should be improved. Currently the reporting of program costs often are estimated incorrectly or just ignored. Also, the total value of government assets is not precisely known.
27. Project reporting needs to be improved especially as it involves financial information and meeting milestones.
28. The use of performance measures should be greatly expanded so that the federal government knows what it is getting for its money and the impact it is having on individuals, the society, and the economy.
29. Federal cash management should be improved. For example, basic tasks, such as agencies reconciling their financial records with the Treasury Department, should be done routinely. Disbursements should be made in a timely manner as required by federal law.
30. Accounts receivables and delinquent accounts should be managed to collect monies promptly. Problems that exist include unclear definition of delinquencies, not establishing allowances for loan losses, and failing to record promptly amounts due.

Other Reform Possibilities

31. The U.S. postal system should be privatized.
32. Amtrak should be privatized.

33. Military commissaries should be turned over to the private sector or at least the benefits should be limited to on-duty military personnel.

34. The federal regional electrical power authorities should be converted to private ventures.

35. The U.S. air traffic control system should be privatized.

36. The Coast Guard functions of non-life-threatening search and rescue, short-range navigation aids, and commercial vessel safety should be privatized.

37. A federally charted corporation should be created to manage independently the Social Security programs, with the full faith and credit of the U.S. government to back up the liabilities of the corporation.

38. Surplus federal properties, including military bases, should be sold and converted to tax generating activities.

39. Where possible and practical, private companies should contract, maintain, and operate roads, highways, and bridges on a franchise basis.

CONCLUSION

These 39 recommendations are presented to provoke thought and to help policy makers realize that much more can be done to change the existing federal budget and financial management processes. Unfortunately the political climate does not yet exist that permits a serious improvement. Thus the debate on reform shall continue until such time as new effective reforms can finally be attempted.

INDEX

CONTRIBUTORS

RALPH BLEDSOE is Professor and Director, Washington Public Affairs Center, University of Southern California, Washington, D.C.

STANLEY B. BOTNER is Professor of Public Administration, College of Business and Public Administration, University of Missouri, Columbia.

SAMANTHA L. DURST is a graduate assistant, Center for Congressional and Presidential Studies, School of Public Affairs, American University, Washington, D.C.

JOHN FORRESTER is Assistant Professor of Public Administration, College of Business and Public Administration, University of Missouri, Columbia.

W. BARTLEY HILDRETH is Associate Professor, Public Administration Institute, Louisiana State University, Baton Rouge.

THOMAS D. LYNCH is Professor of Public Administration, College of Urban and Public Affairs, Florida Atlantic University, Ft. Lauderdale.

LAWRENCE L. MARTIN is Assistant Professor, School of Public Administration, College of Urban and Public Affairs, Florida Atlantic University, Ft. Lauderdale.

RONALD POINTS works for the Office of Government Services, Price Waterhouse, Washington, D.C.

JAMES A. THURBER is Professor and Director, Center for Congressional and Presidential Studies, School of Public Affairs, American University, Washington, D.C.

JOSEPH WHITE is a research associate, Governmental Studies Program, Brookings Institution, Washington, D.C.